STUDIES IN CHRISTIAN HISTORY AND THOUGHT

The Immanent Person of the Holy Spirit from Anselm to Lombard

Divine Communion in the Spirit

STUDIES IN CHRISTIAN HISTORY AND THOUGHT

The Immanent Person of the Holy Spirit from Anselm to Lombard

Divine Communion in the Spirit

Matthew Knell

Foreword by Dennis Ngien

WIPF & STOCK · Eugene, Oregon

Wipf and Stock Publishers
199 W 8th Ave, Suite 3
Eugene, OR 97401

The Immanent Person of the Holy Spirit from Anselm to Lombard
Divine Communion in the Spirit
By Knell, Matthew
Copyright©2009 Paternoster
ISBN 13: 978-1-60899-162-4
Publication date 10/6/2009
Previously published by Paternoster, 2009

This Edition published by Wipf and Stock Publishers by arrangement with Paternoster

Series Preface

This series complements the specialist series of *Studies in Evangelical History and Thought* and *Studies in Baptist History and Thought* for which Paternoster is becoming increasingly well known by offering works that cover the wider field of Christian history and thought. It encompasses accounts of Christian witness at various periods, studies of individual Christians and movements, and works which concern the relations of church and society through history, and the history of Christian thought.

The series includes monographs, revised dissertations and theses, and collections of papers by individuals and groups. As well as 'free standing' volumes, works on particular running themes are being commissioned; authors will be engaged for these from around the world and from a variety of Christian traditions.

A high academic standard combined with lively writing will commend the volumes in this series both to scholars and to a wider readership.

Series Editors

Alan P.F. Sell, Visiting Professor at Acadia University Divinity College, Nova Scotia, Canada

David Bebbington, Professor of History, University of Stirling, Stirling, Scotland, UK

Clyde Binfield, Professor Associate in History, University of Sheffield, UK

Gerald Bray, Anglican Professor of Divinity, Beeson Divinity School, Samford University, Birmingham, Alabama, USA

Grayson Carter, Associate Professor of Church History, Fuller Theological Seminary SW, Phoenix, Arizona, USA

For Emily,

who has brought more joy than I could wish for ...

Contents

Foreword by Dennis Ngien	xiii
Acknowledgements	xv
Abbreviations	xvii

Chapter 1
Introduction and the State of Current Research	1
Introduction	1
The Theological Climate	2
The Importance of the Holy Spirit	3
The Focus of the Book	4
The Writers	5
The Structure of the Book	6
The Twelfth Century in the Context of Previous Western Thought on the Holy Spirit	7
The State of Current Research	7
Works on Medieval Thought	7
Works on the Holy Spirit	9
Studies of Individual Authors	11
Works on Specific Issues in the Twelfth Century	21
Conclusion	22

Chapter 2
Anselm of Canterbury and Anselm of Havelberg	24
Anselm of Canterbury	26
The Monologion and Proslogion	26
De Processione Spiritus Sancti	30
Anselm of Havelberg	36
Conclusion	41

Chapter 3
Peter Abelard	43
Abelard's 'Heresies' Concerning the Person of the Holy Spirit	45
Power, Wisdom, Goodness	46

The World Soul	49
Abelard's Orthodoxy Concerning the Holy Spirit	53
Unity in Trinity	53
The Holy Spirit as Love, Will, Gift, Unity	54
The Procession of the Holy Spirit	58
Conclusion	59

Chapter 4
William of St. Thierry and Bernard of Clairvaux — 61

The Disputes with Peter Abelard and William of Conches	62
The Holy Spirit as World Soul	62
The Holy Spirit as the Goodness or Will of God	64
The Person of the Holy Spirit	65
Unity	66
Love	70
Sweetness, Embrace, Kiss	71
Gift	72
Will	73
Goodness	74
William and Bernard's Overall Understanding of the Holy Spirit	76
Conclusion	77

Chapter 5
Hugh and Richard of St. Victor — 79

Power, Wisdom, Goodness	81
Hugh	81
Richard	83
Love	85
Hugh	85
Richard	87
THE HOLY SPIRIT AS MUTUAL LOVE	87
PROVING THE TRINITY FROM LOVE	88
GIVING AND RECEIVING LOVE: THE PROCESSION AND MISSION OF THE HOLY SPIRIT	91
Union	93
Conclusion	95

Chapter 6
Peter Lombard — 96

The Procession of the Holy Spirit	97
Primacy in Procession	98
Mode of Procession	99
Love	102
Gift	108
Goodness	110
Conclusion	112

Chapter 7
Love — 113
Augustine — 113
The Holy Spirit as the Mutual Love of the Father and Son — 115
Expansion of the Idea of Love — 117
Sweetness, Embrace, Kiss — 117
Complaceo and Condilectio — 118
Equality of the Spirit with the Father and the Son — 119
On Whether Mutual Love Implies that there are Two Spirits — 120
Owing Love — 121
On Whether Father and Son Love with the Love that Proceeds from Them — 122
Analogies Involving the Holy Spirit as Love — 124
Blasphemy Against the Holy Spirit — 125
The Economic Role of the Holy Spirit as Love — 125
Conclusion — 127

Chapter 8
Goodness — 129
The Power, Wisdom, Goodness Debate — 129
Goodness as the Primary Concept of the Holy Spirit — 132
Goodness and the Procession of the Holy Spirit — 133
Goodness and the Blasphemy Against the Holy Spirit — 134
Goodness Linked to Other Concepts About the Holy Spirit — 136
Goodness and the Economic Role of the Holy Spirit — 138
Conclusion — 140

Chapter 9
Will — 141
Augustine — 141
Use of Augustine's Thought on Will in the Twelfth Century — 143
Twelfth-Century Descriptions of the Holy Spirit as Will — 145
Will and Love — 145
Will and Goodness — 146
Will and Unity — 147
Will and Blasphemy Against the Holy Spirit — 148
Will and the Economic Role of the Holy Spirit — 148
Conclusion — 150

Chapter 10
Gift — 151
Augustine — 151
The Role of the Holy Spirit as Gift in the World — 154
The Holy Spirit as Gift in His Immanent State — 156
The Holy Spirit: Eternally a Gift — 156

Gift as a Relative Term for the Immanent Holy Spirit — 158
On Whether the Holy Spirit can be said to Give Himself — 159
Conclusion: The Procession of the Holy Spirit as Gift — 160

Chapter 11
Union — 163
Augustine — 164
The Holy Spirit as Union in Twelfth-Century Thought — 166
Association of Unity with Love in the Person of the Holy Spirit — 170
The Holy Spirit as Union in His Economic State — 172
Conclusion — 174

Chapter 12
The Procession of the Holy Spirit — 176
Basic Processional Issues — 176
The Dual Procession of the Holy Spirit — 176
Primacy in Procession — 177
Unique Relationships Within the Trinity — 178
The Equality of the Holy Spirit in His Procession — 179
The Mode of Procession of the Holy Spirit — 180
The Holy Spirit Proceeding as the Unity of Father and Son — 181
The Holy Spirit's Procession as Mutual Love — 182
Other Processional Terms Regarding the Holy Spirit — 183
A Twelfth-Century Perspective of the Procession of the
    Holy Spirit — 183

Chapter 13
Conclusion — 186

Bibliography — 191

Index — 207

Foreword

This book concentrates on various twelfth-century theologians and their discussions concerning the immanent person of the Holy Spirit and his procession from the Father 'and the Son', which is known as *filioque*. Major thinkers including Anselm of Canterbury, Anselm of Havelberg, Peter Abelard, William of St. Thierry, Bernard of Clairvaux, Richard and Hugh of St. Victor, and Peter Lombard are carefully studied and coherently presented. Augustine's mutual-love theory is extended by the medievalists to include Will, Unity, Goodness and Gift so as to affirm that the Spirit is the communion of the first two persons and that it is as this that the Spirit proceeds. The focus of Matthew's book is the immanent state of the intra-relation which the Spirit has with the Father and the Son. How God is in and for himself, rather than how God is for us, occupies this book. The Spirit's position and relation within the immanent Godhead, as this book unfolds, serves as a corrective to an overemphasis on the temporal mission of the Holy Spirit in many of the contemporary theological discourses on pneumatology. Bold and perceptive, this book is a remarkably able systematic piece of historical theology. It furnishes a comprehensive and accurate evaluation of a neglected perspective on the immanent person of the Holy Spirit held by various thinkers in an important period of theological traditions. Thus it fills a lacuna in medieval studies with regard to the Holy Spirit. The book also serves as a counter-balance to an over-emphasis in current studies that remain focused on traditional issues in the period, such as Anselm's theory of atonement, or general discussions on divine attributes in medieval theology.

Broadly speaking, this book also contributes to current issues in Trinitarian studies as well as ecumenical dialogues by bringing to light the important work done in the 12th century on the nature, identity and attributes of the Holy Spirit in his immanent and economic relations as the One proceeding from both the Father and the Son as their mutual communion and love. The crux of the issue is whether the Son is also the ontological source of the Holy Spirit, along with the Father; and whether the Son imparts the divine essence to the Holy Spirit along with the Father, or whether the Spirit derives the divine essence solely from the Father.

Matthew's book displays an extensive knowledge of the principles and materials related to the subject, lucidity in communicating that knowledge, originality and independence in applying them. It provides evidence of a significant awareness of related scholarly literature. Matthew possesses a talent for sound theological exposition, and an analytical gift to unpack this deep Trinitarian vein in the history of theology. It is my wish that Matthew's work will have the impact it deserves, and will be welcomed by those who are concerned that the *filioque* doctrine continues to receive a full hearing.

Dennis Ngien
Research Professor of Theology
Tyndale Seminary
Toronto, Ont., Canada.

Acknowledgements

I would like to start by thanking the writers I have lived with for the past three years: Anselm, Anselm, Peter Abelard, William of St. Thierry and Bernard of Clairvaux, Hugh and Richard of St. Victor, and Peter Lombard. Whatever others may think when they hear I have been studying twelfth-century thought for so long, I know that you have interested, excited and amused me with your legacy, and I will forever be in your debt.

As for more recent times, I need to thank all at Schloss Mittersill over the many years I have spent there for making me the man I am today (although I accept you may not wish such damning praise), and most especially Norm HG for exemplifying how life can truly be lived to the full. Carl Armerding's belief in me from my first visit to the castle has always been a strong motivation as my studies have progressed. I am also thankful to those at Kendal Road Baptist Church and Redcliffe College for their support of me in my studies over the past three years.

Tony Lane has been a model supervisor in the guidance that he has given my research and the determination for excellence in every respect that I have done my utmost to come close to. David Coffey has taught me in his writings on the person of the Holy Spirit through history, and encouraged me early in my journey to undertake this present work.

My greatest thanks go to my family for the challenge they always present to do the best with what God has given you. My parents have supported me not only through the thesis, but in all the projects and moves I have undertaken in life (and I should additionally thank both mum and Katia Gourmete, an American friend, for their help refining translation of Latin and Italian, respectively).

Finally, I cannot think of what life would be like without the loving support of my wife, Ieva, who inspires all the good that I do and teaches me by her life that it is always possible to choose to live in the best way.

Abbreviations

AHDLMA	*Archives d'Histoire Doctrinale et Littéraire du Moyen Age.*
AP	*Analecta Praemonstratensia.*
CCCM	Corpus Christianorum Continuatio Mediaevalis.
DTC	Dictionnaire de Théologie Catholique (eds. A. Vacant, E. Mangenot, É. Amann. Paris: Letouzet et Ané, 1930-1950).
ETL	*Ephemerides Theologicae Lovanienses.*
FZFPT	*Freiburger Zeitschrift Für Philosophie und Theologie.*
JEH	*The Journal of Ecclesiastical History.*
JMRS	*The Journal of Medieval and Renaissance Studies.*
JRH	*The Journal of Religious History.*
JTS	*Journal of Theological Studies.*
PL	Patrologia Latina (ed. J.P. Migne. Paris: Vrin, 1844-64).
RB	*Revue Bénédictine*
RMAL	*Revue de Moyen Age Latin.*
RSPT	*Revue des Sciences Philosophiques et Théologiques.*
RTAM	*Récherches de Théologie Ancienne et Mediévale.*
SJT	*Scottish Journal of Theology.*
ST	*Studia Theologica.*
TS	*Theological Studies.*
ZFKT	*Zeitschrift Für Katholische Theologie.*

CHAPTER 1

Introduction and the State of Current Research

Introduction

This study of the immanent person of the Holy Spirit in early twelfth-century thought is in many ways overdue. The third person of the Trinity has been absent from most studies that have looked at the period, or at specific writers, despite the obvious importance of the Spirit in both the theology and spirituality of the time. The intellectual climate created by the arrival of scholasticism, and its clashes with more traditional approaches to study, made the twelfth century formative for future Western theology - Peter Lombard's *Sentences* becoming the theological textbook for the medieval period - and yet the varied teaching on the Holy Spirit at the time has not been carefully studied.

The absence of a deep, systematic study of the period is more surprising given that there was more discussion of the immanent state of the Holy Spirit at this time than there has generally been in the history of pneumatology, which has concentrated for long periods on the economy of the Spirit. The more recent debates that have returned to the issue of immanence both in Western thought, and in renewed relevance to Eastern concepts, deserve a more complete picture of twelfth-century thought than has been presented thus far. Bernard McGinn has written that, "the history of twelfth-century theology of the Holy Spirit remains to be written, but it can be argued that this era was a particularly vibrant one for pneumatology".[1]

This study will, therefore, provide useful material for theological thought in the twelfth century; it will offer a more complete context for the contributions of individual writers; it will show the broad understandings about the Holy Spirit within the different approaches; and it will offer a new perspective for the ongoing discussion about the immanent state of the Holy Spirit. The conclusion that will be reached is that Augustine's "mutual love" theory was not only appropriated, but even extended by strengthening his notions of will, goodness and gift to teach that the Holy Spirit is the communion or fellowship of Father

---

[1] B. McGinn, 'The Role of the Anima Mundi as Mediator between the Divine and Created Realms in the Twelfth Century', in J.J. Collins and M. Fishbane, *Death, Ecstasy, and Other Worldly Journeys* (New York: State of New York Press, 1995), pp.285-316, at p.294.

and Son, and that it is as this that He proceeds.[2]

The Theological Climate

The study of Christianity was transformed by the writings of Anselm of Canterbury and his attempts to investigate God and the truths of Christianity from the standpoint of reason. For the most part, thought had been limited before Anselm to that which had been revealed in scripture and interpreted by the Church Fathers and the councils.[3] The challenge set by Anselm was to use reason to reinforce and supplement what was believed. The authors that will be examined in this study continued with the Christian faith as the basis of their studies, although Peter Abelard and, to a lesser extent, William of Conches were accused of subverting faith to reason. This accusation was undeserved, however, as these two writers continued to be guided by accepted teaching in their theology, albeit with a willingness to push the boundaries of what was received from tradition.[4] The writings of all those studied in this book demonstrate a reliance on that which had gone before.

One consequence of Anselm's approach would be the creation of three separate, influential groups in the first half of the twelfth century. The first of these contained those writers who reacted against the new method, and were wary of anything that seemed to go beyond the teachings of scripture and the Fathers. William of St. Thierry and Bernard of Clairvaux were two of the major figures in this, both belonging to the Cistercian tradition in their thought. The second set consisted of the purer academics, of whom Peter Abelard was the prime example, who, although accepting the authority of previous writings, were not bound by the limits of these works nor by the teachings of any particular school. Peter Lombard also belonged to this group, although he was less prepared to challenge tradition than was Abelard. The third group of writers was engaged in study in one of the early schools that would conglomerate to form universities. The two greatest schools at this time were the Victorines and the Chartrains.

These three attitudes to the study of Christianity provided a fascinating blend of ideas, somewhat radical on either extreme but moderated by the monastic schoolmen. The limited geographical spread of learning at the time allowed knowledge of, and interaction between, the various schools of thought. The impact of these thinkers on each other, and the effect of the combined approach to the Holy Spirit, has been neglected by studies conducted on the

---

[2] Personal pronouns referring to members of the Trinity will be capitalised in this thesis in order to give greater clarity to the reader.

[3] There were some exceptions to this, notably Erigena and Boethius, but these men were not part of a major movement in the church and society of their time as happened in the twelfth century. The twelfth century has thus been termed a 'renaissance' by writers such as Haskins and Brooke: C.H. Haskins, *The Renaissance of the Twelfth Century* (Cambridge, Massachusetts: Harvard University Press, 1927); C. Brooke, *The Twelfth Century Renaissance* (London: Thames and Hudson, 1969).

[4] The supremacy of reason over faith was an accusation aimed at later scholasticism.

writers both individually and collectively.

The Importance of the Holy Spirit

The issue of the personhood of the Holy Spirit was the cause of much debate in the late eleventh and early twelfth centuries between the Western and Eastern churches, as well as within Western theology. While this book concentrates on thought in the West, the discussion with the East will be mentioned both as it helps to clarify the Western position, and also in indicating how this position might comment on the continuing divide between the two churches.

The conflict with Eastern thought was over the addition of the *filioque* to the Nicene Creed, creating dual procession of the Spirit from both Father and Son. This addition had two problems: firstly, it was enacted without the authority of an ecumenical council, which was considered necessary for changes to major points of doctrine; and secondly, the relations within the Trinity were altered, and the monarchy of the Father was called into question. The Eastern Church held that both Son and Spirit proceeded equally, but in different ways, from the Father, who was the source of the godhead. With the reopening of this debate at the Council of Bari, Western theologians were aware in their writings of their need to defend this position on the dual procession. They not only did this, but also sought at times to reach out to persuade the Greeks of the legitimacy of this teaching.

The Western position on the Holy Spirit had been largely defined by Augustine, who had not only put forward clear teaching on the dual procession of the Spirit that led to the adoption of *filioque*, but also used analogies for the Trinity that associated terms such as love, will, gift and communion with the third person. It is not clear to what extent Augustine thought that these terms represented the Spirit in His immanent state and could be transferred directly from the analogies. What is clear is that the concept of the Holy Spirit as love took root in Western thought, particularly based on Romans 5:5: "God has poured out His love into our hearts by the Holy Spirit".

Despite this acceptance, the concept of attributes of divinity being ascribed to one of the Trinitarian persons has not been unquestioned in the West. There have been two main objections: the first stems from Greek, and this largely Platonic, thought that God was the highest Good, and that the divine persons must each in themselves be the highest Good, with all the attributes of power, wisdom, love and goodness that can be associated with this idea. This raised objections against the thought that one person could be considered as particularly one element of overall divinity. The second objection has come from Boethius' definition of a person as "an individual substance of a rational nature".[5] Although this has not been generally seen as applicable to a Trinitarian person, the idea that a person is something more substantial than a

---

[5] Boethius, *Contra Eutychen* 3 in H. Stewart, E. Rand and S. Tester's *Boethius: The Theological Tractates* (Cambridge, Massachusetts: Harvard University Press, 1978), p.85.

force between two other persons does result from the Latin terminology, although it does not necessarily arise from the Greek *hypostasis* adopted for the Nicene Creed.

These problems greatly affected some twelfth-century thinkers (such as Gilbert of Poitiers), who refused to discuss the persons as separate entities and who are therefore omitted from this study. The question of attributes will be discussed at length throughout this book. That of personhood in Boethian terms will not be addressed in the main book, but the conclusions reached from twelfth-century writings will indicate that within the Trinity, concepts of "person" need not be bound by notions drawn from human existence, particularly since each member of the Trinity is essentially spirit.

The Focus of the Book

It would be a large task to provide a summary of all teaching on the Holy Spirit in the period from Anselm of Canterbury to Peter Lombard. It has therefore been necessary to set boundaries for the subject to be studied in order to allow suitable depth of study in the given area whilst retaining a topic of profundity as a contribution to thought on both the Holy Spirit and the twelfth century.

The focus of this research will be the immanent state of the Holy Spirit, rather than His economy. There are a number of reasons for this choice. Firstly, it is the initial concentration of the authors being studied, whose works begin with the Trinity, and the Spirit's position and relations within the godhead, before they proceed to examine and reflect on His mission in the world. The questions raised by Augustine's terminology in the new climate of discussion, and by the debate with the Greeks over the processional model, caused a greater focus on the issue of the intra-Trinitarian relations of the Holy Spirit than has been the case for most periods in history. This decision to focus on the immanent has meant that some major twelfth-century writers, such as Rupert of Deutz and Hildegard of Bingen, have been excluded from the study because of their writings' devotion to the economy of the Spirit.

The second reason for the focus of this study is to provide a balance to the amount of thought that has gone into examining the temporal role of the Holy Spirit, both in studies of the twelfth century, and in modern thought, often without reference to concepts of the immanence of the Spirit. It would seem that discussions on the economic role of the Holy Spirit would be helped if there were clearer ideas about His place within the godhead and the means and mode of His procession. There will certainly be clarifications for twelfth-century thought in this examination; the conclusions reached here should also impact the wider chronological understanding of the person and work of the Holy Spirit.

A third point that needs to be made about the balance of this work is that, although the concentration will be on the immanence of the Spirit, this will not, indeed cannot, be done to the exclusion of His economy. The Scriptural record, from which both the Church Fathers and twelfth-century writers drew their thoughts on the person of the Holy Spirit, has little to say explicitly about the eternal relations within the godhead. Any discussion of this issue must therefore gain lessons from teachings about the mission of the Spirit, which is the focus of most of the biblical writings. It is true that the twelfth century saw the beginnings of rational enquiry beyond the bounds of scripture, with Anselm's ontological argument and Abelard's quest for Trinitarian understanding in the philosophers. However, these explorations were not undertaken apart from scripture, but retained the Bible's teachings as a basis for knowledge. This study will therefore include the writings of the authors studied on the economy of the Holy Spirit, but only as they impact their views on His immanence.

The Writers

There are two sets of men whose work will be studied in this book: those whose writings are of such breadth and depth concerning the person of the Holy Spirit that they are indispensable for this study, who break down into the three groups outlined above; and those who warrant inclusion because of the importance of their teaching on the Spirit, although these passages are fewer because of the extent or the focus of their work. Included in the latter group are William of Conches, who was influential in the debate on the Holy Spirit as World Soul, but whose writings have not survived in great quantity; and men like Robert Pullen, Robert Melun and Walter of Mortagne whose more copious works do not contain large, influential sections on the immanent person of the Holy Spirit.

The major writers begin with Anselm of Canterbury and Anselm of Havelberg. Both of these were heavily involved in the dispute with the Greeks over the procession of the Holy Spirit: Anselm of Canterbury at the Council of Bari in 1096, and Anselm of Havelberg in discussion with Archbishop Nicetas in 1136. In addition, Anselm of Canterbury is significant as the father of scholasticism, seeking to use reason in addition to faith to search out the Trinity without referring to scripture.

Peter Abelard was certainly the most controversial writer of the twelfth century, and used reason in his theology beyond any of his medieval peers or predecessors. He was a radical thinker seeking to stretch the human mind to its utmost in searching out the godhead. Peter Lombard was a later academic with Abelard's thoroughness, but without some of Abelard's brilliance and much of his radical thoughts. Lombard's *Sentences* constituted the most complete theological document of the time, a fact shown by later generations' study of it. The greatest difference between Abelard and Lombard was the latter's respect for the authority of the Fathers that Abelard had seemed to question in his *Sic et Non*. Hill describes the development of scholasticism by Abelard and Lombard as follows:

> The scholastic movement was well and truly launched at the beginning of the twelfth century by two Peters, Peter Abelard and Peter Lombard. They had their precursors to be sure, notably St Anselm of Canterbury. But he, like Peter Abelard's great contemporary and adversary, St Bernard of Clairvaux, was still firmly in the older literary and rhetorical tradition of the Fathers. The two Peters,

by contrast, were professional academics through and through.[6]

On the opposite side of the methodological divide from Peter Abelard were the Cistercians. The two greatest writers on the Holy Spirit in this camp were William of St. Thierry and Bernard of Clairvaux. The Holy Spirit can be one of few areas where Bernard was not the most significant Cistercian voice, but his work does support the positions taken by his friend. William's position as a Cistercian could be questioned given that he was initiated, and spent much of his life, as a Benedictine; but the tenor of his works show the desire that he expressed in life to be considered a Cistercian, which ultimately he became in every way. The Cistercians were devoted to the witness of faith found in the Bible and the Fathers, particularly Augustine, and expressed concern whenever a teaching seemed to depart from these bases. Their writings are more "spiritual" than "academic", but contain profound theological insight nonetheless, and are a very significant contribution to overall thought on the Holy Spirit in this period.

In-between these two groups are the monastic schoolmen, of whom the Victorines were the most important for their views on the immanent Holy Spirit. Of these, Richard is the most varied, original and noteworthy writer, taking and extending the thoughts of his predecessor, Hugh. The school at Chartres was highly Platonic in its thought, with the result that there was less teaching on the individual, immanent persons of the Trinity. However, Thierry of Chartres and William of Conches were two writers who did include some interesting perspectives on the Holy Spirit, and these sections will be addressed in relevant parts of the book.

The Structure of the Book
In order to retain clarity amidst the complexities of debate and depth of thought, it has been decided to divide the book into two major sections. After an analysis of the state of current research, which will form part of this introduction, the most important writers will be studied in turn to show the various pictures that are built up of the Holy Spirit in their writings. Some of these - the two Anselms, the Cistercians and the Victorines - will include two writers in the same section either because, in the Anselms' case, they directly relate to each other on a single issue, or because two writers reflect the same position on the personhood of the Holy Spirit. In this way, individual positions will be shown in their entirety to inform the second part of the book.

This will examine the person of the Holy Spirit from a thematic perspective over all the writers. There are many attributes or names that are used to refer to the Holy Spirit: love, goodness, will, gift and communion. Each of these will be examined in all areas of writing in the period to build up a comprehensive

---

[6] E. Hill, *The Mystery of the Trinity* (London: Geoffrey Chapman, 1985), p.148.

picture of the Holy Spirit in twelfth-century thought. These will be brought together in the chapter on the processional model of the Holy Spirit, which can be created from the ideas expressed. The two separate sections are necessary to present comprehensible and complete pictures of the thoughts of each of the writers, and to allow a thorough examination of thought over all of the writings, without this confusing individual messages.

This structure should provide clarity in the picture of the Holy Spirit both in each author's work in comparison with the others, and from a wider twelfth-century perspective. It will then be possible to conclude what was thought on the Holy Spirit at this time, as well as suggesting how this position might impact the broader debate about the immanent state of the Spirit.

The Twelfth Century in the Context of Previous Western Thought on the Holy Spirit

One point needs to be clarified on references to thought on the Holy Spirit outside the period under study. The dependence of twelfth-century authors on the teaching and work of Augustine has already been noted. However, because the writers did not simply repeat Augustine's ideas, but worked with and developed them in the new philosophical climate, there will not be a definition of Augustine's overall pneumatology at the beginning of this study. Each of the terms applied to the Holy Spirit had some basis in the work of Augustine,[7] but all of them received new insight in this period.

In order to facilitate clarity on each point, Augustine's views on individual themes will form brief introductions to each of the chapters in the second half of this book. In this way, it is easier to assess how the writers of the twelfth century engaged with, and expanded upon, the legacy of Augustine.

The State of Current Research

This review of works which deal, or should deal, with the person of the Holy Spirit in the twelfth century will be split into four sections: those written about the twelfth century or medieval thought in general; surveys of ideas about the Holy Spirit in history; studies of the writings of authors who will be examined in the book; and finally works which deal specifically with one theme or issue concerning the Spirit in this period.

Works on Medieval Thought

The most disappointing books for the current study are those that purport to write on the Holy Spirit at this time, and yet do little or no justice to the discussions of the twelfth century about the intra-Trinitarian position and

---

[7] Indeed, all but 'World Soul' (which will only be dealt with in the first part of the thesis) are words applied directly by Augustine to the Holy Spirit on at least one occasion. Goodness, however, does not receive any significant teaching by Augustine.

relationships of the Spirit. This is perhaps more understandable with an article on "The Lord, the Giver of Life",[8] although the subtitle is rather bold in declaring it a reflection on the "Theology of the Holy Spirit". This study deals with the work of Rupert of Deutz and Hildegard of Bingen, whose concentration on the economy, rather than the immanence, of the Spirit has been noted above. Stanley Burgess also emphasises the work of the Spirit, although he does mention something of the basis for this in summarising the writing of Abelard, Richard and Bernard.[9] Burgess, Rusch and Watkin-Jones all try to cram too much study into insufficient pages (Rusch devoting less than three pages to Anselm, Abelard, Bernard, Richard and Peter Lombard), but the last is at least helpful and balanced in his structure.[10] Wolfram von den Steinen's work entitled *Vom Heiligen Geist des Mittelalters* might lead one to expect some analysis of the person of the Holy Spirit, but he does not discuss either Anselm or Bernard's concept of the Spirit in depth, but simply shows that the Holy Spirit was inspirational in their work:[11] "Ich nenne das Werk "Vom heiligen Geist des Mittelalters" ... weil Anselm und Bernhard für sich allein genug von diesem Geist zu geben vermögen".[12]

One exception to this trend is Dennis Ngien's study of the *filioque* clause in medieval theology.[13] Ngien concentrates on the procession of the Holy Spirit, around which the *filioque* debate revolves, but also shows how western writers used the identity of the Spirit in His immanent and economic states to support their ideas. There is some discussion in this book of the use of Augustine's concepts of gift, love and communion, which relates to this book,[14] and this book also summarises the teaching of Anselm of Canterbury and Richard of St. Victor regarding the issue of dual procession.

The lack of serious study of the person of the Holy Spirit in more general books on the history, philosophy or even theology of the middle ages is less surprising given the multitude of issues and the breadth and depth of thought to

---

[8] W. Zemler-Cizewski, '"The Lord, the Giver of Life:" A Reflection on the Theology of the Holy Spirit in the Twelfth Century', *Anglican Theological Review* 83:3 (2001), pp.547-56.

[9] S. Burgess, *The Holy Spirit: Medieval Roman Catholic and Reformation Traditions* (Peabody, Massachusetts: Hendrickson, 1997), pp.41-69.

[10] W.G. Rusch, 'The Doctrine of the Holy Spirit in the Patristic and Medieval Church', in P.D. Opsahl, *The Holy Spirit in the Life of the Church: From Biblical Times to the Present* (Minneapolis: Augsburg, 1978), pp.66-98, at pp.87-90; H. Watkin-Jones, *The Holy Spirit in the Medieval Church: A Study of Christian Teaching Concerning the Holy Spirit and His Place in the Trinity from the Post-Patristic Age to the Counter-Reformation* (London: Epworth Press, 1922), pp.83-96.

[11] W. Von den Steinen, *Vom Heiligen Geist des Mittelalters: Anselm von Canterbury, Bernhard von Clairvaux* (Darmstadt: Wissenschaftliche Buchgesellschaft, 1968).

[12] *Ibid.*, p.7.

[13] D. Ngien, *Apologetic for Filioque in Medieval Theology* (Milton Keynes: Paternoster, 2005).

[14] *Ibid.*, p.13.

choose from in this period. Where the Holy Spirit is dealt with at all in these works, it is normally one aspect relevant to the overall interests that are presented regarding the twelfth century.

The revived use of Platonic thought is one such area that is discussed to some degree in the context of medieval philosophy, enabling comparisons with the more Aristotelian developments of the thirteenth century. The heated discussions between Peter Abelard and William of Conches, on the one hand, and the monastic writers on the other are covered in two works on philosophy in the middle ages, by Luscombe and Gilson.[15] These surveys do not enter into discussions of more theological topics such as the concept of the Holy Spirit as the mutual love of the Father and the Son.

Those who interest themselves more with theology in the medieval period focus on the emergence of the scholastic method in the twelfth century, and the controversies that this created with the more traditional, monastic devotion to the teachings of the Church Fathers, or examine the Trinity in Boethian concepts of personhood. Anselm, Abelard and Bernard are naturally the figures studied, and little discussion reaches the personhood of the Holy Spirit, except brief references to the ways in which Augustinian analogies for the Trinity were used in the new theological climate. Good examples of these approaches are Pranger's work on authority in the middle ages, and the survey of medieval theologians edited by Gillian Evans.[16]

The lack of attention given to thought on the Holy Spirit in studies of the medieval period is unfortunate given, as will later be shown, the importance of this topic for writers in the twelfth century and the developments that were made in this area at the outset of scholasticism.

Works on the Holy Spirit

Research into historical perspectives on the person of the Holy Spirit has been going through a boom period in the last twenty or thirty years, but has left the thoughts of those in the early scholastic period largely untouched. The focus seems to have moved straight from Augustine to Aquinas, without studying those writers who first applied reason to Augustine's teaching to form it into

---

[15] D. Luscombe, 'Peter Abelard', in P. Dronke, *A History of Twelfth Century Western Philosophy* (Cambridge: CUP, 1988), pp.279-307, at p.297; E. Gilson, *A History of Christian Philosophy in the Middle Ages* (London: Sheed and Ward, 1955), pp.162-63.

[16] B. Pranger, 'Patristic Authority between Refusal and Acceptance: Anselm of Canterbury, Peter Abelard and Bernard of Clairvaux', in I. Backus, *The Reception of the Church Fathers in the West: Volume 1* (Leiden: E.J. Brill, 1997), pp.165-93; G.R. Evans (ed.), *The Medieval Theologians: An Introduction to Theology in the Medieval Period* (Oxford: Blackwells, 2001). In the latter work, there is one article by Stiegman on the Cistercians that does engage with thought on the Holy Spirit. E. Stiegman, 'Bernard of Clairvaux, William of St. Thierry, the Victorines', pp.129-55.

scholastic theology, and who formed the basis for Aquinas' thought.[17]

Not only is there this gap in the historical pneumatology, but the teaching of the twelfth century can be influential in one area of modern debate on the Holy Spirit - His procession as the "mutual love" of Father for Son and Son for Father. David Coffey has written a great deal in favour of this theory, drawing from the Bible, Augustine and Aquinas as support.[18] Jürgen Moltmann, among others, has argued against this position on the philosophical grounds that it creates a "Binity", not a Trinity, but he fails to engage with the historical foundations, weakening his position.[19] The conclusions of this book will support Coffey's position, but will extend the idea of the Holy Spirit as love with ideas of goodness, will, gift and ultimately union.

One of the most comprehensive historical surveys on the Holy Spirit is Yves Congar's three-part work, *I Believe in the Holy Spirit*.[20] Congar does engage with Anselm of Canterbury's metaphysical application of Augustine's Trinitarian analogies as the basis for the medieval western position, but moves too quickly then to Aquinas' position without showing the development of

---

[17] One of Aquinas' most important works was his commentary on Peter Lombard's *Sentences*. Marsh finds roots for Aquinas' thought in the writings of Anselm, Abelard, Lombard and Richard of St. Victor. T. Marsh, *The Triune God. A Biblical, Historical and Theological Study* (Connecticut: Twenty-Third Publications, 1994), p.143.

[18] D. Coffey, 'The Holy Spirit as the Mutual Love of the Father and the Son', *TS* 51.2 (1990), pp.193-229; *Grace: The Gift of the Holy Spirit* (Sydney: Catholic Institute of Sydney, 1979); *Deus Trinitas: The Doctrine of the Triune God* (New York, Oxford: OUP, 1999); 'The Roman 'Clarification' of the Doctrine of the Filioque', *International Journal of Systematic Theology* 5:1 (2003), pp.3-21; 'Spirit Christology and the Trinity', in B.E. Hinze and D.L. Dabney, *Advents of the Spirit: An Introduction to the Current Study of Pneumatology* (Milwaukee, Wisconsin: Marquette University Press, 2001), pp.315-38; 'A Proper Mission of the Holy Spirit', *TS* 47.2 (1986), pp.227-50; 'The "Incarnation" of the Holy Spirit in Christ', *TS* 45.3 (1984), pp.466-80.Additional support has been given to this position by the study on biblical data by Von Balthasar (H. Von Balthasar, *Spiritus Creator* (Einsiedeln: Johannes Verlag, 1967), pp.106-22) and in other work on Augustine's position: G. Bray, 'The Filioque Clause in History and Theology', *Tyndale Bulletin* 34 (1983), pp.91-144; J. Burnaby, *Amor Dei: A Study of the Religion of St. Augustine* (London: Hodder and Stoughton, 1938), especially pp.173-77.

[19] J. Moltmann, 'The Trinitarian Personhood of the Holy Spirit', in B.E. Hinze and D.L. Dabney, *Advents of the Spirit: An Introduction to the Current Study of Pneumatology* (Milwaukee, Wisconsin: Marquette University Press, 2001), pp.302-14. Karl Rahner is another theologian whose Trinitarian thought conflicts with Coffey's position because Rahner does not allow for major distinctions in the invisible Trinity, focusing instead on their economic functions. K. Rahner, *The Trinity* (tr. J. Donceel. Tunbridge Wells, Kent: Burns and Oates, 1986).There has been a novel procession formula proposed by Weinandy (T. Weinandy, *The Father's Spirit of Sonship: Reconceiving the Trinity* (Edinburgh: T & T Clark, 1995)) in which the Son proceeds from the Father and the Holy Spirit, but the attempts to support this from Aquinas are weak, and there is little other basis for the theory in historical theology.

[20] Y. Congar, *I Believe in the Holy Spirit* (tr. D. Smith. New York: Seabury Press, 1983), Vol.1, pp.115-25; Vol.3, pp.79-115.

Anselm's thought in the two or three generations after him. Three other works have similar faults: Mühlen passes to Aquinas without any major study of the depth of twelfth-century ideas; Fortman gets side-tracked on Boethian concepts of personhood, and devotes most of his study of the twelfth century to Gilbert of Poitiers, who largely denies any distinctive personality to the three persons; Heron does note the basics of the position in the twelfth century, but his analysis lacks depth into the complexities of thought and debate.[21] Badcock engages with Richard of St. Victor from the twelfth century regarding the idea that the Holy Spirit is love in God, comparing Richard with Augustine. However, this is only a brief passage in a work that quickly moves onto the Reformation.[22]

The historical survey of the Holy Spirit that perhaps most interacts with the twelfth century is McDonnell's *Other Hand of God*, which, sadly for this study, deals almost exclusively with the economy of the Trinity, when looking at the medieval writers, and does not seriously investigate theories of the immanence of the Spirit. This may contribute to the belief that Richard of St. Victor's "writings on the Trinity are probably the most distinguished Trinitarian contribution between Augustine and the time of Bonaventure and Thomas Aquinas", ignoring the influence of Anselm, Abelard and Hugh on the Victorine.[23] In light of the omission of a wider study of the person of the Holy Spirit, the attempt to construct a "theology of the Holy Spirit" seems misguided. These surveys of historical thought on the Holy Spirit would seem to suggest a lack of substantial or influential thought in the twelfth century, which this book will show to be incorrect.

Studies of Individual Authors

One book which perhaps sums up the attitude of scholars to the Holy Spirit at this time is Gillian Evans' *Anselm and Talking About God*.[24] This supposedly goes through Anselm of Canterbury's works piece by piece drawing out what is said about the godhead, and is reasonable in its assessments. What is remarkable is that there is no chapter devoted to Anselm's *De Processione*

---

[21] H. Mühlen, *Der Heilige Geist Als Person: Beitrag zur Frage nach der dem Heiligen Geiste Eigentümlichen Funktion in der Trinität, bei der Inkarnation und im Gnadenbund* (Munster: Aschendorffsche Verlagsbuchhandlung, 1963); E.J. Fortman, *The Triune God: A Historical Study of the Trinity* (London: Hutchinson, 1972); A. Heron, *The Holy Spirit: The Holy Spirit in the Bible in the History of Christian Thought and in Recent Theology* (Philadelphia: Westminster, 1983), pp.90-94.

[22] G. Badcock, *Light of Truth and Fire of Love: A Theology of the Holy Spirit* (Grand Rapids: Eerdmans, 1997), pp.246-49.

[23] K. McDonnell, *The Other Hand of God: The Holy Spirit as the Universal Touch and Goal* (Collegeville, Minnesota: Liturgical Press, 2003), p.26. McDonnell does have some teaching on the Cistercians' concept of unity regarding experience of the divine, but the focus here remains on the economy of the Spirit.

[24] G. Evans, *Anselm and Talking About God* (Oxford: OUP, 1979).

Spiritus Sancti, which is only ever mentioned in passing.[25] That one of Anselm's major works, with such a clear reference to God in the title, should be overlooked is surprising, but also evidence of the status of the Holy Spirit in historical thought concerning the twelfth century.

The major focus in studies on Anselm has been the ontological argument, particularly since Kant's refutation of it. With interest also aroused by the "fides quaerens intellectum" approach, and the resulting soteriology of the *Cur Deus Homo*, there has not been much serious study of Anselm's pneumatology.[26] The Holy Spirit only really appears in Anselmian studies in the context of Trinitarian relationships or imagery, which are both addressed in the *Monologion* and *Proslogion*, although there is significant relational teaching in the *De Processione*.[27]

The potential importance of the *De Processione* for Trinitarian relations is highlighted by Bertold's article on the *filioque* controversy, but this study falls too quickly into summaries of Anselm's argument without instructive commentary.[28] The relationship significance is also picked up in Deme's study of christology in Anselm, and in Gemeinhardt's examination of the *Filioque*;[29] the latter raises problems with the rational constructions of Anselm. In Gemeinhardt's view, the reliance of Anselm on logical arguments detracts from the relational models that are produced. Alistair Heron has written a very interesting article regarding Anselm's *De Processione* from the perspective of a Greek reader, which highlights some of the problems inherent in Anselm's work.[30] These faults differ from those found by the same writer in Augustine's theory of dual procession.[31] Dennis Ngien presents a more unified picture of the *filioque* theory from the writings of Anselm.[32] Importantly, Ngien provides an analysis of the positions taken by Anselm in his various works, and yet he does not stress the differences which will later be shown between the logically-based *De Processione* and the more rounded presentation of the Holy Spirit in the

---

[25] *Ibid.*, pp.10, 54, 109, 195, 196, 197.

[26] An excellent example of this is Hopkins' thorough study, *A Companion to the Study of Anselm* (Minneapolis, Minnesota: University of Minnesota Press, 1972), which never gets beyond theories of divine personhood to the person of the Holy Spirit in particular.

[27] This will be discussed in the chapter on Anselm's contribution to twelfth-century pneumatology.

[28] G.C. Bertold, 'Saint Anselm and the *Filioque*', in G.C. Bertold, *Faith Seeking Understanding: Learning and the Catholic Tradition* (Manchester, New Hampshire: Saint Anselm Press, 1991), pp.227-34.

[29] D. Deme, *The Christology of Anselm of Canterbury* (Aldershot: Ashgate, 2003), pp.121-48; P. Gemeinhardt, *Die Filioque-Kontroverse zwischen Ost- und Westkirche im Frühmittelalter* (Berlin: Walter de Gruyter, 2002), pp.463-64.

[30] A. Heron 'Anselm and the *Filioque*: A Responsio pro Graecis', *Anselm Studies* I (Milwood, New York: Kraus International, 1983), pp.259-64.

[31] A. Heron, '"Who proceedeth from the Father and the Son": the problem of the Filioque', *SJT* 24.2 (1971), pp.149-66.

[32] Ngien, *Apologetic for Filioque*, pp.23-50.

Monologion.

Gillian Evans is the most important recent scholar to have analysed Anselm's works and, despite the omission in *Anselm and Talking About God,* she does bring out some of Anselm's teaching on the Holy Spirit, always within a Trinitarian context. The relations with Father and Son are examined in *Anselm* and in *Anselm and a New Generation*; the latter work also deals with the images that Anselm used for the Trinity, which are further examined in 'St. Anselm's Images'.[33] Included in this is a comparison of Anselm's use of the watercourse image as a processional model with the teaching on this given by Anselm of Havelberg. This was crucial to both writers' understanding of the dual procession of the Holy Spirit, and Evans does not include any serious reflection on the implications of Anselm of Canterbury's writings for the immanent person of the Holy Spirit.

The richness and complexity of Peter Abelard's thought has meant that general studies of the man and his work have not always addressed the major issues concerning the Holy Spirit, although the two most significant, on the World Soul and a trinity of power, wisdom and goodness, had enough impact on Abelard's life that they are normally at least mentioned. Study of Abelard is not helped by the fact that so little of his major work has been translated from the original, although the first *Theologia* has now been translated into German.[34]

It is interesting that two of the best studies of Abelard's philosophy, by Luscombe and Marenbon, deal more with the areas affecting the Holy Spirit than does the comprehensive life study by M.T. Clanchy.[35] This is not surprising in the case of the teaching on the World Soul, with the implications for continuing Platonic thought in the twelfth century, but is more significant in picking up on Abelard's trinity of power, wisdom and goodness which he saw revealed in scripture and creation. Sikes' earlier study on Abelard is a good survey of both life and thought that does include some discussion of these issues, in contrast to Clanchy.[36] Grane includes in his study of the man and his philosophy an assessment both of Abelard's analogy of a bronze seal, as well as something of his teaching on the Holy Spirit as love, which is largely overlooked in Abelard's writing.[37]

---

[33] G. Evans, *Anselm* (London: Geoffrey Chapman, 1987); *Anselm and a New Generation* (Oxford: OUP, 1980); 'St. Anselm's Analogies', *Vivarium* 14 (1976), pp.81-93.

[34] Peter Abelard, *Theologia Summi Boni: Tractatus de unitate et trinitate divina* (tr. U. Niggli. Hamburg: Felix Meiner Verlag, 1997).

[35] D. Luscombe, *The School of Peter Abelard: The Influence of Abelard's Thought in the Early Scholastic Period* (Cambridge: CUP, 1969), pp.103-42; 'Peter Abelard', in P. Dronke, *A History of Twelfth-Century Western Philosophy* (Cambridge: CUP, 1988), pp.279-307; J. Marenbon, *The Philosophy of Peter Abelard* (Cambridge: CUP, 1999), pp.233-50; M.T. Clanchy, *Abelard: A Medieval Life* (Oxford: Blackwells, 1999).

[36] J. Sikes, *Peter Abailard* (Cambridge: CUP, 1932), pp.61-75.

[37] L. Grane, *Peter Abelard: Philosophy and Christianity in the Middle Ages* (London: George Allen and Unwin, 1970), pp.92-100.

Constant Mews has done a great deal of work to iron out the complexities of the various extant copies of Abelard's work, as well as the confusion over the charges that were made against Abelard at Soissons.[38] This has made an examination of what Abelard, rather than his school, actually taught on various issues of theology more manageable, although Mews himself has not written much on the Holy Spirit beyond a few comments in his re-examination of the latter two *Theologia*.[39]

One study that contains a good empathy for Abelard's thought on the Spirit is Weingart's examination of soteriology.[40] This not only shows Abelard's link between goodness and love that is at the root of his Trinitarian nomenclature, which is not noted by many in the debate on this issue, but also conveys the balance that Abelard sought to communicate in his writings on the philosophers. Weingart shows the number of "pagan" writers that Abelard cites to support his case, and states that Abelard did not see their witness as conclusive evidence.[41] This is backed up by Abelard's statement that revelation, even to Biblical writers, was only partially understood, and that philosophers must also have been limited in their comprehension, even of what they themselves were writing.

Brower's study of the Trinity in Abelard is generally disappointing in its depth, merely contextualising Abelard's thought which extended the traditional distinctive attributes concerning procession into differences in definition or property.[42] Brower seems to take Chartrain thinking rather than Augustine's more developed thought as the "traditional" position, as the distinctions stated are those of begetter, begotten, proceeding.[43] Abelard went far beyond these in differentiating the Trinitarian persons, expanding even on the attributes that Augustine had applied to the persons.

Despite the disputes with William of St. Thierry and Bernard of Clairvaux

---

[38] C.J. Mews, *The Development of the Theologia of Peter Abelard* (Oxford: DPhil Thesis, 1980); 'The List of Heresies Imputed to Peter Abelard', *RB* 95 (1981), pp.73-110; 'On Dating the Works of Peter Abelard', *AHDLMA* 52 (1985), pp.73-134; 'Peter Abelard's (*Theologia Christiana*) and (*Theologia 'Scholarium'*) re-examined', *RTAM* 52 (1985), pp.109-58; 'The *Sententiae* of Peter Abelard', *RTAM* 53 (1986), pp.130-84; 'In Search of a Name and Its Significance: A Twelfth-Century Anecdote about Thierry and Peter Abaelard', *Traditio* XLIV (1988), pp.171-200; 'A neglected gloss on the *Isagogue* by Peter Abelard', *FZFPT* 31 (1984), pp.35-55.

[39] Mews, 'Peter Abelard's (*Theologia Christiana*) and (*Theologia 'Scholarium'*) re-examined', pp.84-85.

[40] R. Weingart, *The Logic of Divine Love: A Critical Analysis of the Soteriology of Peter Abailard* (Oxford: OUP, 1970).

[41] Weingart, *The Logic of Divine Love*, p.15.

[42] J.E. Brower, 'Trinity', in J.E. Brower and K. Guilfoy, *The Cambridge Companion to Abelard* (Cambridge, CUP, 2004), pp.223-57, at p.224.

[43] This is not meant to imply that Augustine did not use these terms. However, Augustine did not limit his processional understanding to these ideas, but extended them in his use of attributes which the school at Chartres did not include as a major part of their understanding of the procession of the Trinitarian persons.

that Abelard began with his developments of the personal attributes of the divine persons, he was not the first to move beyond the processional model for understanding the persons. This had not only been done by Augustine, but had become common since the time of Anselm. Buytaert undertakes an interesting study of the Trinity in the three *Theologiae*, but is rather confused in his assessment of the *Summi Boni*, first stating that the doctrine contained therein is only economical, before stating that the eternal properties of the persons are considered.[44]

The interest raised by Abelard's life and the controversies that were caused by some of his teachings have meant that, although there is little available in translation, there have been many studies undertaken. This goes against David Bell's rule that "it is a well known fact that the number of post-graduate dissertations dealing with any author increases in direct proportion to the degree in which that author appears in translation".[45] Peter Lombard, although his work aroused as much interest at the time, and far more in the centuries afterwards with the copious number of commentaries, has suffered more from the lack of translation of his *Sentences*, which is perhaps better known from studies on the commentaries made on them by Aquinas and others than for its own merits.

That said, there have been two major recent studies on Lombard that may, in conjunction with the translation being undertaken by the Franciscan Archive, provide the stimulus for more work in the future.[46] The most comprehensive appraisal of Peter Lombard has been written by Marcia Colish, who undertakes a systematic assessment of Lombard's contribution to twelfth-century thought in her two-volume work, comparing at each point the relevance of the Lombard's teaching to other major thinkers of the period.[47] This is a very helpful approach, but is hindered by the omission of Anselm, the Cistercians, and Richard of St. Victor from the discussion. As this present study will show, these writers are crucial to an overall understanding of thought on the Holy Spirit in the period. Colish's attention is clearly elsewhere, however, as the large amounts devoted to the person of the Spirit in the *Sentences*, noted even in the brief study on the Lombard in the *Dictionnaire de Théologie Catholique*,[48] is directly addressed in only ten pages of Colish's study.[49]

The second, more recent study, on Peter Lombard also fails to draw out the

---

[44] E.M. Buytaert, 'Abelard's Trinitarian Doctrine', in E.M. Buytaert, *Peter Abelard: Proceedings of the International Conference Louvain May 10-12, 1971* (Leuven: Leuven University Press, 1974), pp.127-52, at pp.129, 133-34.

[45] D.N. Bell, *The Image and Likeness: The Augustinian Spirituality of William of St. Thierry* (Kalamazoo: Cistercian Publications, 1984), p.13.

[46] This translation is available online at: http://www.franciscan-archive.org/lombardus/index.html#writings.

[47] M. Colish, *Peter Lombard: Volumes 1 & 2* (Leiden: E.J. Brill, 1994).

[48] "La théologie du Saint-Esprit, très developpée dans le *Livre des Sentences*" in the article on Peter Lombard by J. de Ghellinck in *DTC* 12(2):1941-2019.

[49] Colish, *Peter Lombard* 1, pp.253-63.

significance of the teaching on the Holy Spirit. Despite noting that there is an "exceptionally long and rich pneumatology" covering thirty-eight chapters of the *Sentences*, Philipp Rosemann devotes only five pages to his analysis of this subject.[50] Rosemann is useful in understanding Lombard's concept of the Holy Spirit as love, but does not enter into the power, wisdom, goodness debate, which receives a large portion of Colish's work.

Two other studies also merit mention for their work on Lombard's concept of love, and particularly the phrase, "Quod Spiritus sanctus est caritas, qua diligimus Deus et proximum", which Schupp notes is "Die berühmte Sonderlehre" of Lombard.[51] Schupp's study on grace in Lombard has an excellent section on the understanding of the Holy Spirit, and relates this teaching to that found in Anselm, William of St. Thierry and Hugh of St. Victor - the very sources not included in Colish. The other writer who examines Lombard's view of love is Saarinen, who provides a comparison with the teaching of Martin Luther.[52] It is interesting to note that Rosemann, Schupp and Saarinen all disagree with Marcia Colish on this issue of the Holy Spirit as love, as will later be shown.

The writings of the Cistercians, and particularly those of William of St. Thierry, have received most attention from secondary commentators concerning their thoughts on the person of the Holy Spirit in this period. This is because of the mystical and experiential nature of much of their writings, although William is equally concerned with establishing a correct view of the immanence of the Spirit for his pneumatology and for the church,[53] as was shown in the accusations against the teaching of Peter Abelard and William of Conches. This strength of William is not always reflected in studies of his work, which normally focus on his teaching of the experience of the Spirit, but it is impossible to review William's thought without including something of his foundational concepts of the Spirit's person.

One outstanding study of William's pneumatology is David Bell's *The Image and Likeness*.[54] The "image" and "likeness" of the title refer to the work of the Spirit in restoring these features in man to their original, created state, and thus the thrust of the work is about man's relationship to God; this does not prevent Bell from engaging fully with William's concept of the Spirit's role

---

[50] P. Rosemann, *Peter Lombard* (Oxford: OUP, 2004), pp.85-90.

[51] J. Schupp, *Die Gnadenlehre des Petrus Lombardus* (Freiburg im Breslau: Herder, 1932), pp.216-30.

[52] R. Saarinen, 'Ipsa Dilectio Deus Est: Zur Wirkungsgeschichte von 1. Sent. dist. 17 des Petrus Lombardus bei Martin Luther' in *Thesaurus Lutheri: Auf der Suche nach neuen Paradigmen de Luther-Forschung* (Helsinki: Vammalan Kirjapaino Oy, 1987), pp.185-204.

[53] Renna notes the reliance of the early Cistercians on the writings of Augustine in his article 'Augustine and the Early Cistercians', in F. Van Fleteren, J. Schnaubelt and J. Reino, *Augustine: mystic and mystagogue* (New York: Peter Lang, 1994), pp.379-400, at p.382.

[54] Bell, *The Image and Likeness*, especially pp.89-124.

within the godhead, from which he draws out the operation of the Spirit in man. Bell helpfully compares his own view with that of M.-M. Davy, who seeks to weaken William's concept of the Spirit as love;[55] Bell shows that William is clear in his teaching, and that this idea is central to an understanding of the temporal mission of the Spirit.

Another scholar who has drawn out the overall importance of William's pneumatology is Odo Brooke, who has written about the Holy Spirit as union and has discussed the controversial "amor intellectus est" passage, as Bell also does.[56] Brooke shows the struggle in dealing with William's writing in his article on 'Speculative Development', as he shows the paradox in William's denunciation of Abelard's terminology in the context of his own thought on the Spirit as love and union.[57] Sadly, the article does not note the different positions taken by William in the separate parts of his works.

Verdeyen's examination of William's mystical theology combines the different teachings of William in one work, summarising the position on the persons as that of unity in nature, "alterité" in person.[58] Verdeyen realises the importance of the immanent nature of the Spirit for William, despite his concentration in this book on the temporal mission. He compares William with Bernard in this aspect of his pneumatology: "Plus que l'abbé de Clairvaux, Guillaume s'interesse aux conditions et a la structure théologique de la rencontre humano-divine."[59] *The Mystical Theology* is clear in summarising the relationship for William between the immanent and the economic position of the Holy Spirit: "Dans la Trinité, le Saint-Esprit *est* la charité et l'unité mutuelle des Personnes; en nous, il *fait* ou il *realise* la même charité et unité d'Esprit".[60]

The book on William's life and work by Dechanet concentrates naturally more on those parts of his thought which most profoundly affected his public life, which teach the inseparability of the three persons under any aspect whatsoever.[61] Only rarely does Dechanet indicate that William distinguishes between the persons on the basis of attributes, and the former does not discuss in these sections the relevance of this fact to the main focus of the book, with the result that an incomplete picture of William's pneumatology is presented.

---

[55] M.-M. Davy, *Théologie et Mystique de Guillaume de Saint-Thierry* (Paris: J. Vrin, 1954), p.162.
[56] O. Brooke, 'The Trinitarian Aspect of the Ascent of the Soul to God in the Theology of William of St. Theirry', *RTAM* 26 (1959), pp.85-127; Bell, *Image and Likeness*, pp. 217-49.
[57] O. Brooke, 'The Speculative Development of the Trinitarian Theology of William of St. Thierry in the *Aenigma fidei*', *RTAM* 27-28 (1960-1), pp.193-211, 26-58.
[58] P. Verdeyen, *La Théologie Mystique de Guillaume de Saint-Thierry* (Paris: FAC-editions, 1990), pp.54-58.
[59] *Ibid.*, p.43.
[60] *Ibid.*, p.93 (Verdeyen's italics).
[61] J.M. Dechanet, *William of St Thierry: The Man and his Work.* (Spencer, Massachusetts: Cistercian Publications, 1972).

There are three studies that are helpful in showing the relative position of the Cistercians, and particularly Bernard of Clairvaux, to the theological climate of the twelfth century. The first of these is Butler's work on *Western Mysticism*, and compares the Cistercian approach to that of the Victorines.[62] Butler indicates that Bernard was "pre-scholastic" in his theology, holding onto the approach that had been used at least until the time of Anselm, whereas Richard of St. Victor managed to write a scientific treaty of mystical theology.[63] The second work is Sommerfeldt's article on Bernard and scholasticism, which challenges the accepted position by showing how Bernard was not only in amicable contact with scholastic writers, but actually used the scholastic method himself in some of his works.[64] This shows that, while there was a divide between the Cistercians and some of the leading figures in the scholastic movement, these men cannot be totally divorced from the academic climate that surrounded them. The third study is Bredero's work on Bernard, which briefly compares Bernard's approach to God with that of Abelard.[65] Bredero indicates Abelard's commitment to theology as an intellectual exercise, which Bernard saw as an attack on faith, and therefore on monastic spirituality, which held more tightly to Scripture and the teachings of the Church Fathers.

Two works on Bernard bring out the importance in his work of the concept of the Holy Spirit as love, particularly in his *On Loving God* and the sermons on the Song of Songs. Elizabeth Dreyer concentrates on the latter in her article, which is mostly about the work of the Spirit in the life of the believer, but also draws out the intra-Trinitarian relationships of Father, Son and Holy Spirit.[66] Etienne Gilson draws on Bernard's writing about the Holy Spirit as both love and unity in his study, *Mystical Theology*, which also has useful material on William of St. Thierry.[67] There is some discussion here of the relationship between the Holy Spirit as God's gift of love and the reciprocal love leading to unity from man, but Gilson does not go beyond a presentation of Bernard's writings to make a judgement on an overall position that might be concluded from this.

Study on the work of Richard of St. Victor may have been more harmed than helped by the translation only of book three of his *De Trinitate*.[68] This

---

[62] C. Butler, *Western Mysticism: The teaching of SS. Augustine, Gregory and Bernard on Contemplation and the Contemplative Life* (London, New York: Keegan Paul International, 2000), pp.137-38.

[63] *Ibid.*, pp.125-26.

[64] J. Sommerfeldt, 'Bernard of Clairvaux and Scholasticism' in *Papers of the Michigan Academy of Sciences, Arts and Letters* 48 (1963), pp.265-78.

[65] A.H. Bredero, *Bernard of Clairvaux: Between Cult and History* (Grand Rapids: Eerdmans, 1996), pp.194-200, 219-47.

[66] Dreyer, 'An Advent of the Spirit' in *Advents of the Spirit*, pp.123-62.

[67] E. Gilson, *The Mystical Theology of St. Bernard* (tr. A.C. Downes. Kalamazoo: Cistercian Publications, 1990), pp.60-154.

[68] G.A. Zinn, *Richard of St. Victor: The Twelve Patriarchs, The Mystical Ark, Book Three of the Trinity* (London: SPCK, 1979).

most famous part of Richard's treatise, seeking to provide a proof of the Trinity from the concept of love, has caught the imagination of many studies of the Holy Spirit, and not only of the medieval period.[69] One problem with this is that, although Richard does provide this teaching, it is done in the context of the remainder of the *De Trinitate*, which is founded on concepts of goodness in the immanent Trinity, providing the basis for the argument in book three. Another problem is that the teaching found in this major work is backed up and clarified in many other works, of which only *De quatuor gradibus violentae charitatis* has received any significant comment.[70] The concentration on this aspect of Richard's teaching is not surprising in modern works; that it becomes the major factor in Bligh's assessment of the theology in the *De Trinitate* is unacceptable.[71]

The most thorough study of Richard's overall theology is Nico Den Bok's *Communicating the Most High*, although this could have provided more of a balanced view over the corpus of Richard's work than it does, with its focus on the *De Trinitate*.[72] Den Bok analyses the social trinity that is built up in Richard's work in comparison to the mental trinity found in Augustine, upon which much medieval thought was based. In this, the attributes of goodness and love, as applied to the Holy Spirit, are discussed, but there is more treatment of the nature of the attributes than there is of how these pertain to the relevant persons in the godhead. There is also exploration of the concept of *personae* within the Trinity and Richard's use of this terminology, but this is not related to the issue of attributes. There is thus a lot of informative writing concerning the Trinitarian persons without too much application of the various discussions to build up coherent pictures of the persons themselves.

There has, of course, been more recent scholarship on Augustine than on any of the major twelfth-century writers featured in this book. Given the focus of this work on the later period, it is impossible to survey completely the vast amount that has been written on the work of Augustine. However, it is necessary to refer to those works that are most important in analysing Augustine's thought in relation to the issues that will be dealt with in the main body of this book. Many of the works on Augustine will be referred to in other

---

[69] For example: C. Pinncok, *Flame of Love: A Theology of the Holy Spirit* (Downers Grove: IVP, 1996), pp.33-34; G. McFarlane, *Why Do You Believe What You Believe About the Holy Spirit?* (Carlisle: Paternoster, 1998), pp.88-92.

[70] The edition of the *De Trinitate* used for this thesis is that edited by Jean Ribaillier (Paris: J. Vrin, 1958). His other works can be found in Migne's *Patrologia Latina*, volume 196; references for the *De Trinitate* will also be given for the Migne version. Richard's other important works on the Holy Spirit are: *De tribus appropriatis personis in Trinitate, Quomodo Spiritus Sanctus est amor Patris et Filii, Sermo de missione Spiritus Sancti, De spiritu blasphemiae* and *De gradibus charitatis*.

[71] J. Bligh, 'Richard of St. Victor's *De Trinitate*: Augustinian or Abelardian?', *Heythrop Journal* 1 (1960), pp.118-39.

[72] N. Den Bok, *Communicating the Most High: A Systematic Study of Person and Trinity in the Theology of Richard of St. Victor* (Paris: Brepols, 1996).

sections of this analysis of current research because of their relevance to particular issues. There are other works that merit attention that need to be mentioned here.

One of the most important for this book is Joseph Ratzinger's article which discusses the use of *communio* by Augustine as a concept relevant to the person of the Holy Spirit, especially given the importance of this for twelfth-century writers, and the sparse use that Augustine directly gives to this idea.[73] Ratzinger also discusses Augustine's thought on the Holy Spirit as both love and gift, thus putting his ideas on *communio* into the overall context of Augustine's work.

Mary Clark has also written on Augustine's picture of the Holy Spirit in her book covering his life and work, and in an article in *The Cambridge Companion to Augustine*.[74] It is interesting that when Clark writes about the Trinity in Latin Christianity, she takes Richard of St. Victor as a prime example of this viewpoint, extending Augustine's idea of "mutual love" to the concept of "shared love".[75] This choice is slightly surprising given the different structure of the *De Trinitate* from other theological works of Latin Christianity, as well as some of the unique teachings that it contains.

Two works deserve mention regarding Augustine's use of love in his theology. Arendt's study on *Love and Saint Augustine*, whilst it is a thorough account of thought on the love that people have for each other and God, does not discuss the idea that the Holy Spirit should be thought of particularly as love in the godhead.[76] Canning's study of *The Unity of Love for God and Neighbor* nearly falls into a similar trap, only getting round to discussing the Spirit's identity on page 301.[77] The following pages provide a useful overview of Augustine's teaching on this point that engages with the earlier discussion, but it is surprising that this idea is not more foundational in the book as a whole, reflecting its importance for Augustine.[78]

---

[73] J. Ratzinger, 'The Holy Spirit as Communio: Concerning the Relationship of Pneumatology and Spirituality in Augustine', *Communio* 25 (1998), pp.324-39.

[74] M. Clark, *Augustine* (London: Continuum, 1994), pp.68-72; '*De Trinitate*' in E. Stump and N. Kretzmann, *The Cambridge Companion to Augustine* (Cambridge: CUP, 2001), pp.91-102. The latter work is disappointing for the most part in the number of chapters that deal with the Trinitarian persons in Augustine's work. S. McDonald wrote one chapter on 'The Divine Nature', but this does not focus on the persons of the godhead (*The Cambridge Companion*, pp.71-90).

[75] M. Clark, 'The Trinity in Latin Christianity', in B. McGinn and J. Meyendorff, *Christian Spirituality: Origins to the Twelfth Century* (New York: Crossroad, 1987), pp.276-90, at pp.286-87.

[76] H. Arendt, *Love and Saint Augustine* (Chicago: University of Chicago Press, 1996).

[77] R. Canning, *The Unity of Love for God and Neighbor in St. Augustine* (Louvain: Augustinian Historical Institute, 1993).

[78] In comparison, Studer's short article on Augustine's pneumatology does focus on the Spirit's identity as love, comparing this with the Son being called the Word of God. B. Studer, 'Zur Pneumatologie des Augustinus von Hippo (*De Trinitate* 15, 16, 17-27, 50)', *Augustinianum* 35:2 (1995), pp.567-86, at pp.569-70.

Works on Specific Issues in the Twelfth Century

The Platonic concept of *Anima Mundi*, and its appropriation by Abelard and William of Conches, has received some treatment in secondary literature.[79] Bernard McGinn provides a good background study of the World Soul, particularly in its Platonic understanding, but is rather brief in the use made of this by Abelard, William of Conches and Thierry of Chartres.[80]

The debate between Abelard and William of St. Thierry over this issue has received a lot of attention, partly because William's simplistic rendering of Abelard's case, that Abelard taught that the Holy Spirit is the World Soul (*Quod Spiritus Sanctus sit Anima Mundi*), had such a major impact on Abelard's life. Many scholars have jumped to Abelard's defence, focusing on the use of *Involucrum* as Abelard's protection against William's claim. Earlier scholarship, such as Sikes' study,[81] had not brought this out, but Luscombe, Moonan, Dronke and Ott all seek to clarify Abelard's actual position against that which was claimed against him.[82] There is also an interesting study that informs this debate by Zerbi, which shows the different allegations made by William (of Sabellianism) and Bernard (of Subordinationism).[83]

A second issue that has received some treatment is that of the applicability of the terms power, wisdom and goodness to the Trinitarian persons, although surprisingly this has generally not focused on William's problems with Abelard's terminology. Marcia Colish devotes a large amount of her study of Peter Lombard to this issue;[84] Horst makes some comments about this analogy

---

[79] Tulio Gregory, a major writer on the World Soul, is disappointingly brief in all of his works which might have dealt more fully with twelfth-century thought on this issue: T. Gregory, *Anima Mundi: La Filosofia di Guglielmo di Conches e la Scuola di Chartres* (Firenze: G.C. Sansoni, 1956); 'The Platonic Inheritance', in P. Dronke, *A History of Twelfth-Century Western Philosophy*, pp.54-80; 'Le platonisme du XIIe siècle', *RSPT* 71:2 (1987), pp.243-59.

[80] McGinn, 'The Role of the Anima Mundi', pp.295-300.

[81] Sikes, *Peter Abailard*, pp.67-68. It must be noted in Sikes' defence that he did not believe that Abelard taught equivalence of the Holy Spirit with the World Soul.

[82] Luscombe, *The School of Peter Abelard*, pp.123-27; L. Moonan, 'Abelard's Use of the Timaeus', *AHDLMA* 56 (1986), pp.7-90; P. Dronke, *Fabula: Explorations into the Uses of Myth in Medieval Platonism* (Leiden: E.J. Brill, 1974), pp.55-67; L Ott, 'Die platonische Weltseele in der Theologie der Frühscholastik' in K. Flasch, *Parusia: Studien zur Philosophie Platons und zur Problemgeschichte des Platonismus* (Frankfurt: Minerva, 1965), pp.307-31. This issue will receive extended discussion in the main body of the thesis.

[83] P. Zerbi, 'William of St. Thierry and His Dispute with Peter Abelard', in J. Carfanton, *William, Abbot of St. Thierry: A Colloquium at the Abbey of St. Thierry* (Kalamazoo: Cistercian Publications, 1987), pp.181-203.

[84] Colish, *Peter Lombard 1*, pp.100-31. Other elements of Abelard's language are also discussed in these pages.

in his study of Robert Melun;[85] while Knoch only seriously remarks on this in relation to Hugh of St. Victor.[86] This book will address the issue of the Holy Spirit as goodness as part of the debate that took place in the twelfth century, and will thus attempt to fill in some of the gaps in this area of study.

A final issue that has received some comment in more general study is that of the Holy Spirit as the union of Father and Son. This is linked to the idea of the Spirit as love, which has been shown above to be a part of modern debate in pneumatology. The concept of the Spirit as bond or union is found most clearly in the work of William of St. Thierry, and is dealt with in studies on his work, but is also present in the work of many other writers in the twelfth century. McGinn and Tomasic do not extend their studies of this beyond the Cistercians;[87] Heron, in a wider examination of thought on the Holy Spirit in Christian history, notes the importance of unity more widely in western thought, but particularly in this period.[88]

Conclusion

This review shows both that there has not yet been any comprehensive study of the person of the Holy Spirit in the twelfth century, and that such a study has something to add to concepts of twelfth-century thought as well as modern debates in pneumatology. The richness of debate that took place with the advent of scholasticism, and its clashes with more traditional approaches to Christian study, raised issues about western conceptions of the Spirit that were both grounded in scripture and the Church Fathers' writings, and thoroughly tested by reason and debate.

Study of thought on the Holy Spirit in the twelfth century, when it has been included in works, has been limited: either by concentration on the economy of the Spirit, which was applied from concepts of His immanence by writers in this period; or by focusing on individual authors, or writers from a particular tradition, which need contextualising in light of the alternative positions that were present at the time. No study shows the breadth of thought that existed on the person of the Spirit, or attempts to resolve the different views that were expressed.

It is the purpose of this book to show the relations of the variant authors to

---

[85] U. Horst, *Die Trinitäts- und Gotteslehre des Robert von Melun* (Mainz: Matthias-Grunewald-Verlag, 1964), pp.119-32.

[86] W. Knoch, '"*Deus unus est Trinus*": Beobachtungen zur frühscholastischen Gotteslehre', in M. Bohnke and H. Heinz, *Im Gesprach mit dem Dreieinigen Gott: Elemente Einer Trinitärischen Theologie* (Dusseldorf: Patmos Verlag, 1985), pp.209-30.

[87] B. McGinn, 'Love, Knowledge and Mystical Union in Western Christianity: Twelfth to Sixteenth Centuries', *Church History* 56.1 (1987), pp.7-24; T. Tomasic, 'Neoplatonism and the Mysticism of William of St. Thierry', in P. Szermach, *An Introduction to the Medieval Mystics of Europe* (Albany: State University of New York Press, 1984), pp.53-76.

[88] Heron, *The Holy Spirit*, pp.91-94.

the overall context of twelfth-century pneumatology in order to understand better their individual positions; to draw out the attributes that were applied to the person of the Holy Spirit separately and in relation to each other in order to build up a more complete and cohesive picture of teaching on the Spirit in this period; and to attempt to resolve the seeming differences in approach and content to suggest an overall pneumatology from the twelfth century that can be of use in the current debate on this important theological issue.

CHAPTER 2

Anselm of Canterbury and Anselm of Havelberg

This chapter will examine the thoughts of two Latin scholars who both engaged with the Orthodox church over the issue of the procession of the Holy Spirit and the Western addition of *filioque* to the Nicene Creed, which had contributed to the schism between Rome and Constantinople. Both men taught that dual procession, from Father and Son, was correct because of the intra-Trinitarian identity and relationships of the Holy Spirit. This basis for their arguments will be studied in detail not only to show the relevance to the question of procession, but also for its wider application in the context of this book. The chapter will first examine Anselm of Canterbury's works, showing how he built up a well-defined identity of the immanent person of the Spirit, and then assessing how he adapted this to his presentation of the issue of the *Filioque*; and secondly, there will be a study of Anselm of Havelberg's account of his discussion with Nechites.

The chapter will conclude that although Anselm of Canterbury, in his more varied writings, was able to study the person of the Holy Spirit more closely, he was less successful in integrating this study into his account of the procession; Anselm of Havelberg's ideas are more clearly connected in his presentation to the Greeks, and thus provide a much more convincing case for acceptance of dual procession.

There has been a great deal of interest in Anselm of Canterbury because of his position at the outset of Scholasticism, and the genius that is demonstrated in his writings.[1] He advocated a balanced used of reason in regard to things of faith, exemplified in his "I do not seek to understand so that I may believe; but I

---

[1] Perhaps the best overall treatment of Anselm's life is Richard Southern's *Saint Anselm: A Portrait in a Landscape* (Cambridge: CUP, 1990).

believe so that I may understand";[2] whilst at times he went beyond this to arguments based solely on reason, with "nothing whatsoever to be argued on the basis of the authority of Scripture".[3]

One of Anselm's greatest contributions to theology was his ontological argument for the existence of God, which has been the primary topic of interest in studies on Anselm. This is found in one of Anselm's early works, the *Proslogion*. In this work and its earlier companion, the *Monologion*, are found Anselm's thought not only about the existence of God, the Supreme Good, but also the form that this Supreme must exist in. Anselm, not satisfied in proving that God must exist, seeks to show that there must be three persons in one God and explains the relations and attributes of these three. The depth of teaching on the Trinitarian persons makes the *Monologion* and *Proslogion* foundational documents for understanding Anselm's position on the person of the Holy Spirit.

The other major work of Anselm's that has significant content on the Spirit is the *De Processione Spiritus Sancti*. This was a result of his attendance at the Council of Bari in 1098, where he was asked by the Pope to provide a defence of the Latin position on the procession of the Spirit in the face of Greek opposition. Anselm was sufficiently interested in the issue to write up his thesis and publish it in 1102, around twenty-five years after the *Proslogion*.[4]

This later work is very different in its content on the person of the Holy Spirit compared with Anselm's earlier teachings. The metaphysical appropriation of Augustine's analogies that formed the basis of the attributes ascribed to the Spirit in the *Monologion* is entirely absent from the *De Processione*, which concentrates instead on a relational model of the Trinity. Whilst this in itself is a fascinating insight into Anselm's thoughts on intra-Trinitarian relations, the lack of teaching on the mode of procession greatly weakens the argument of this later work. It is unfortunate that no Greek

---

[2] Anselm of Canterbury, *Proslogion* 1, Vol.1.p.100 in *Opera Omnia* Vols.1-6 (ed. F.S. Schmitt. Edinburgh: Thomas Nelson, 1946-49) and p.87 in B. Davies and G.R. Evans' translation *Anselm of Canterbury: The Major Works* (Oxford: OUP, 1998). From here on in the footnotes, Anselm of Canterbury will be referred to as Anselm C, and Anselm of Havelberg as Anselm H. References to Anselm of Canterbury's work will all come from the Schmitt edition and Davies' and Evans' translation (the latter page numbers will be in brackets). This system will be used even when quotations are given from the translation edition, and will also be applied to other primary sources, where translations are available.

[3] Anselm C, *Monologion*, Prologue, Vol.1, p.7 (p.5). This refers to his proof for the existence of God. The same method was used at times in the *Cur Deus Homo* to show the logical necessity of God becoming man to die for men's salvation. Gillian Evans, when discussing Anselm's methodology, writes that he discussed the Trinity "by pagan principles" (G. Evans, *Anselm and a New Generation*, p.5). For a broad survey of Anselm's approach to theology, see R. Campbell's 'Anselm's Theological Method', *SJT* 32:6 (1979), pp.541-62.

[4] This dating is taken from Evans' and Davies' introduction to Anselm's works, *Anselm of Canterbury*, pp.viii-ix.

response to Anselm survives from which it would be possible to gauge the effectiveness of his presentation.[5]

Anselm of Havelberg was the ambassador of Emperor Lothar in Constantinople. In this role, he conducted a debate with Nechites, one of the twelve *didascali* of the university of Constantinople, about the procession of the Holy Spirit from the Greek and Latin perspectives, which Anselm himself wrote up as part of the work *Dialogi*.[6] This is the only major source for the ideas of Anselm of Havelberg on the person of the Holy Spirit. The views of Anselm of Havelberg, as they are presented in this work, combine the two elements of relationships and attributes of the Spirit in response to the Greek position, in contrast to Anselm of Canterbury's *De Processione*.

Much more is known of Anselm of Canterbury's life, and a greater quantity of work written by him exists today, and this will be reflected in the comparative length of study of the two authors below. Both writers agree in their thoughts on the person of the Holy Spirit, but Anselm of Havelberg displays greater conciseness in bringing together the elements contained more widely in Anselm of Canterbury's works. This is helpful for understanding both the overall identity of the Holy Spirit, and the relation of this to the Greek understanding of the procession.

Anselm of Canterbury

This review of Anselm of Canterbury's teaching on the Holy Spirit will be divided into two sections: the first will deal with the *Monologion* and *Proslogion*, which include Anselm's views on the immanent person of the Spirit in the godhead; the second will examine how Anselm uses these ideas in his defence of the *Filioque* clause in the *De Processione*.

The Monologion and Proslogion

Both of these works consider the godhead from a rational point of view, excluding scriptural authority and the writings of the Church Fathers.[7] The *Monologion* is described in the preface as a meditation "upon the essence of the divine",[8] while the *Proslogion* is a search for "one single argument ... to prove

---

[5] Although we do now have a modern response from the Greek position to the *De Processione* written by Alistair Heron, 'Anselm and the *Filioque*'.

[6] Anselm H, *Dialogi* 2 (PL 185:1163-1210). Naturally, there must be some care taken as this report was written up by one of those involved in the debate. However, the account does appear to be reasonably balanced in its expression of the Greek side, including at one stage a contradiction by Nechites that Anselm was not able to answer (this will be noted in the main text).

[7] Although it should be noted that Pranger believes that, in the *Monologion*, "Anselm offers a theology of the Trinity which is entirely based on Augustine's *De Trinitate*". Pranger, 'Sic et non', p.173.

[8] Anselm C, *Monologion*, Prologue, Vol.1, p.7 (p.5).

that God really exists".⁹ As such both begin with thoughts about the divine essence, before moving on to the existence of persons within the godhead that correspond to Father, Son and Holy Spirit. It is Anselm's belief that not only can the existence and nature of God be rationally comprehended without scripture, but also the Trinity of persons that exists within the godhead.

The *Monologion* makes clear the basis for the discussion about God's existence in its opening chapter, which declares that "of all the things that exist, there is one nature that is supreme".¹⁰ Anselm develops this thought along standard Platonic lines, arguing that everything that has a positive quality (such as justice or goodness) is not this quality in itself, but participates in a greater goodness. This greater good must exist of itself, as "nothing that is good through something other than itself is equal to or greater than that good which is good through itself".¹¹ The logical conclusion that Anselm draws from this is that there must be one supremely great being that exists through itself. Anselm's teaching on God in the *Monologion* is all derived from this understanding of God as the supreme good.

Having taken as his view of God that He is the supreme spirit that contains within itself completeness of every perfection, such as goodness, justice and power, Anselm later rationalises a second person within the godhead who is the Word or wisdom of God by which God expresses himself eternally.¹² Because this Word is God's self-expression, it comes from the very essence of God and so is both coeternal and consubstantial with God. In these thoughts on the Word of God, Anselm establishes a plurality of persons in the godhead, a processional model for creating this, and the concept of relations between these persons. Although no appeal has been made to scripture, Anselm's thought is clearly directed towards establishing the Christian doctrine of the Trinity.

In creating this view, Anselm is relying on the analogy given by Augustine, who saw the Trinity as memory, knowledge and love reflected in the human mind.¹³ However, Anselm is not seeking to use these terms analogously in the *Monologion*, but is attributing the qualities to the immanent divine persons.¹⁴

---

⁹ Anselm C, *Proslogion*, Preface, Vol.1, p.93 (p.82).

¹⁰ Anselm C, *Monologion*, 1, Vol.1, p.13 (p.11).

¹¹ *Ibid.*, 1, Vol.1, p.15 (p.12).

¹² *Ibid.*, 29, 37-40, Vol.1, pp.47, 55-57 (pp.45, 52-54).

¹³ Augustine, *De Trinitate*, 9 (ed. W. Mountain. Turnholt: Brepols, 1968), pp.292-310 (and in *The Trinity* (ed. J. Rotelle, tr. E. Hill. Brooklyn: New City Press, 1991), pp.270-82). References from Augustine's *De Trinitate* will be from both the Latin and (in brackets) English editions.

¹⁴ It is unclear how far Augustine himself would have seen these attributes pertaining to the respective persons of the Trinity. The *De Trinitate* is, however, far more circumspect in its language than the *Monologion*. Schmaus claims that Anselm was the first to seriously apply these terms to the Trinitarian persons as more than a metaphor based on a psychological study. M. Schmaus, 'Die theologiegeschichtliche Tragweite der Trinitätslehre des Anselm von Canterbury', *Analecta Anselmiana* 4:1 (Frankfurt: Minerva, 1975), pp.32-33.

Watkin-Jones writes about Anselm's balance in teaching that the Holy Spirit "flows whole" from both the Father and the Son as their love, and yet how, within the *memoria, intelligentia, amor* triad, all three members of the Trinity are each of these attributes individually.[15]

This is the context in which Anselm introduces the person of the Holy Spirit, moving on from his thoughts on the self-knowledge and self-expression of God to God's self-love: "For the supreme spirit indeed loves itself, just as it is conscious of, and understands, itself. How absurd to deny it! Even a rational mind can love both itself and the supreme spirit".[16] For Daniel Deme, this idea that the relationship of Father and Son is marked by their love for each other is the "starting-point of Anselm's pneumatology".[17] This mutuality creates further plurality in the godhead.

There is an indication in this section of the *Monologion* that the Holy Spirit is more than the mutual love of Father and Son, as the doxology that begins this teaching reads: "What delight to gaze upon what is proper to Father and Son and what they have in common! And nothing gives me more delight in contemplation than their mutual love".[18] Yves Congar still does not think that Anselm goes so far as to teach that the Holy Spirit is the mutual love of Father and Son, but only that the Father and Son love each other with the Love proceeding from both.[19] Whilst Anselm may not teach mutual love as clearly as other writers of the twelfth century, this idea is at least strongly suggested by his use of language. Given the indications of Anselm's reliance on Augustine's thought, it would seem that he does support Augustine's mutual love theory in the teaching of the *Monologion*.

The initial teaching on love is of a single love of self by the supreme spirit. This love is then transferred to the Father and Son, as Anselm declares, "it is clear that the supreme spirit's love proceeds from its being self-conscious and self-understanding", and this love is said to proceed "equally from the Father and the Son".[20] This development of the concept of love within the supreme spirit includes a processional model that supports dual procession, as love is contingent upon consciousness and understanding. Something can be loved only to the extent that the lover is conscious of it and understands it.[21]

This leads Anselm neatly into a consideration of the relation of love in the supreme spirit to consciousness and understanding. This has two stages: in the

---

[15] Watkin-Jones, *The Holy Spirit in the Medieval Church*, p.84.
[16] Anselm C, *Monologion*, 49, Vol.1, p.64 (p.60).
[17] Deme, *The Christology of Anselm*, p.140.
[18] Anselm C, *Monologion*, 49, Vol.1, p.64 (p.59). Other aspects of the commonality of Father and Son are not explored in the *Monologion*, but are hinted at in the *Proslogion*.
[19] Congar, *I Believe in the Holy Spirit 1*, p.85.
[20] Anselm C, *Monologion*, 50, Vol.1, p.65 (p.61).
[21] Simonis confirms that Anselm upholds the dual procession of the Holy Spirit on the basis of His identity as love in the Trinity. W. Simonis, *Trinität und Vernuft: Untersuchungen zur Möglichkeit einer rationalen Trinitätslehre bei Anselm, Abaelard, den Viktorinern, A. Günther und J. Frohschammer* (Frankfurt: J. Knecht, 1972), p.29.

first, Anselm declares that both Father and Son love themselves and each other with complete intensity because of the fact that each is, as an individual, the supreme spirit;[22] in the second stage, Anselm concludes that the love must be equal in greatness to the Father and Son because they have complete consciousness and knowledge, and therefore love, of themselves and each other.[23]

Anselm recognises that there still needs to be clarification of the position of this love within the supreme spirit. Because the love of God is said to proceed from two members, logic would dictate that there would be two loves. However, Anselm affirms that it is only one love, as it "proceeds from their being one",[24] not from their relation, but from their essence. This reinforces the unity of being of Father and Son, despite a relational model that would seem to create two separate spirits, and shows the Spirit binding the whole godhead together as one.

Following on from the thought that the Son (the Word) is coeternal and consubstantial with the Father because He proceeds from the divine essence, so the Spirit (the love of God) is given the same attributes for the same reason.[25] From this status of coequality with Father and Son, the Holy Spirit is also given all other attributes that Anselm has described as belonging to the supreme spirit, such as wisdom and virtue.[26] The Holy Spirit is thus revealed by Anselm to be equal and identical with Father and Son in every way, yet especially to be seen as the love of God for himself, which is both the Spirit's relational identity as well as the mode of His procession.

The issue of the procession of the Holy Spirit is dealt with again later in the *Monologion*. Anselm brings out two points connected with the name of the third person that support his theory of dual procession.[27] The first of these deals with the mode of procession, that is unlike the begotten Son. Anselm notes that Father, Son and Love are all spirit, but states that the Father and Son are not considered to be the spirit of anything. The term that Anselm uses for the procession of the spirit is 'breathing out' or 'expiration', which is said to be appropriate to the name of the Holy Spirit, and differentiates the Spirit from the Son.

The second point concerns the "lack of a name that is proper to it".[28] "Father" and "Son" are both terms distinguishing them within the Trinity. "Holy Spirit" is, in some senses, not unique to the third person as both Father and Son are holy and spirit. Anselm considers it wholly appropriate that the Spirit should have as a name that which the Father and Son have in common, as

---

[22] Anselm C, *Monologion*, 51, Vol.1, p.65 (p.61).
[23] *Ibid.*, 52-53, Vol.1, pp.65-66 (pp.61-62).
[24] *Ibid.*, 54, Vol.1, p.66 (p.62).
[25] *Ibid.*, 58-60, Vol.1, pp.70 (pp.65-66).
[26] *Ibid.*, 58, Vol.1, p.69 (p.65).
[27] Both points are found in *Ibid.*, 57, Vol.1, pp.68-69 (p.65).
[28] Anselm C, *Monologion*, 57, Vol.1, pp.68-69 (pp.64-65).

"it suggests that Love has the same being as Father and Son, and at the same time derives its being from them".[29] There is also in this another indication that the Holy Spirit is the commonality of Father and Son.

This picture of the Holy Spirit is confirmed in the *Proslogion*, which has less to say on the persons individually, having as its main focus the ontological proof for the existence of God. The Proslogion differs only slightly in the definition of God that is built up, based on the idea that there must be a being "than which nothing greater can be thought",[30] and proceeding from this to the concept of a supreme goodness (whereas the *Monologion* had moved from the quality of goodness to a supremely great being).

In the short section on the persons that follows the teaching that the greatest being is good, there are two notable statements. The first is an incorrect processional statement regarding the person of the Holy Spirit. Anselm follows his summary of the persons of the Father and Son with the statement that, "You are so simple that there cannot be born of You any other than what You are. This itself is the Love, one and common to You and to Your Son, that is the Holy Spirit proceeding from both".[31] There seems to be no reason for Anselm using the word "born" in relation to the Holy Spirit, and this is not developed later. Also interesting in this quote is the idea that this mutual love comes from the unity of Father and Son.

The second statement that requires comment concerns the identical nature of the three persons in the godhead, that "whatever each is singly, that the whole Trinity is together".[32] This is further explained: "each singly is not other than the supremely simple unity and the supremely unified simplicity which can be neither multiplied nor differentiated". The concept of the Holy Spirit making unity in Trinity is important in this book, and this teaching of Anselm about all three persons being unity will be further examined in the second section of the book.

The *Monologion* and *Proslogion* thus create a clear concept of the identity of the Holy Spirit within the godhead, drawn out from an orthodox understanding of the nature of God. The idea of the Holy Spirit as love is central to Anselm's overall understanding, and the importance of this is emphasised by the relational models that are taught in these works. The procession of the Holy Spirit is shown to be from both Father and Son in equal measure, and the third person of the Trinity is shown by this to be equal in every way to the other two.

De Processione Spiritus Sancti

It is surprising given the clarity of these earlier works that Anselm's thesis *De Processione Spiritus Sancti* is turgid and unconvincing in its attempt to

---

[29] *Ibid.*, 57, Vol.1, p.69 (p.65).
[30] Anselm C, *Proslogion*, 2, Vol. 1, p.101 (p.87).
[31] *Ibid.*, 23, Vol.1, p.117 (p.100).
[32] *Ibid.*, Vol.1, p.117 (p.100).

persuade the Greeks of the Latin position on the *Filioque*. What is more, the later work does not make use of the ideas earlier formulated regarding the person of the Spirit. In his work on the procession of the Spirit, Anselm at no point includes mention of the Spirit as the Love of God, of Father and Son, and only uses the concept of breathing regarding Jesus' giving of the Spirit to His disciples, without transferring this into his concept of the eternal procession.

The strength of the *De Processione* is in Anselm's use of reason to provide a logical argument from a common starting ground why the Greeks should accept the principle of dual procession. Anselm at times shows his genius in this work in explaining why the Latin position should be accepted, and inclusion of more of his earlier material could have made this work a wonderful apologetic.

Anselm's main goal is to prove the dual procession of the Spirit. In order to do this, he begins by stating what both Latin and Greek Christians believe concerning the Holy Spirit: that He is God proceeding from God; and that His name designates that He is the spirit of another. In this initial section, Anselm concentrates on the unity of God: "We say that the one God is the Father and the Son and the Holy Spirit, and we may say that they, whether singly or in pairs or all three, are one and the same God".[33] In this, Anselm is providing the foundation for his theory in the relational structure of a triune God, whose persons are identical in their attributes. Anselm has chosen to emphasise this side of divine personhood to the exclusion of the personal properties of consciousness, knowledge and love that had been developed in his earlier work.

The strength of this approach for Anselm is that he can declare that both Son and Holy Spirit must be understood as proceeding from God the Father as from "the unity of the divine nature".[34] This phrase, if accepted, forces the Greeks to conclude that either the Son is from the Holy Spirit, or the Holy Spirit from the Son, as whichever is from God second must come from the unity of the Father and another person. Anselm writes that the Son cannot be from the Holy Spirit, as this would make the Holy Spirit a father (as the Son proceeds by being begotten); and so the Holy Spirit must be from the Son (proceeding in the same way as He does from the Father).[35] Anselm is using the strength of his reasoning that was shown in the *Monologion* and *Proslogion* to attempt to compel the Greeks to accept the Western position by sheer power of logic.

Anselm picks up later on this idea of unity in discussion of the Nicene Creed's statement, "We believe in the Holy Spirit, who proceeds from the Father". The Nicene Creed was the major basis for the Greeks' opposition to the filioque clause, which was added by the Western church without the authority of an ecumenical council, and was thus the focal point for Anselm's thesis.

The concentration on the unity of the divine persons in the *De Processione* is an ideal base from which Anselm can defend the addition of "filioque" to the

---

[33] Anselm C, *De Processione Spiritus Sancti*, 1, Vol.2, p.181 (p.394).

[34] *Ibid.*, 1, Vol.2, p.183 (p.396).

[35] *Ibid.*, 1, Vol.2, pp.183-84 (pp.396-97).

creedal statement. Anselm writes that the creedal declaration cannot mean that the Spirit proceeds from the Father in that He is Father, as that would make the Spirit a Son.[36] Instead, it must be interpreted as being procession from the Father as God, which would therefore include procession from the Son as He is united to the Father in the divine nature:

> For if the Holy Spirit's being from the Father is the reason why he is from God we should, when we say he is from the Father, understand that this is so by reason of the fact that God is Father (i.e. by reason of the Father's relation to the Son), not by reason of the fact that the Father is God (i.e. by reason of the divine substance). Therefore, the Holy Spirit will not have the divine substance from the Father's divine nature but from the Father's relation to the Son. And to say this is very foolish.[37]

Again, Anselm's logic within his own argument seems to be irrefutable, a point he makes himself later.[38]

However, Anselm's thesis has three major problems. The first of these is Anselm's assumption that each member of the godhead must proceed from "the unity of the divine nature", which is the key to the whole argument.[39] This phrase is not creedal, and is therefore not authoritative support for an argument concerning alteration of a creedal clause. There remains some strength in this point because of the concentration of Eastern theologians on the economy of the persons: the individuality of the divine persons in their immanent state was not strongly developed in Eastern theology. Anselm's phraseology regarding the procession of the Holy Spirit challenges the Greeks to clarify their understanding of the nature of the Spirit's procession.

The second problem is that Anselm does not address the Greeks' own position on the relative processions of Son and Holy Spirit. This is connected to the first problem and Anselm's concept of unity in the divine nature. The Greek teaching on procession is not as linearly clear as that of the West, where the Spirit was held to have proceeded after the procession of the Son (not temporally, but in the nature of the divine persons). The Greeks saw the temporal procession of the Spirit coming after that of the Son, and is demonstrated by their teaching that all things come from the Father, through the Son, in the Holy Spirit. However, the Eastern church also held that, in their immanent state, both Son and Spirit proceeded, in different ways, from the

---

[36] Anselm C, *De Processione*, 2, Vol.2, pp.189-90 (pp.403-44).

[37] *Ibid.*, 2, Vol.2, p.190 (p.404).

[38] "Irrefutable logic makes it evident that the Holy Spirit is from the Son, just as he is from the Father, and yet he is not from them as if from two different sources, but as from one". *Ibid.*, 14, Vol.2, p.212 (pp.426-27).

[39] Alisdair Heron notes this weakness in his article on Anselm and the *Filioque*, suggesting that there are "hidden traps concealed in the form of your [Anselm's] affirmations". However, in arguing against the *De Processione* from the Greek standpoint, Heron does not engage with the phrase 'unity of the divine nature' as directly and effectively as he might. Heron, 'Anselm and the *Filioque*', pp.161-62.

Father alone. These processions were seen as equal and eternal, and so there is no necessity for either to have proceeded from the Father and one other person.

The third problem, which is shown up by these first two weaknesses, is Anselm's decision not to enter into any discussion of the relational identities of the persons beyond the source of procession. Because Anselm has based his argument purely on the application of logic to the names of the Trinitarian persons, there is no depth to his case that might prevent the Greeks from a simple denial of his debateable starting point. Anselm does not expand on what it means for the Holy Spirit to proceed from the divine essence, or on the form in which the Holy Spirit proceeds, as he had in the *Monologion*.[40] If Anselm had included his teaching on the Holy Spirit as the mutual love of Father and Son, which would have required Biblical and Patristic authority in addition to the pure use of reason, the Greeks would have been forced to consider to what extent their tradition supported these ideas, and how this element affected their processional model of the Holy Spirit in both His immanent and temporal states.

Anselm uses two analogies in the *De Processione* to support his position in relation to the Greeks. The first analogy that he refers to is that of the sun, its heat and its brightness.[41] This analogy would seem to support the Greek position, that the Son and Spirit proceed cotemporally in eternity from the Father without either needing to proceed from the other; but Anselm rejects its suitability as the procession involved is not like from like (sun from sun) as is the case with divinity in the Trinity. Anselm goes on to declare that, even if the analogy were to be allowed, it is not consistent with the Greek position, which holds that the Holy Spirit does belong to the Son, even if there is not procession from the Son. This would require either heat or brightness to belong to the other in the sun analogy, but in the twelfth century, "no reasoning allows that heat belongs to brightness, or brightness to heat".[42]

Anselm's second analogy, that of the watercourse, is supportive of his position, but is extremely complicated due to its possible application by the Greeks in their favour. This analogy involves a spring (the Father), a river (the Son) and a pool (the Holy Spirit).[43] Anselm had first raised this analogy in a far simpler form in his *On the Incarnation of the Word*.[44] In this instance, Anselm

---

[40] It is interesting that Heron picks up on this weakness in the *De Processione*, but does not seem to realise that Anselm had taught on the Holy Spirit as love in earlier works. Instead he looks back to Augustine for the concept of *vinculum caritatis*. Heron, "'Who proceedeth from the Father and the Son'", pp.149-66.

[41] Anselm C, *De Processione*, 8, Vol.2, pp.200-01 (p.414). It would seem from the way that Anselm refers to this analogy that the Greeks may have used this in support of their case in arguing with Anselm at the Council of Bari. Anselm introduces this analogy as if it came from an opponent ("And to say that"), and rejects it in similar manner ("[this analogy] is not properly alleged as an objection to our position").

[42] Anselm C, *De Processione*, 8, Vol.2, p.201 (p.414).

[43] *Ibid.*, 9, Vol.2, pp.203-05 (pp.416-19).

[44] Anselm C, *De Incarnatione Verbi*, 13, Vol.2, pp.31-32 (pp.256-57).

had not sought to clarify his position on the application of "from", "through" and "in" terminology, which matched the Greek position on the procession of the divine persons.[45]

Anselm notes the Greeks' understanding of this analogy in the *De Processione*:

> the lake does not come from the stream but is collected from it, although the lake has its existing from the stream. Therefore, even if the Holy Spirit should have existence from the Son, we still do not, strictly speaking, say that the Holy Spirit proceeds from the Son; rather, we say that the Holy Spirit proceeds from the Father as his source.[46]

Anselm's response is again to focus on the unity of Father and Son in their essence. When this is transferred into the analogy, it does not allow for the spring and stream to be considered as two separate sources of the lake which can be differentiated in their status as the origin of the lake.

Anselm is most lucid when explaining how he considers the lake to be both from the spring and the stream. The focus here is on the water, that is one and the same water in all three parts of the analogy, as there is one God and three persons:

> Water rising from the depths bubbles up in the spring, descending from the spring flows in the stream, is collected and stays in the lake. Therefore, we understand by the spring the water bubbling up from the depths, by the stream that the water flows from the spring, by the lake that the water then coalesces together.[47]

In this, Anselm comes close to his earlier teaching on the Spirit as that which binds the Father and Son together, primarily in love, but does not further explore the "coalescing" role of the Spirit beyond remarking that the Spirit proceeds in a "singular and ineffable way".

Anselm concludes the analogy clearly, backing up his point about the unity of Father and Son:

> Therefore, as the lake is not such from the condition by reason of which the spring and the stream differ from one another, but from the water in which they are the same, so the Holy Spirit is not such from the condition by reason of which the Father and the Son differ from one another, but from the divine substance in which the Father and the Son are the same.[48]

---

[45] Clanchy notes that Peter Abelard was unhappy with this initial presentation of the analogy in the *Theologia Christiana*. Abelard's criticism lacks strength because he fails to note the corrections that Anselm made in the *De Processione*. M.T. Clanchy, 'Abelard's Mockery of St. Anselm', *JEH* 41 (1990), pp.1-23, at pp.5-6.

[46] Anselm C, *De Processione*, 9, Vol.2, p.203 (p.417).

[47] *Ibid.*, 9, Vol.2, pp.204-05 (pp.418-19).

[48] Anselm C, *De Processione*, 9, Vol.2, p.205 (p.419).

Anselm could at this point have introduced another teaching from his earlier works, concerning the appropriateness of the name "Holy Spirit" for the person who proceeds from the one essence of Father and Son, who are both holy and spirit, but refrains from doing so.

Gillian Evans shows that Anselm of Havelberg criticised Anselm's use of the watercourse image because it was ineffective in showing how the Holy Spirit proceeded according to His relationships, focusing instead on procession from substance or personhood.[49] It is unclear whether Anselm of Havelberg followed Peter Abelard's mistake in concentrating on the presentation in the work *On the Incarnation of the Word*, without realising that Anselm of Canterbury had corrected his ideas in the *De Processione*.[50]

Following this analogy, Anselm turns to the Greek objection that dual procession indicates two Spirits, one proceeding from the Father and the other from the Son, which is not in line with Christian teaching.[51] This is comfortable ground for Anselm, as it is answered by repeating that the Spirit proceeds from Father and Son in that they are one God, not two persons.

One of the highpoints of Anselm's logic comes at the end of the *De Processione*, when he develops his processional model using the names of the three persons to show the uniqueness of each in comparison to the other two:

> There are six differences between the Father and the Son and the Holy Spirit that arise from these names, namely: to have the Father as Father, and not to have the Father as Father; to have the Son as Son, and not to have the Son as Son; to have the Spirit proceeding from oneself, and not to have the Spirit proceeding from oneself.[52]

Each of the persons of the godhead has one of these differences as a proper characteristic that distinguishes them from the other two, and two differences in common with each of the other persons. For example, the Father has the Son as His Son uniquely, but shares not having the Father as Father with the Holy Spirit, and having the Spirit proceeding from Himself as the Son does. This neatly distinguishes the persons from each other in a way that Greek teaching about procession in the Trinity does not allow, and reinforces his logical thought on the dual procession of the Spirit.

To conclude, Anselm's reliance on relational language to argue the Latin position on the procession of the Holy Spirit weakens his argument so that, despite Anselm's logical genius, at no stage of his argument are Greek doubts

---

[49] Evans, *Anselm and a New Generation*, p.46.

[50] Gillian Evans has noted elsewhere that Anselm of Canterbury only reluctantly used analogies in the presentation of his thoughts because they will always be incomplete in the pictures that they draw. Evans, 'St. Anselm's Images', p.47.

[51] Anselm of Havelberg's discussion shows that this was an important point for the Greeks.

[52] Anselm C, *De Processione*, 16, Vol.2, pp.216-17 (p.431).

about dual procession fully answered. It is surprising that Anselm never includes in the *De Processione* his clear teaching on the identity of the Spirit in the godhead that had been lucidly presented in his earlier works, such as the concept of the Spirit as the love of God, of Father and Son for each other, which would provide a deeper and more convincing argument for belief in dual procession. Anselm's presentation of the procession of the Spirit over the whole range of his works, however, creates a deep, cohesive case for accepting dual procession and the place of the Spirit as the mutual love binding Father and Son together.

Anselm of Havelberg

In contrast to Anselm of Canterbury, the remaining works of Anselm of Havelberg are less numerous and less diverse. There is no major work that systematically studies the eternal properties and relations of the Trinitarian persons as the *Monologion* does. However, it is possible to discover his belief in the person of the Holy Spirit from the account of his dispute with Nechites, archbishop of the Nicomedians. In this, we can see the difference between his presentation and that of Anselm of Canterbury in the lucidity of their approach to the procession of the Holy Spirit in the face of Greek objections to the Latin position.[53]

The problems posed by the Greeks to Anselm of Havelberg are similar to those that Anselm of Canterbury attributes to his opponents in his *De Processione*. The central and recurring objection is that the principle of dual procession indicates two Spirits, as the same Spirit cannot flow from two different sources. Nechites says that the idea of two sources either means that one is insufficient, or that one is superfluous; he further declares that to admit two sources for the Holy Spirit is "against all reason".[54] The Greek position is thus firmly stated that the Father is the one principle of both Son and Holy Spirit, one by generation, and one by procession.

Anselm of Havelberg's response is based on logic, but included in this logic is the Biblical teaching that Father and Son are one (John 10:30). If this is accepted, as it must be, by the Greeks, Anselm questions whether it is possible to hold that the Holy Spirit proceeds from the Father, if the Spirit does not also proceed from the Son: "For if, according to, we must believe that he does not proceed from the Son, we must also believe, according to you, that he does not

---

[53] Gillian Evans shows that Anselm of Canterbury and Anselm of Havelberg were superficially similar in their approaches to resolving the *filioque* issue, both using received doctrine and common points. The analysis then reveals how Anselm of Canterbury defined the issue as narrowly as possible, whereas Anselm of Havelberg gives a broad discussion of all the related issues, including (as Peter Abelard would do), specific teachings of earlier writers from both Eastern and Western traditions, which are absent from the *De Processione*. Evans, 'Anselm of Canterbury and Anselm of Havelberg' pp.164-65.

[54] "Porro si duo essent principia, vel utrumque insufficiens esset, aut alterum superfluum esset ... quod est contra omnem rationem". Anselm H, *Dialogi*, 2.2 (PL 188:1165).

proceed from the Father, for the Father and the Son are one".[55] Anselm of Havelberg thus teaches that the Spirit does not flow from Father and Son as they are separate, but from their divine essence, phraseology reminiscent of Anselm of Canterbury's "unity of the divine essence".

Although this concept of dual procession theoretically answers the Greek problem of two spirits, there remains a question about the mode of the procession of the Holy Spirit from both Father and Son which cannot be answered only by logic. There are deeper issues in the personhood of the Spirit that need to be incorporated into the processional model to provide a comprehensive defence of the Latin position. Anselm of Havelberg undertakes this secondary explanation in contrast to his predecessor. The case is weakened by Anselm's initial concession that it is not possible to know in what manner the Holy Spirit proceeds, just as it is impossible to know in what way the Son is generated, or how the Father exists ingenerate: "That just as it is unknown in what way the Father is ingenerate and the Son is generated, so also the eternal procession of the Holy Spirit is unknown".[56] Anselm challenges Nechites to explain the nature of the Father and the procession of the Son, in order to reinforce the depth of mystery which they are discussing. Whilst this may show that the Greeks are not on completely solid ground on these points, the uncertainty raised on the processions would seem to undermine Anselm's own attempts to explain the procession of the Holy Spirit.

Anselm's discussion of the eternal person of the Holy Spirit does not only concentrate on His relations with Father and Son, but also includes an assessment of the appropriateness of attributes for the third person in relation to the other members of the godhead. He examines why the Holy Spirit is so-called, when all agree that both Father and Son are holy and spirit.[57] This is the point that Anselm of Canterbury made in the *Monologion* as part of his teaching in that book about understanding the person of the Holy Spirit, but was not included in the *De Processione*.

Anselm of Havelberg continues this line of thought by noting that the Spirit is said to be breathed out by the Father and Son,[58] and concludes from this that it is the Holy Spirit that creates unity in the Trinity:

> And perhaps for that very reason the Holy Spirit alone is rightly called the Holy Spirit, since by his breath he joins both members of the godhead and in himself connects them in one essence, unity in Trinity and Trinity in unity, ineffably distinguished and wonderfully conjoined.[59]

From this, Anselm goes on to list attributes of the Holy Spirit in eternal relation to Father and Son, that He is their connexion, communion, concord, love,

---

[55] Anselm H, *Dialogi*, 2.3 (PL 188:1170).
[56] *Ibid.*, 2.5 (PL 188:1171).
[57] *Ibid.*, 2.7 (PL 188:1172-73).
[58] Also a line of thought that is found in the *Monologion* but not in the *De Processione*.
[59] Anselm H, *Dialogi*, 2.7 (PL 188:1173).

sweetness and holiness.[60] In teaching this, Anselm of Havelberg explores beyond the mutual love teaching of Anselm of Canterbury, expanding on the Holy Spirit's role as the commonality of Father and Son. There is also a stronger unifying role given to the Holy Spirit in comparison to Anselm of Canterbury's writing in the *Proslogion* that all three persons are simple unity and unified simplicity.

This is a remarkable feature of the discussion because, while the Latin church accepts these terms on the authority of Augustine, it is unclear to what extent they would be acceptable to members of the Greek church.[61] It is noticeable that at no point does Nechites argue against the truth of these attributes regarding the eternal person of the Holy Spirit. Given the reasonable balance found in Anselm's account of the debate, it would be surprising if he were to leave out an attack on this position.

In the midst of Anselm's presentation of the Holy Spirit as the communion of Father and Son, there is a discussion about how the Spirit is given, whether by the Father alone or by both. Nechites asserts that two givers would indicate two gifts, to which Anselm replies by repeating his position on procession that the giving is done by Father and Son as they are one.[62] Anselm also notes that the Greek position of the Spirit being given by the Father through the Son gives the Son a middle position ("media relatione") regarding the Spirit as neither giver nor gift, which he declares to be incomprehensible.[63] Although this issue concerns the temporal procession of the Spirit, Anselm's point on the position of the Son is important for the overall debate. The problem that is raised for the Greeks is the difference between the immanent procession of the Spirit which is from the Father alone, and the economic procession in which the Son is involved in this uncertain middle role. This contrasts with the Western position that is stronger in reflecting the immanent procession than the economic.

The discussion of the Holy Spirit as connexion of Father and Son moves onto new ground with Anselm speaking about the concept of blasphemy against the Holy Spirit as being the unforgivable sin, far worse than blasphemy against Father or Son. Whoever offends against the Son, according to Luke 10:16, also offends against the Father; and Anselm believes that the opposite is also the

---

[60] "Est itaque Spiritus sanctus coaeterna amborum connexio, amborum communio, amborum concordia, amborum charitas, amborum suavitas, amborum sanctitas." Throughout this section, Anselm consistently presents the Holy Spirit as, for instance, the sanctity of Father and Son without suggesting that the Spirit is the holiness by which Father and Son are holy: "Sanctus spiritus ... coaeterna amborum sanctitas est". *Ibid.*, (PL 188:1173).

[61] It is disappointing that Gillian Evans does not engage with this point in her article on Anselm of Havelberg and ecumenicism, concentrating instead on Anselm's better methods of engaging with the Greeks than those found in the *De Processione* of Anselm of Canterbury. Evans, 'Unity and diversity: Anselm of Havelberg as ecumenist', *Analecta Praemonstratensia* 67 (1991), pp.42-52.

[62] Anselm H, *Dialogi*, 2.10 (PL 188:1178-79).

[63] *Ibid.*, 2.11 (PL 188:1180).

case. However, Anselm goes on to say that blasphemy against the Holy Spirit, because of His relational identity in the Trinity, is blasphemy against the whole Trinity.[64] This shows the strength of the unifying power of the Holy Spirit in the godhead in Anselm's position.

Thus far, it is possible that the Greeks would accept Anselm's position, as this concept is never formally opposed. The blasphemy against the Holy Spirit has caused much discussion, and many opinions were offered in the twelfth-century.[65] However, Anselm then goes on to show his need for instruction in ecumenical discussion, as he declares in light of this finding: "What is a greater blasphemy against the Holy Spirit, than to believe and to teach that the Holy Spirit does not proceed from the Son?"[66]

It is hardly surprising that this statement drew a passionate response from Nechites. Nechites responded by noting the Greek attitude to the person of the Holy Spirit in giving worship and glory equally with the Father and the Son, which correct practice shows that the Greek church cannot be in the position that they can never be forgiven.[67] Anselm does not follow up this point, and so he may have allowed the validity of this response. It is disappointing that Anselm took such an aggressive line on this point, as the response of Nechites to the initial claim that blasphemy against the Holy Spirit involved blasphemy against the whole Trinity would have been instructive for the Greek reaction to the unifying place of the Spirit.

Instead of following up this point, Anselm of Havelberg provides an interesting analogy to show the equality of procession of the Spirit from Father and Son. The analogy chosen is that of Adam, Eve and Abel.[68] Anselm notes that Eve came from Adam in the creation narrative, but after Eve's creation, she and Adam together produced a son, Abel. There are some problems with this analogy: the issue of Cain first, and the negative connotations associated with him; the problem of time between the two processions which is not helpful regarding divine procession; and the differences between the processions in the analogy (from the rib of Adam followed by a son) and in the godhead (a Son and then procession of the Spirit). However, the strength of the analogy is that it does grant equality of procession of the third person from the first two, which mirrors the Western position on the procession of the Holy Spirit.

This analogy also touches on the question of whether primacy in procession of the Holy Spirit should be granted to the Father. Augustine had granted

---

[64] Anselm H, *Dialogi*, 2.12 (PL 188:1181). Anselm does not here include any discussion on the unity of the divine nature regarding the person of Father or Son. This is because the idea of unity has now been attributed to the person of the Holy Spirit.

[65] Some of the theories about the blasphemy against the Holy Spirit will be studied later in the thesis, as they pertain to concepts that writers held about the personal identity of the Spirit in relation to Father and Son.

[66] Anselm H, *Dialogi*, 2.12 (PL 188:1181). "Quae enim major blasphemia in Spiritum sanctum, quam credere et docere Spiritum sanctum, a Filio non procedere?".

[67] *Ibid.*, 2.11 (PL 188:1181-82).

[68] *Ibid.*, 2.20 (PL 188:1191-94).

primacy to the Father, whilst affirming dual procession: "The Father is called the one from whom the Word is born and from whom the Holy Spirit principally proceeds".[69] Anselm of Canterbury stressed that the Holy Spirit proceeded from divine unity, thereby seeming to disagree with Augustine. Anselm of Havelberg follows Augustine's line, stating that, although there is dual procession, the Holy Spirit "is found to proceed rightly and principally from the Father".[70] The reason for principal procession from the Father is that the Son received the capacity to have a divine person proceeding from Him in His own procession. This is shown in the analogy, as the creation of Eve makes possible the production of Abel from both Adam and Eve.

Anselm of Havelberg's position is backed up by quotes from Jerome and Augustine. Anselm used quotations from Church Fathers not only to support this position, but also in his basic argument for dual procession of the Holy Spirit: from the Greek side, Anselm quotes Didymus, Cyril and Chrysostom, while he also quotes the Latins Augustine, Jerome, Ambrose, Isidore and Hilary.[71] Together, these quotations seek to show that dual procession was believed by both East and West, and that belief in dual procession pre-dated the Nicene Creed that is at the centre of the *filioque* debate. Anselm shows a greater sense of his opponent's feelings in the course of this argument, referring to the Greek Fathers as "sapientissimi Graecorum" in using their writings.[72]

Anselm of Havelberg is thus very broad in his presentation of the dual procession of the Spirit. Not only does he seek to show the relational demand for this belief, he also finds the grounds for the relationship in eternal attributes of the Spirit, such as His being the connexion of Father and Son. Whilst he may not have been uniformly tactful in his presentation of his case, Anselm does also allow the authority of the Greek Fathers, and uses his knowledge of their writings to support his case, and find greater credence in the eyes of his opponents.

Anselm concludes his account of the debate with Nechites by writing that the Greek teacher accepted the validity of the Western position that the Holy Spirit proceeded from the Father and from the Son, "and said that one of the ecumenical councils led by both emperors and the pope should define the doctrine of the Trinity once and for all".[73] Although nothing formal resulted

---

[69] Augustine, *De Trinitate*, 15.17, pp.503-04 (p.419).

[70] Anselm H, *Dialogi*, 2.25 (PL 188:1205).

[71] *Ibid.*, 2.24 (PL.188:1202-05).

[72] *Ibid.*, 2.24 (PL 188:1205).

[73] W. Berschin, 'From the Middle of the Eleventh Century to the Latin Conquest of Constantinople' in *From Greek Letters and the Latin Middle Ages: From Jerome to Nicholas of Cusa* (tr. J. Frakes. The Catholic University of America Press, 1988) published on the *Myriobiblos* website (March 2005, http://www.myriobiblos.gr /texts/english/Walter_Berschin_35.html).

from this discussion,[74] the acceptance of Anselm's basic principles for understanding dual procession by Nechites shows the power of integrating the theological and logical teachings which had been put forward by Anselm of Canterbury.

Conclusion

Given the general clarity of the thought of Anselm of Canterbury, it is surprising how unconvincing was his argument for the dual procession of the Spirit. The teaching that is found in the *Monologion* and *Proslogion* shows that Anselm of Canterbury's overall understanding of the person of the Holy Spirit was the same as, and in some ways deeper than, that of Anselm of Havelberg.

It is possible that the differences in audience of the two writers affected the organisation of their work. It is clear that Anselm of Havelberg had knowledge of the Greek method of thinking from his prolonged period in Constantinople that may have aided him in knowing how to reply to Greek objections. It is less obvious how much contact Anselm of Canterbury had with the Greeks. It appears that there were Greeks at the Council of Bari, where Anselm was asked to present the Latin position, but his work does not indicate that Anselm spent much time in dialogue with these men.[75] Rather, the *De Processione* appears to be a work written from Anselm's perspective, relying on his logical strength, and suggesting objections that Greeks may make when Anselm wishes to consider these points. Experience and audience both seem to lend Anselm of Havelberg an advantage that affects the clarity and appropriateness of his presentation.

Anselm of Canterbury's work was intended to convince the Greeks of the validity of the Latin position. There is no indication that he came anywhere near achieving this goal. Anselm of Havelberg claims success in his discussion,

---

[74] Anselm did not write up the debate for thirteen years, and did not undertake another disputation until 1154, with Basil of Achrida. Nothing resulted from this second discussion.

[75] Although Bertold, in his essay on Anselm, writes that the Greeks present at the Council of Bari accepted the argument that Anselm presented, and thus the overall Western position (Bertold, 'Saint Anselm and the *Filioque*', p.228). The authority for this comes from Eadmer's autobiography of Anselm: "he was induced by the pope to confute the Greeks, who erred on the procession of the Holy Spirit, in asserting that He proceeded from the Father but not from the Son. Having accomplished this in a reasoned and catholic disquisition, he was held in great honour by all and established as a man worthy of the highest veneration". Eadmer, *The Life of St. Anselm, Archbishop of Canterbury* (ed., tr. R.W. Southern. Oxford: OUP, 1962), p.113. There is little evidence external to Eadmer to support the success of Anselm at Bari. Indeed, Gillian Evans writes in her comparison of the two Anselms that "Anselm of Canterbury had almost certainly not held formal discussions with advocates of the Greek viewpoint" even at the Council of Bari. G. Evans, 'Anselm of Canterbury and Anselm of Havelberg: the controversy with the Greeks', *AP* 53 (1977), pp.158-75, at pp.158-59.

although the proposed ecumenical council did not occur.[76]

The work of Anselm of Havelberg was thus far more successful both in its theological presentation as well as in its reception (according to his own accounts) by the desired audience. Gillian Evans writes of Anselm's conclusion that, "he presents them as reasonable and willing to come together with the Latins provided the whole Church can agree together on the disputed points".[77] The relevant documents show the need for the inclusion of belief concerning the person of the Spirit in attempting to understand the source and mode of His procession. While Anselm of Canterbury was able to establish the identity of the Spirit, he was unable, or unwilling, to include this in his work on the procession to the Greeks, which was a barrier to this gaining either internal cohesion or external acceptance.

---

[76] One reason for this may be that Anselm undertook the debate as the Emperor's ambassador, rather than as an advocate for the papacy. It was not until there was a new pope, Eugenius III, that Anselm was asked to write up his account of the debate.
[77] Evans, 'Unity and Diversity', p.52.

CHAPTER 3

Peter Abelard

Peter Abelard was one of the outstanding individuals of the twelfth century. Possessed of an intellect and clarity of thought beyond most of his peers, he continues to be remembered more for an affair and his subsequent castration than for his work, which had a profound impact on the development of Christian theology.[1] His thoughts on the Holy Spirit, as part of his rational study of the Trinity, contributed to his two public condemnations in 1121 and 1140. Abelard was seen as a radical man for his times in both lifestyle and thought, and yet this chapter will show that essentially he taught an orthodox theology of the Holy Spirit.

This chapter will begin with an overview of Abelard's life, which will show the large scope of his writings, and also indicate some of the doctrinal troubles in which Abelard became embroiled, in addition to his ethical failures. The next part of the chapter will deal with Abelard's two teachings that concern the Holy Spirit for which he received criticism and ultimately condemnation - his teaching on the World Soul and his personification of the Spirit as the Goodness of God - noting both Abelard's arguments and his detractors' criticisms. In the last major part of the chapter, Abelard's orthodoxy will be defended over the whole corpus of his writings considering the person of the Holy Spirit in the context of the development of thought in the twelfth century.

The chapter will conclude that Abelard was an exceptional thinker attempting to use his gifts and training for the use of the church; that at times the elevation of Abelard's thought shocked more conservative elements in the church; but that ultimately Abelard did not stray far beyond the limits that orthodox thought of the time should have allowed concerning the Holy Spirit.

We are fortunate in studying the life of Abelard because he is one of the few men in the medieval period to write an autobiography, his *Historia Calamitatum*, or "Story of my misfortunes". Many men had biographies written about them, but these were generally hagiographical and thus not very trustworthy. Other men's lives must be constructed from histories and surviving letters.

However, Abelard's autobiography cannot be taken completely at face value. As the title suggests, the work is partly a defence of his hardships, as well as an account of his life. Abelard seeks to put his view on the events

---

[1] Indeed, as will be explained more fully below, the term 'theology' regarding Christian studies, which Abelard used, was not welcomed by some of his contemporaries.

narrated, and occasionally omits details, such as the fact that he was taught by Roscelin of Compiegne in his youth. Roscelin was a man who had earlier disputed about theological matters with Anselm of Canterbury, and was someone for whom Abelard later developed "utter contempt".[2]

Abelard was trained as a logician, and this training continued to shine throughout his life in works such as his *Logica, Dialectica* and *De Intellectibus*. Abelard had a love of argument, and this was best displayed in his work *Sic et Non*, a discussion of the writings of the Church Fathers intended to show how the contradictions in this body of revered works could be handled. Abelard was an excellent student, and boasts at the outset of his autobiography that he outshone his master, William of Champeaux, early in his time at Paris. His success and confidence led him to set up his own school.[3]

Abelard's first obvious fall from grace was his affair with Heloise, his pupil, the niece of Fulbert, canon of Notre Dame. This episode is so well chronicled that it needs little mention here. Abelard was forced to marry Heloise, then sent her off to a convent, after which he was forcibly castrated. He left Paris, the centre of academic thought in the twelfth century, to teach in a disreputable school in St. Gildas.[4] Abelard was thus not the typical intellectual of his time, but was well-known for this infamous incident, as well as for his theological views.

While Abelard continued to teach throughout his life, it was his writings, and the reactions to them, that dominate our knowledge of his later years. Abelard wrote on a variety of issues, but his works that concern this book, in addition to the already-mentioned *Sic et Non*, were his *Theologiae*. Abelard wrote three major "theologies": the *Summi Boni, Christiana* and *Scholarium*.[5] Bernard of Clairvaux ridiculed Abelard's idea of "theology" on the basis that it was impertinent to think that one could study God. Bernard renamed Abelard's "Theology", "which Abelard was so proud to have contributed to scientific discourse, as 'Stupid-ology'".[6] In these works, Abelard presented studies of the Trinity, and it was on this issue that he was twice convicted of heresy - at Soissons in 1121 and at Sens in 1140.

The opposition to Abelard was begun by William of St. Thierry, who was concerned at what he understood Abelard to be saying, and prosecuted by William's closest confidant, Bernard of Clairvaux. Constant Mews has studied the various extant lists of charges against Abelard to decide what the actual charges probably were. Those concerning the Holy Spirit are as follows:

---

[2] J. Marenbon, *The Philosophy of Peter Abelard* (Cambridge: CUP, 1997), p.9.

[3] Abelard, *Historia Calamitatum* (ed. J. Monfrin. Paris: J. Vrin, 1967), p.64.

[4] Abelard was appointed to be the abbot of the monastery at St. Gildas to remove him from Paris.

[5] For examination of the major developments in the theologies, as well as comment on the various versions, see Constant Mews' 'The Development of the Theologia'. The *Theologia Scholarium* is also known as the *Introductio ad Theologiam*.

[6] Clanchy, *Abelard: A Medieval Life*, 6.

1. That the Father might be complete power, the Son some power, and the Holy Spirit no power.
2. That the Holy Spirit might not be from the substance of the Father or the Son.
3. That the Holy Spirit might be the soul of the world (anima mundi).
14. That to the Father, because he is from no one, rightly and particularly pertains power, and not wisdom and kindness.[7]

These charges will be studied in depth during the course of this chapter. It should be noted at this point that Abelard refuted each of these in his *Responsio Petri Abelardi Contra Calumnias Objectorum* as being misinterpretations of what he had written.[8]

Abelard unsuccessfully defended himself at Soissons, and refused to answer the call to the second trial at Sens - instead appealing to Rome, and seeking and receiving refuge at the hands of Peter the Venerable in the monastery of Cluny, where Abelard lived out the last two years of his life. It would seem from this short account of his life that Abelard was constantly at odds with the moral and theological convictions of his day. Whilst this may be true of his behaviour with Heloise, this chapter will show that Abelard did not seek to offend with his thoughts on the Holy Spirit, but to explore further the truths handed down by tradition.

Abelard's 'Heresies' Regarding the Person of the Holy Spirit

This first section on Abelard's teaching on the Holy Spirit will examine those elements for which Abelard received criticism and condemnation. There were two main teachings on the nature and persons of the Trinity, and the Holy Spirit in particular, for which Abelard was denounced: his use of the attributes power, wisdom and goodness as appropriate names for the Father, the Son and the Holy Spirit respectively; and his seeming equivalence of the Holy Spirit with Plato's World Soul. One would expect these teachings to be radical departures from accepted thought, yet both will be shown to be explorations founded on accepted ideas about the Holy Spirit, and that the criticisms levelled at Abelard were based on incorrect readings of his views.

Abelard sought to back up his teaching by citing references from the Old Testament and pagan philosophers, in order to show that the persons of the godhead were revealed to the world in creation, before the writings of the New Testament. The use of pagan philosophers to support his argument was one reason why contemporaries were wary of agreeing with his ideas, although, as Weingart notes on the *Theologia Scholarium*, Abelard "marshals the same parade of witnesses - Plato, Macrobius, the Platonists, Virgil - to evidence the extent of the revelation of the Trinity, but *does not claim* that it was rationally inferred by any of them".[9]

---

[7] Mews, 'The List of Heresies', p.73-110.
[8] Abelard, *Responsio Petri Abaelardi Contra Calumnias Objectorum* (PL 180:330).
[9] Weingart, *The Logic of Divine Love*, p.15 (my italics).

Power, Wisdom, Goodness

One of the major charges against Abelard was his teaching that the attributes of power, wisdom and goodness could be applied to the Trinitarian persons as their particular qualities. This was seen to imply incomplete divinity in each of the persons. It was this belief that was the basis of charges 1 and 14 (above): that the Holy Spirit has no power (as the Father has full power, and the Son some power); and that the Father does not have wisdom and kindness as particular qualities of himself (as these belong to the Son and the Spirit).

The problem with this teaching, as is shown by the charges made against Abelard, is that to designate each of the persons as being particularly one of these qualities would seem to indicate that the other two members of the godhead are somehow lacking in that attribute. Thus, if the Father is power, the Son and the Holy Spirit must be somehow deficient in their power. This point can be defended on the grounds that the Father is the ultimate origin of the Trinity, being the only person who does not is some way derive His being from another. There are greater problems with the concept of the Son being wisdom, as if the Father were not this in himself, although it is difficult to argue against Abelard on this point because of the use that Augustine had made of the term wisdom in relation to the second person of the Trinity, as well as Biblical references that imply this idea (such as descriptions of Jesus as the Word of God in John 1). The relation of the Holy Spirit to goodness has the greatest problem because there is little in the traditional teaching of the church to make this direct connection. An additional problem for opponents of Abelard was the extent to which this whole approach related to the traditional teaching of the church, that each of the three persons was the fullness of God, and that as such they were identical in their divine nature.

Although there would seem to be problems raised by these ideas, Abelard begins each of his *Theologiae* with this model as the basis for his understanding of the Trinitarian persons: "The majesty of divine power is specially expressed in the name of Father God, just as the wisdom of God is signified by the name Son or Word ... And indeed his charity or kindness is expressed by the name Holy Spirit," or again, "such therefore are the three persons of God, which are the Father and the Son and the Holy Spirit, and if we say that the divine substance is power, wisdom, kindness, it is even this power, this wisdom, this kindness ".[10] Abelard's opening statement on this point in his first *Theologia*, the *Summi Boni*, is so straightforward that it appears he would not expect any opposition to these ideas. It is treated as though it were one of the major

---

[10] References from Abelard's *Theologiae Christianae and Scholarium* will come from CCCM 12-13 (ed. E.M. Buytaert. Turnholt: Brepols 1969, 1987) and will cite the work, the section of the work, and then the volume and page number from Buytaert in brackets. References from the *Theologia Summi Boni* are from the edition by U. Niggli (Hamburg: Felix Meiner, 1997). Abelard, *Introductio ad Theologiam*, 1.30 (Vol. 3, p.330); *Theologia Summi Boni* 1.2, p.4. Abelard states later in the *Summi Boni*, "proprium est patris posse, filii discernere, spiritus sancti benignum esse", *Summi Boni* 2.4, p.142.

teachings of the Church Fathers on the persons of the Trinity.

The explanation for this is found in the reasoning that Abelard gives for his nomenclature. One of the founding statements on which Abelard bases his doctrine of the Holy Spirit as goodness is that this quality is suitably attached to that person whose work it is to dispense grace and charity: "That which holds to the operation of divine grace and the goodness of divine charity we ascribe to the Holy Spirit ".[11] The link between goodness, on the one hand, and grace and charity, on the other, is a logical step that backs up Abelard's overall point. This teaching is based on the work of the Holy Spirit in creation, and is supported by Abelard with comments on the presence of the Spirit in the creation narrative. In this, Abelard sees the Holy Spirit as the "good" that God saw when He created the world.[12] Nielson states that, for Abelard, the Holy Spirit proceeds from the Father and Son as love between God and creation, founded in goodness.[13] There does remain a weakness in this approach in that it is unclear how this temporal role of the Spirit proceeds from an eternal status as "goodness" in the godhead.

This is addressed by Abelard by looking at established teaching about the Holy Spirit's immanent personhood. Abelard draws on Augustine's teaching that the Holy Spirit is the love of God, which was accepted by western theologians in the twelfth century, and uses this doctrine to back up his concept of the Holy Spirit as the goodness of God.[14] Augustine himself uses the words "love" and "will" interchangeably regarding the Holy Spirit when discussing properties of the Trinitarian persons; Abelard inserts his "goodness" term as an equivalent to love that fits best into his presentation of the Trinity. There is here a similar logical step as was taken from the Spirit's work of charity and grace. As the Holy Spirit can be conceived of as love in the Trinity, He can also be considered goodness, as goodness pertains to love.[15] Abelard uses this goodness/love link in his *Apologia* to Bernard, accusing Bernard of stating that the love of God has no power, if impotence is a result of the power, wisdom, goodness model.[16]

Another reason why Abelard must have thought himself on safe grounds is that he makes it clear in his work that, while seeing these attributes as particularly relevant to the respective persons, he does not see them as exclusive to those persons. William of St. Thierry's charge that Abelard denies some power to the Son and all power to the Holy Spirit is against the clear

---

[11] Abelard, *Introductio*, 1.64 (Vol. 3, p.343).

[12] "Et vidit Deus quod esset bonum. Bonitas Dei quam Spiritum sanctum dicimus, insinuatur", Abelard, *Introductio*, 1.72 (Vol. 3, p.347).

[13] Nielson, 'Peter Abelard and Gilbert of Poitiers', in Evans', *The Medieval Theologians*, p.113.

[14] Abelard, *Introductio*, 1.32-33, 64-68 (Vol.3, pp.331-32, 343-45).

[15] "Benignitas autem ad amorem pertinet, ut quem benignissimum habemus, potissimum diligamus". Abelard, *Theologia Christiana* 1.6 (Vol. 2, p.74).

[16] Abelard, *Apologia Contra Bernardum*, 8 (ed. E.M. Buytaert. Turnholt: Brepols, 1969) p.362.

backing that Abelard gives in each of his *Theologiae* to the statement found in the Athanasian Creed: "The Father is omnipotent, the Son is omnipotent, the Holy Spirit is omnipotent", which Abelard states "seems to be greatly confirmed".[17] This teaching does come later in the *Theologiae* and is not stressed to the same extent that the initial model receives. However, the presence of this in Abelard's work shows that the accusations that were made against him were not based on a thorough study of his ideas.

Abelard is quick to point to this balance in his teaching in his defence to the charges which were levelled against him, in his article *Responsio Petri Abaelardi Contra Calumnias Objectorum*, in which he states that not only did he not write about a lack of power in the Son or the Holy Spirit, but that such a concept was abhorrent to him:

> Therefore, that which has been attributed to me through malice or error – that I have written about God that the Father has complete power, the Son some power and the Holy Spirit no power – these words, not so much human as diabolical, I abhor and detest, as is most just.[18]

Abelard also notes in this work that his appropriation of the three terms to the persons does not denote exclusivity of one characteristic to one person, as each of the persons is equally powerful, wise and kind, which is part of their very nature as God: "I confess that God the Father has equal wisdom, and the Son equal kindness as the Holy Spirit, because it is not possible for one of the persons to differ from the others in any fullness of goodness nor in any glory of dignity".[19] Abelard stresses that he is not going beyond established and accepted teaching on the nature of divinity in the persons, and yet maintains that it is possible for each of the persons within the godhead to have a particular affinity with one or other characteristic of divinity. In this, Abelard places himself alongside Augustine in his method of treating the persons; but Abelard prefers the term "goodness" to that of "love" in describing the person of the Holy Spirit both as a more complete term for that person, and because he thinks that power, wisdom and goodness together provide a more complete image of God.

It is clear that Abelard's teaching on this issue created a large amount of opposition, prompting the great Bernard of Clairvaux himself to take the lead in the trials against him. Twice, Abelard was condemned: against the first condemnation, Abelard wrote a defence; he avoided the second by seeking sanctuary. Yet Abelard maintained his position throughout his life, and was supported by many in the church using the same terminology (though they did not necessarily speak up in Abelard's defence), such as Hugh of St. Victor.[20]

The concept of the Holy Spirit as the goodness of God was one of the key

---

[17] Abelard, *Theologia Summi Boni*, 3.11, p.190.
[18] Abelard, *Responsio Petri Abaelardi Contra Calumnias Objectorum* (PL 180:330).
[19] *Ibid.*, (PL 180:332).
[20] As will be shown in later chapters.

areas of discussion about the third person in the twelfth century, and as such will be thoroughly discussed over the whole range of authors in the chapter on "Goodness" in the second part of the book. Peter Abelard was one of the first and foremost proponents of this position, using this as the basis for his understanding of the Holy Spirit within the Trinity, backed up both by logic and the authority of Augustine.

The World Soul

A second doctrine of Abelard's that was attacked was his linking of the Holy Spirit to the World Soul found in Plato's *Timaeus*. Peter Abelard consistently included this teaching in his *Theologiae*,[21] as he had his thoughts on the Holy Spirit as goodness, but ultimately the connection between Holy Spirit and World Soul remained confined to Abelard and members of the Chartrain school of thought who had a strongly Platonistic basis to their philosophy.[22]

The charge that was made against Abelard was that he had written, "that the Holy Spirit might be the soul of the world". This was an attempt by William of St. Thierry to condense and distil Abelard's teaching into a single statement, and, as with the charges concerning the attributes and the persons, William was incorrect in his interpretation of Abelard in a way that would inflame opposition against him. Abelard never equated the Holy Spirit with the World Soul, recognising at all times the limitations of the similarity; but he did remain interested in the resonances that Plato's thought had with Christian teaching about the godhead.

It is slightly surprising that Abelard devotes so much space in his *Theologiae* to the concept of the Spirit as World Soul given that, as John Marenbon has noted, Abelard in earlier work "criticizes those who identify the Platonic World Soul with the Holy Spirit ... [and] describes Plato's doctrine of the World Soul as a 'fiction utterly removed from the truth'".[23] In the *Dialectica*, Abelard states that "[the soul of the world] is not coeternal, but gains his origin from God in the manner of creatures", whereas the Holy Spirit "consists in the perfection of the divine Trinity, just as the Father and the Son are consubstantial and coequal and coeternal, which should be doubted by none of the faithful".[24] It is never made clear at what point Abelard's view changed, but he strongly defends the comparison of World Soul with Holy Spirit in his *Theologiae*. Abelard has two bases for his identification: the work that both the Holy Spirit and the World Soul are said to perform in the world; and the mode of procession that each has

---

[21] Bernard McGinn thinks that Abelard may have been engaging with a problem current in schools at the time when writing about the *anima mundi* in the first of his *Theologiae*. McGinn, 'The Role of the Anima Mundi', p.295.

[22] Because this concept was not more widely examined by those writers featuring in this thesis, discussion of this theory about the Holy Spirit will take place here, and in the chapter on William for his views, and will not have a separate thematic treatment in the second half of the thesis.

[23] Marenbon, *The Philosophy of Peter Abelard*, 42.

[24] Abelard, *Dialectica* (ed. L. De Rijk, Assen: Van Gorcum, 1956), Tractatus 5, p.559.

at their origin.

The main work which is seen as being common to both Spirit and World Soul is that of giving life to all creation through being diffused in all that has been created: "The soul of the world, which implies the Holy Spirit, confers onto animals a spiritual life by the distribution of his gifts, so that there are single souls for their bodies".[25] Abelard sees a further level of quickening that is hidden in Plato's thought but brought out in scripture, which is that of the love of God which the Holy Spirit stimulates in men to do the good work of God.[26] The World Soul is also pictured by Plato as being involved in the creation of the world, and Abelard is thus able to draw strong parallels between the temporal work of the Holy Spirit and the role that is ascribed to the World Soul.

Abelard strengthens the link between Spirit and Soul by looking at the mode of procession. Plato describes a trinity coming from God of mind, nous or intelligence, and World Soul.[27] The World Soul is seen as a third person who exists through himself and operates through His effects, proceeding not directly from the mind and nous but somehow from between them. This differs from the procession of the Holy Spirit in Christian understanding because of the concept that the three divine entities are persons in relation to each other, but the concept of one third in proceeding who works the will of the godhead in creation remains similar to the Christian Trinity. The processional model that Plato had put forward thus works well in relation to the temporal procession of the Holy Spirit.

Although Abelard insisted that Plato had some understanding of the Trinity in his mind, nous, World Soul construct, it was recognised that Plato had not grasped the full nature of the Trinity, as is immediately apparent because of the lack of any eternal element to teaching on the World Soul. Abelard consistently used the word *involucrum* to refer to Plato's understanding, implying that it was veiled or cloaked, and not complete.[28] Therefore, for William of St. Thierry to make the charge that Peter Abelard had declared "Quod Spiritus Sanctus sit anima mundi" shows that he was reacting against the notion that a "pagan" philosopher had knowledge of the Christian Trinity. William was not prepared to engage with Abelard on the possibility of partial revelation of the truth about the nature of God to the human mind through those things that can be observed, which was at the basis of Abelard's thought on this point.[29]

---

[25] Abelard, *Theologia Summi Boni*, 1.6, p.38-40. The 'ipsis animabus' referred to is the quickening of life in the body that the human soul is said to create.

[26] "Caritas dei, quam spiritum sanctum dicimus, cordibus humanis per fidei sive rationis donum primates infusa quondam vivificat ad bonorum fructum operum nos promovendo". *Ibid.*, 1.6, p.40.

[27] It is easy to see the parallels between this and the image of the Trinity that St. Augustine found in mind, knowledge of self and love of self.

[28] Most clearly in *Introductio*, 1.166 (Vol.3, pp.386-87).

[29] Abelard was interested in the extent to which God's invisible qualities mentioned in Romans 1:20 could be discerned and understood without direct, Christian revelation.

The importance of understanding *involucrum* in studying Abelard's views on the World Soul has been stressed by many authors in recent scholarship. Two authors have been particularly clear in explaining Abelard's thought on this point, and the consequent impact this should have had on his contemporaries. Tulio Gregory has written that:

> Dans l'interprétation des textes platoniciens ce parallélisme [between Plato's thought and Biblical imagery] trouve peut-être son application la plus vaste chez Abélard qui use du thème de l'*involucrum* ou *integumentum* pour ramener à la foi chrétienne les textes les plus difficiles de Platon.[30]

Moonan is equally clear about Abelard's intentions: "More than once Abelard goes out of his way to emphasise that what Plato had been saying, had at any rate not to be taken over and understood as sober doctrine".[31] He goes on to argue that, for Bernard to accuse Abelard of teaching *Quod Spiritus Sanctus sit anima mundi*, "was unjustifiable on Bernard's part, because Abelard had more than once taken pains to explain why that could not be held by a Christian".[32]

Abelard noted that Plato's World Soul was limited by its existence being linked to the temporal things of the world. One solution that he offered to this problem was to say that the World Soul accurately reflected the temporal procession of the Holy Spirit, while the eternal procession was not visible to all through creation but must be revealed by God. Bernard McGinn summarises Abelard's teaching in the *Theologia Christiana*: "There is an eternal procession of the Spirit according to love (affectus), because he willed in this way from eternity; there is a temporal procession of the soul according to what has been made (effectus)."[33] The author of the *Epitome Theologiae Christianae*, a work written by someone in the school of Abelard, though almost certainly not by Abelard himself,[34] shows how Abelard took the seven-fold Spirit of God and the effects described, and applies this to the World Soul, while retaining the name Spirit for the eternal third person of the godhead:

> Secundum igitur hunc septiformem effectum, per quem effectuum cunctorum universitas designatur, quae in creaturis efficiuntur, Spiritus sanctus anima mundi dictus est, quia anima et creata censetur, quia ipse Spiritus creaturas vivificat. Eadem ergo substantia et Spiritus sanctus et anima dicitur, spiritus ex bonitate, anima ex vivificatione, Spiritus sanctus ex affectu, anima ex effectu,

---

[30] Gregory, 'Le platonisme du XIIe siècle', pp.246-47.

[31] Moonan, 'Abelard's Use of the *Timaeus*', p.58.

[32] *Ibid.*, p,60. Marenbon and Chenu are two other writers who stress this importance of a correct understanding of Abelard's teaching about the World Soul: Marenbon, *The Philosophy of Peter Abelard*, p.57; Chenu, 'La Théologie au Douzieme Siècle', p.123.

[33] McGinn, 'The Role of the Anima Mundi', pp.295-6.

[34] Luscombe, who has done a great deal of research, thinks that the most likely author of the *Epitome* is Master Hermann. Luscombe, *The School of Peter Abelard*, p.158. Luscombe notes that the work is "clearly a valuable source of Abelard's teachings".

Spiritus in sua aeternitate, anima in administratione temporali.[35]

Peter Abelard was not the only thinker in the twelfth century to be intrigued by the similarity between the Platonic and Christian trinities.[36] Two members connected to the school at Chartres also wrote comparing the Holy Spirit to the World Soul: Thierry of Chartres and William of Conches.[37] Thierry wrote in his *De Sex Dierum Operibus* that Plato has the World Soul, Virgil has a "nourishing spirit", the Jews had the spirit of God, and the Christians have the Holy Spirit, all of whom do the same task in the world and are to be equated with each other.[38] Thierry was not condemned as Abelard and William of Conches were.

William of Conches taught about the World Soul in his *Philosophia Mundi* and in his *Glosae Super Consolationem Boethii*. In the *Glosae*, William wrote, "The World Soul is the natural energy by which some things have the power only to be moved, others to grow, others to sense, others to judge. Ask what that energy is? It seems to be that the natural energy is the Holy Spirit, that is, the divine and beneficent concord from which all things possess being, movement, growth, sensation, life and judgement".[39] William of St. Thierry wrote to Bernard of Clairvaux about William of Conches on the same lines as he had done against Peter Abelard in the letter *De Erroribus Guillelmi De Conchis Ad Sanctum Bernardum*.[40] William of Conches seems to have been less certain of his ground than Abelard as the teaching on the World Soul is missing from his later work such as the *Dragmaticon*.[41]

While Abelard was able to defend himself from the charge of equating the Holy Spirit with the World Soul, his ideas on this link between philosophers and Christianity did not have any major effect on Christian thought in the Middle Ages. This may have been due to the growing role of philosophies other than Platonism from the late twelfth century onwards,[42] and was also a result of

---

[35] Hermann?, *Epitome Theologiae Christianae*, 18 (PL 178:1721).

[36] The best survey of teaching on the 'anima mundi' in the twelfth century is Bernard McGinn's article 'The Role of the Anima Mundi'.

[37] William of Conches had been taught by Bernard of Chartres.

[38] Thierry of Chartres, *De Sex Dierum Operibus*, 27, in *Commentaries on Boethius by Thierry of Chartres and his school* (ed. N. Häring. Toronto: Pontifical Institute of Medieval Studies, 1971), pp.566-67, quoted by McGinn in 'Role of the Anima Mundi', pp.300-01.

[39] William of Conches, *Glosae Super Consolationem Boethii* quoted by B. McGinn in 'Role of the Anima Mundi', p.298. The quote is taken from R. Southern's *Platonism, Scholastic Method and the School of Chartres* (Reading, Reading University Press, 1979), p.23, n.27.

[40] William of St. Thierry, *De Erroribus Guillelmi De Conchis Ad Sanctum Bernardum* (PL 180:333-40).

[41] Noted by McGinn in his article 'The Role of the anima mundi', p.300.

[42] From the twelfth century onwards, there was an ever-growing awareness of the thought of Aristotle as well as an awareness of Arabic thought.

the imperfect comparison, because Plato did not conceptualise an eternal World Soul.

Abelard's Orthodoxy Concerning the Holy Spirit

Having taken the major charges of heresy against Abelard and shown his desire to remain orthodox whilst seeking as great a knowledge of eternal things as his mind would allow him, it is now time to back up this theory that Abelard was not a thinker opposed to the church and its tradition by looking at a number of areas where he followed the teaching of those before and after him concerning the person of the Holy Spirit. This is important both to consolidate Abelard's own position on the Holy Spirit in his theology, and as a contribution to the overall purpose of this book, examining thought on the person of the Spirit in the twelfth century.

Unity in Trinity

One of the most important doctrines concerning the Trinity for medieval theologians was the equality of all three persons in all things. Most of the major heresies that the church had faced had attempted to devalue either Son or Spirit as being less than the Father in some way on account of their procession from His being.[43] As has been noted above, Abelard was suspected of heresy on similar lines due to his use of the terms power, wisdom and goodness to refer to the Trinitarian persons. However, not only was he orthodox in his assignation of these terms because they could be seen as especially relevant to the particular persons, but Abelard also stressed throughout his works that the Trinity was indivisible, coeternal, consubstantial and coequal, which church tradition had taught.

Abelard showed his knowledge of the classical formulation of the Trinity most clearly in his *Sic et Non*. While this purpose of this work is not to teach Abelard's own opinion on the matters discussed but purely to show the discrepancies in the writings of the Fathers, the organisation of the material does give stress at times to one or other side of the argument. The sections on the unity of the godhead are prime examples of this, where the bulk of the material, enclosing arguments against unity, supports the position that all three are equal in every way:

> That it is one in its substance and is not able to be separated, although it is not of a singular nature, but is united. Singularity pertains to the person, unity to the nature.
> All three persons are coeternal and coequal.
> In the divine Trinity, there is noting dissimilar, nothing unequal.[44]

---

[43] Many other heresies sought to show that the concept of one God denied the existence of three persons, which were seen as modes of the being of God. Abelard's orthodoxy on this point will be discussed below in the section "The Procession of The Holy Spirit".

[44] Abelard quoting Ambrosius, Athanasius and Pope Leo IX in *Sic et Non*, 5, 7, 11 (PL 178:1358, 1359, 1367).

The *Sic et Non* was not written as an attempt to discredit the Church Fathers, but to show that there were different opinions found in their writings on a range of issues. Abelard fully upheld the authority of the Fathers, and he confirmed this in his *Theologiae* by the many times that he quoted them, and particularly Augustine, in support of his arguments.

In all of the versions of his work on the Trinity, Abelard continues to stress the unity of the three persons on the basis of their common substance. Commenting on Athanasius in his first *Theologia*, the *Summi Boni*, Abelard asks "who would even dare to deny that each of the persons is power and wisdom and kindness?"[45] It may have been wiser to stress this belief earlier in the work, which instead launches immediately into the appropriateness of specific names for the persons before showing a true basis in their unity of being. It is surprising that in the *Christiana* and *Scholarium*, there is no major change to link this line of thought at the outset of the presentation on the Trinitarian persons.

The *Theologia Christiana* does however contain a greater and clearer statement on the unity of the persons, although again it is placed after discussion of the individual terms appropriate to each. In book 3 of the *Christiana*, Abelard declares, "Est itaque harum trium personarum una et eadem omnino substantia, et individua penitus et simplex essentia, una prorsus potentia, una gloria, una majestas, una ratio, una voluntas, eadem operatio, non divisa."[46] There can hardly be a more complete statement of unity in Trinity than this, which covers both eternal and temporal; and words which were previously used to describe each of the persons individually, here applied to the persons corporately in their divinity: potentia (Father), ratio (Son), voluntas (Holy Spirit).

All of these references show William of St. Thierry's mistakenness in his second charge, "Quod Spiritus Sanctus non sit de substantia Patris aut Filii", which was made at Soissons after the publication of all three *Theologiae*. Abelard addresses this point directly in dealing with the nature of the three persons in their substance and relation, noting that "For neither is the Father what the Son is, or the Holy Spirit, nor is the Holy Spirit who the Son is; but, however, what the Father is, that also the Son and the Holy Spirit are and vice-versa."[47] On the issue of unity in Trinity, therefore, Abelard showed over the course of his works that he believed that each of the Trinitarian persons had the fullness of divinity in themselves, which he could hold alongside the particular applicability of certain terms.

The Holy Spirit as Love, Will, Gift, Unity

One of the major assaults on Abelard, discussed above, was on his

---

[45] Abelard, *Theologia Summi Boni*, 3.1, p.190. "Quis etiam negare queat, quin unaquaeque personarum potens sit et sapiens et benigna?"

[46] Abelard, *Theologia Christiana*, 3.61 (Vol. 2, p.220).

[47] Abelard, *Introductio*, 1.20 (Vol. 3, p.327).

appropriation of the term goodness to the Holy Spirit. However, the concept of taking qualities of God and applying them to individual persons was established in Christian tradition in the West, and Abelard followed his predecessors' use of other terms in his own theology. Goodness as a specific quality of the Holy Spirit may have been one that Abelard used more centrally than any previous writer had, but many of the other words used for the Holy Spirit show that the concept of goodness was eminently suitable for application to the third person of the Trinity. Abelard was thus clear and orthodox in his thought on the person of the Holy Spirit that proceeded from the Father and Son; it was this decision that the best term to bring together all elements of the Spirit's personhood was goodness that caused his opponents to speak against him. No writer in the twelfth-century applied only one of these terms as being *the* word which described the immanent person of the Spirit to the exclusion of the others.

As with his concept of unity in Trinity, Abelard shows his knowledge of the traditional use of terms regarding the Holy Spirit in his *Sic et Non*. In this work there are quotations from the Fathers saying that the Spirit is the love of the Father and Son, the gift of God, and the communion of Father and Son.[48] All of these terms are quoted from the work of Augustine, who was the Church Father whose writings about the Trinity were key to understanding the person of the Holy Spirit in relation to Father and Son; but Abelard also shows that these words were used by other Fathers, as he includes Jerome's description of the Spirit as *dilectio*.[49] The *Sic et Non* is useful for showing Abelard's knowledge of traditional teaching on the person of the Holy Spirit. However, it is important that Abelard not only showed his awareness of these terms, but also used them in his *Theologiae* as part of his understanding of the Holy Spirit in his theology.

The term "love" is the one most used by Abelard when he does not use goodness.[50] There are three Latin words for love used in the Vulgate: *amor*, the neutral term for love; *charitas*, which is chaste love, loving God because of God; and *dilectio*, which implies love of conscious preference.[51] Abelard uses all three of these terms to describe the love that the Holy Spirit is in the Trinity. Love was the primary term that had been used by Augustine to describe the Holy Spirit, and was also important in the work of Anselm of Canterbury, with whose work Abelard was familiar. In the *Introductio ad Theologiam*, Abelard

---

[48] Abelard, *Sic et Non*, 24 (PL 178:1384-85).

[49] *Ibid.*, 24 (PL 178:1384).

[50] Indeed, as was shown above, Abelard linked his teaching on the Holy Spirit as goodness to the idea of love. Nielson writes that Abelard saw God's goodness springing from his love, which resides in Him and effects others. Despite the apparent problem in this linking the Holy Spirit to creation, Nielson states that Abelard saw the love of God residing in Him eternally, thus allowing for the connection of this term to the person of the Spirit. Nielson, 'Peter Abelard and Gilbert of Poitiers', p.113.

[51] These definitions are taken from Bell's *The Image and Likeness*, p.56-57. Renna notes that William of St. Thierry uses a different progression of terms in his mystical theology from *amor* (an inclination of the will towards God) through *dilectio* (union with Him) to *caritas* (the enjoyment of God). Renna, 'Augustine and the Early Cistercians', p.388.

introduces the concept of the Holy Spirit as kindness alongside the accepted word, love: "But indeed, his love or kindness are expressed in the name of Holy Spirit".[52] Weingart notes the association of love and goodness in Abelard's work in his study, *The Logic of Divine Love*, and states that, for Abelard, love was "the special characteristic of the third person of the Trinity".[53]

Also in the *Introductio*, the concept of the Holy Spirit as love is used in two more important ways. Firstly, it is shown to be one reason for considering the Spirit as equal to Father and Son. Abelard writes linking love to the gift of God, which is the Holy Spirit, and concludes, "what follows more than that that love which is called God is also from God".[54] It is important that Abelard uses love in this context, as it shows that his understanding of "goodness" as a particular term for the Holy Spirit is to be understood as including terms like love, as love is used here as a fundamental reason for believing in the coequality of all three divine persons.

Secondly, Abelard writes that it is partly as love that the Holy Spirit binds the Father and Son together: "The Spirit proceeding from the Father and the Son joins them together in love".[55] This same message is repeated from another angle: "If the affection (*charitas*) by which the Father loves the Son and the Son loves the Father ineffably shows the union of them both, what is more convenient than that that spirit should be called love which is the union of them both?"[56] This section links two words, love and union, which were both applied to the person of the Holy Spirit, and uses these terms to explore the procession of the Spirit from the Father and Son. Again, we see that Abelard is not limiting his definition of the Spirit by the word "goodness", but shows how his use of that term includes and allows other elements of the person of the Spirit to be worked into his theology.

There are three more terms which Abelard used to describe the Holy Spirit. The use Abelard made of the term "will" is most clearly shown as it is reported in the *Epitome Theologiae Christianae*. Here, the reference comes in the midst of discussion about the procession of the Spirit. Noting that wisdom is a product of power, and does not create power, the writer then goes on to say that the will is dependent on what is possible and known: "procedit a potentia et sapientia haec voluntas, quia ideo vult Deus omnia quae facit, quia potest, quia scit, non autem ideo potest quia scit, vel quia vult".[57] This passage uses the same terms, power and wisdom, for the Father and the Son as were used in

---

[52] Abelard, *Introductio*, 1.32 (Vol. 3, p.331).

[53] Weingart, *The Logic of Divine Love*, p.152.

[54] Abelard, *Introductio*, 1.66 (Vol. 3, 344), quoting from Augustine's *De Trinitate*, 15.19, p.513 (p.424).

[55] *Ibid.*, 2.160 (Vol. 3, p.485). This is a quote from Chrysostom's *Homily* 28.

[56] *Ibid.*, 1.66 (Vol. 3, p.344) "Quod si charitas qua diligit Pater Filium, et Patrem diligit Filius ineffabiliter communionem amborum demonstrat, quid convenientius quam ut ille proprie dicatur charitas quae spiritus est communis amborum?" This is another quote from Augustine's *De Trinitate*, 15.19, p.513 (p.424).

[57] Herman?, *Epitome*, 15 (PL 178:1717).

Abelard's original section on the Trinitarian persons, but in using will for the Holy Spirit, another coherent model for the procession of the Holy Spirit is given, consistent with those found in Abelard's thought. This model stresses the need for dual procession from Father and Son, because it is only to the extent that someone is able to do something and knowledgeable of it, that they are able to will to do it.

"Gift" would seem at face value to be a term describing the temporal mission of the Spirit. There is no sense in which the Father and Son eternally give the Holy Spirit to each other, although He may be said to be the love that they have for each other. Augustine liked using the term gift, and in order to make this part of the eternal person of the Spirit, concluded that the Spirit proceeded eternally as giveable, although only temporally was He given as a gift.[58] In the description of the Holy Spirit as love, Abelard stated that love is the greatest gift of God, of Father and Son, and used this as part of his basis for confirming the coequality of the Spirit in the Trinity.[59] Abelard deals with Augustine's gift/giveable problem in treating of the World Soul. In passages quoted above, Abelard used Spirit to refer to the eternal state, and soul to refer to the temporal state of the third person. The language of gift is inserted into this framework, as being part of the temporal mode of procession of the Spirit, observed by philosophers, and called by them soul:

> What therefore is surprising when we say that the Spirit proceeds in two modes, if on accound of one mode of procession He is called Spirit by us, and on account of another he is called soul by the philosophers?[60]

While this interpretation does solve the problem of a person of God proceeding as "giveable", and thus potential rather than actual, it might imply a change in the Spirit from His eternal state at the creation of the world. Abelard was satisfied that this corresponds to the incarnation of Jesus, and thus did not entail any change in the Spirit's eternal state.

The final term describing the Holy Spirit that Abelard uses comes again from the writings of Augustine, and is used mainly in direct, lengthy quotation without any major commentary from Abelard. The word used is *communio*, and signifies that the Holy Spirit is in some way the fellowship of Father and Son. This has been noted above in the context of the Holy Spirit as the love which joins the Father and Son together.

The passage of Augustine in which this term is used looks at the name of the Holy Spirit in the context of His being the gift of the Father and the Son. Abelard quotes this context in full. Augustine declares that as both Father and Son are holy and spirit in themselves, the signification of the name Holy Spirit must be that He is the person who draws Father and Son together in fellowship: "The Holy Spirit is the ineffable communion of the Father and the Son, and

---

[58] Augustine, *De Trinitate*, 5.16, p.224 (p.200).
[59] Abelard, *Introductio*, 1.66 (Vol.3, p.344).
[60] *Ibid.*, 2.178 (Vol. 3, p.494).

perhaps for that reason he is so called, since that name is able to join the Father and the Son".[61] Abelard seems to accept both Augustine's teaching here, and the approval which this teaching has found in the minds of his readers.

It is perhaps a little disappointing that Abelard did not choose to elucidate more on this idea himself to show its significance for his overall Trinitarian thought. In the *Theologia Christiana*, he presents this quotation at the end of his outline of the Trinity before going on to look at the Trinity in the Old Testament prophets and then the pagan philosophers. It seems therefore to take the place of a concluding remark to satisfy his orthodoxy on the person of the Holy Spirit at the end of this initial outline. It is to be regretted that Abelard at no point assesses the place of union language in the context of his thought on the Spirit as goodness, which he has placed as the most important descriptive term for the third person.

Abelard's orthodoxy was called into question because he appropriated the term "goodness" as particularly relevant to the Holy Spirit. However, it becomes clear when Abelard's work is studied that this nomenclature was a result of considered study of accepted terminology regarding the Spirit, and that it fits into the tradition on this subject. However, Abelard does not bring together his thoughts on the various names which he applies to the Holy Spirit to provide a clear, logical description of the third person of the Trinity.

The Procession of the Holy Spirit

Another area in which Abelard shows his orthodoxy is in his presentation of the procession of the Holy Spirit. The best example of this is his discussion in the *Introductio ad Theologiam*, in which he affirms the dual procession of Spirit from Father and Son, noting the relevancy of the terms *ingenitum*, *genitum* and *non genitum* to distinguish the relative states of the three persons.[62] These three terms cover the respective origins of the persons, and distinguish between the processions of the Son and the Spirit in their procession from the Father. In this section, Abelard quotes from Augustine, Gennadius and Gregory the Great, showing that he is following the traditional line on the procession of the Holy Spirit as it had been received in the twelfth century.

Abelard uses another line in the *Introductio* concerning the procession of the Holy Spirit which is the quotation of Greek sources to support the equal, dual procession. This is not found in the writing of Anselm of Canterbury on the subject, though it was part of the discussion reported by Anselm of Havelberg. Abelard quotes from Cyril, Didymus, Chrysostom and Athanasius to show that these Greeks taught dual procession.[63] This analysis of writers from the Greek side shows that Abelard was not only orthodox from a Western perspective, but also that his teaching was in line with that of the whole church before the issue of the Spirit's procession divided East from West.

---

[61] Augustine *De Trinitate*, 5.11, p.219 (p.197), quoted by Abelard in *Theologia Christiana* 1.36 (Vol. 2, p.87).

[62] Abelard, *Introductio*, 1.22 (Vol. 3, p.327-28).

[63] Abelard, *Introductio*, 2.157-60 (Vol. 3, p.483-85).

In teaching on the dual procession of the Holy Spirit from Father and Son, Abelard brings in many of the terms that he had used to describe the person of the Holy Spirit: *bonitas, benignitas, charitas, voluntas*.[64] Abelard shows in this that these terms all have applicability in relating the Spirit to the Father and the Son: goodness is used in relation to the qualities of power and wisdom; love shows that the Holy Spirit must have come from both other members of the godhead, as, citing Gregory the Great, Abelard states that "It is not possible to have love between less than two".[65]

One area of slight controversy in Abelard's writing on the procession of the divine persons concerns the analogy that he created of a seal. The image begins with the bronze object (Father) from which a seal, or an image (Son), is made; the sealing that then happens can thus be seen to come from both the bronze and the seal.[66] Bernard of Clairvaux objected to the analogy,[67] claiming that it was one area in which Abelard inferred that the Son had only some power, and the Holy Spirit none. Sikes responds to this that such criticisms miss the object of Abelard's analogy, which is intended to concentrate on the possibility of the divine processions.[68]

Abelard showed in his teaching on the procession of the Holy Spirit that he had fully grasped all the important positions taught by the Church Fathers, and that he accepted them as they were taught. What is more, he was able to use a wide range of terms used to describe the Holy Spirit in a short passage to explain how the Spirit proceeds from both the Father and the Son. This processional teaching is important for understanding Abelard's earlier writing on the Holy Spirit as goodness and World Soul, as he clearly does not want to teach anything which undermines this standard position. Abelard is unfortunate that those who were concerned about parts of his teaching did not read these sections in the context of Abelard's overall thought on the Holy Spirit.

Conclusion

It is apparent, therefore, that Abelard did not see himself attempting to change the traditional position of the church on the person of the Holy Spirit, despite the apparent novelty of the views which he presented on the relation between

---

[64] *Ibid.*, 2.122-26 (Vol. 3, p.468-71). Watkin-Jones notes that Abelard worked with the name Holy Spirit, that this suggested the love of divine goodness proceeding equally from the first two persons. Watkin-Jones, *The Holy Spirit in the Medieval Church*, pp.92-96.

[65] *Ibid.*, 2.123 (Vol. 3, p.469) quoting from Gregory the Great, *Homiliae in Evangelica* (PL 76:1139). Grane writes that, for Abelard, the Holy Spirit proceeds from the passion of the love of the Father and Son (Grane, *Peter Abelard*, p.97).

[66] *Ibid.*, 2.112 (Vol. 3, pp.462-63). Grane provides a useful explanation of this analogy in his book, *Peter Abelard*, p.96-97. Clanchy writes that this was Abelard's equivalent of Anselm of Canterbury's watercourse analogy (Clanchy, *Abelard: A Medieval Life*, pp.282-83).

[67] Bernard of Clairvaux, *Epistola* 190 (*Opera Vol.VIII*) pp.17-40.

[68] Sikes, *Peter Abailard*, p.155.

the Spirit and Plato's World Soul, and the idea that the term "goodness" is especially relevant to the third person. These were intended to be instructive, broadening insight into the immanent person of the Spirit because of their exploration into new lines of thought.

Abelard's own natural mental ability, coupled with his training as a logician and grammarian, and a taste for discussion and argument, meant that he sought to dig deeper into the mysteries of God than had been accepted up to his time. His findings on two major issues concerning the Holy Spirit brought serious reaction from some members of the church who feared the novelty of his teaching and did not fully understand his argument on these points. This was not helped by the prominent position that they held in the *Theologiae*, nor by the fact that Abelard did not provide explicit defences for these new teachings, but included them as major parts of his theology. It is understandable that a reader of Abelard's work in the twelfth century would have been drawn to these teachings, and yet there is also a large amount of material showing that Abelard was searching out new ideas in the context of previously held beliefs.

Abelard's thoughts on the World Soul were not as definite as his opponents alleged, linking this concept only to the temporal mission of the Spirit. However, the incompleteness of this comparison, together with its roots in pagan philosophy, meant that the concept was not followed up by the church, but only by the Abelardian school. The remainder of Abelard's teaching, as this book will show, followed the standard lines of thought on the Holy Spirit in the twelfth century, and was not even at odds with those very men who condemned him for his views.

Abelard must therefore be seen to be faithful to the Christian tradition concerning the person of the Holy Spirit, as he demonstrated throughout his writings; and recognised as a key figure in the growing movement to apply reason more fully to the faith that was upheld by the church in the twelfth century. The controversy that surrounded Abelard in his life and work does not affect the contribution that he made towards understanding on the Holy Spirit in this period.

CHAPTER 4

William of St. Thierry and Bernard of Clairvaux

William of St. Thierry was one of the most significant writers on the person of the Holy Spirit in the twelfth century, concentrating much of his teaching on man's relationship to God through the Spirit, and basing this on the eternal attributes of the Spirit which make this possible. Because of the importance of the activity of the Spirit to his overall theology,[1] William was greatly concerned to establish a correct view of the Holy Spirit in His eternal state and relations with the Father and the Son. In doing this, William denounced what he saw as the errors of Peter Abelard and William of Conches, but also provided a great deal of interconnected thought on the various attributes of the Spirit.

Bernard of Clairvaux wrote less about the eternal nature of God, which he viewed as a mystery largely beyond the comprehension of the human mind.[2] However, when he taught on this issue, Bernard used the same concept of the Spirit as William did in his writings. Bernard was called upon because of his status within the church by William as a defence against what William saw as heretical teaching, further showing their agreement on the eternal identity of the Spirit. William's reliance on Bernard in this matter is insightful into their relative positions in the church, as their writings show William to be the more prepared critic of Abelard's positions.

William and Bernard represent a monastic, mystical reaction against the budding scholasticism that had started under Anselm of Canterbury and that had been taken to disturbing heights by Peter Abelard, according to the mystics.[3] The use of reason to explore faith, advocated by Anselm, was seen as

---

[1] David Bell shows in his work how the Holy Spirit is the 'key' to William's mystical theology (Bell, *Image and Likeness*, p.234).

[2] Verdeyen believes that this is one of the causes for the more structured relationship in William's work between the godhead and people: "Plus que l'abbé de Clairvaux, Guillaume s'interesse aux conditions et a la structure théologique de la rencontre humano-divine" (Verdeyen, *La Théologie Mystique*, p.43).

[3] This is the accepted view, as shown in Pranger's article 'Sic et non: Patristic Authority between Refusal and Acceptance: Anselm of Canterbury, Peter Abelard and Bernard of Clairvaux'. However, Sommerfeldt has argued against this in his article 'Bernard of Clairvaux and Scholasticism'. He believes that Bernard's relationship with Abelard should not be taken as a guideline for Bernard's attitude to the scholastic method: "Bernard did not hesitate to examine God Himself and did so with the aid of dialectical tools" (p.270). Sommerfeldt shows that Bernard was well acquainted with many of the early scholastic theologians, and that he supported the work that they were doing.

perverted into the dominance of reason over faith in the writings of Abelard. Bernard reacted particularly strongly against this concept of "theology", renaming it "Stupid-ology".[4] Abelard was seen as prying too deeply into the hidden mysteries of the godhead. William and Bernard essentially wanted a more experiential pneumatology reflecting the emphasis of the Bible on the work of the Holy Spirit.

However, as this chapter will show, both William and Bernard had definite ideas about the status and relationships of the persons of the godhead which permeated their teachings, and not only followed some of the errors they denounced in Abelard's work, but even went beyond their contemporary writers in defining the person of the Holy Spirit. The chapter will begin with an analysis of the disputes with Abelard and William of Conches from the perspective of the Cistercians, showing the extreme positions of the two sides in their approaches to theology; the next stage of the chapter will be a thematic study of the Holy Spirit in the writings of William and Bernard. Finally, the chapter will show the strength of William's definition, in particular, of the person of the Holy Spirit binding His immanent and economic identities and roles.

William of St. Thierry will be the main focus of the chapter throughout because of the mass of material that he wrote concerning the person of the Holy Spirit, while the writing of Bernard will be considered as it supports the positions that William taught. Of Bernard's works, the most significant for this chapter was his *Sentences*, while the works *On Loving God* and his *Sermons on the Song of Songs* also provide some useful comment. Most of William's works will be analysed: his more theological *Mirror* and *Enigma of Faith*; his contemplative *On Contemplating God* and *Meditations*; his commentaries on Romans and on the Song of Songs; and his accusations against Peter Abelard and William of Conches.

The Disputes with Peter Abelard and William of Conches

It is important to study these disputes from the point of view of both Peter Abelard (in the chapter above) and the Cistercians, because the debate illuminates their overall views on the person of the Holy Spirit. The focus will be on William of St. Thierry's critiques, as these were the basis of the opposition. This analysis will be briefer than that concerning Abelard (because the context and issues have been considered in the treatment of Abelard's views) and will show how William of St. Thierry saw traditional pneumatology being attacked by what Abelard and William of Conches had written.

The Holy Spirit as World Soul

The first area of dispute that will be examined here was the connection that Abelard and William of Conches saw between the person of the Holy Spirit and the World Soul found in Plato's *Timaeus*. William of St. Thierry was concerned about these references to the philosopher found in works of Christian theology,

---

[4] Clanchy, *Abelard: A Medieval Life*, 6.

and wrote to Bernard detailing those errors which he saw in the works of the two writers. The greater volume of material was written against Abelard and this will be focused on, although, as Marcia Colish has noted, there is no great difference between the teachings of Abelard and William of Conches.[5]

Abelard's thought on the World Soul comes in the context of teaching on the revelation of God before the coming of Christ, and the recognition of this by the prophets and the philosophers. Abelard states that the trinity of Mind, Nous and World Soul found in the writings of Plato is a recognition of the Trinitarian nature of God. The key to understanding Abelard's presentation of this is noting his use of the word "involucrum", a word helpfully translated by Ludwig Ott as "allegorische Einkleidung".[6]

It is this cloaking of meaning which makes Plato's trinity acceptable to Abelard as a veil through which the Christian Trinity can be seen, and which William of St. Thierry views as a wall that Christians should not look beyond. William focuses in his *Disputatio Catholicorum Adversus Dogmata Petri Abaelardi* on the impossibility of viewing the Holy Spirit as the World Soul because of the temporal nature of the latter.[7] In the charges with which Bernard ultimately accuses Abelard at Sens in 1140 is the statement that Abelard taught "Quod Spiritus Santus sit anima mundi".[8] It was possible for Abelard to defend himself against the charge of having taught equality of the World Soul with the Holy Spirit; however, it would appear that William of St. Thierry was unhappy with any suggestion that a Trinitarian person could be likened to something that was not fully divine.

William of Conches is far more direct in his association of the Holy Spirit with the World Soul, stating that the World Soul, understood to be the Holy Spirit, is the means by which all things live, and relating to what he terms the "naturalis vigor". These teachings are based on the fact that the Holy Spirit can be seen as the goodness and love of God, which themes are discussed earlier in his work *Philosophia Mundi*;[9] in the *Glosae* on Plato's *Timaeus*, William wrote that it was wrong to state that the World Soul was created, because it was said to be the Holy Spirit, which proceeds: "And it is good that it says "thought out" and not "created", because the soul is said to be the Holy Spirit. And the Holy

---

[5] Colish, *Peter Lombard: Volume 1*, p.100.

[6] Ott, 'Die platonische Weltseele', p.309. *Involucrum* is difficult to translate into English. Dronke provides some options (covering, analogy, figurative) without providing a concept as clear as that in German. Dronke, *Fabula: Explorations into the Uses of Myth*, p.61.

[7] William of St. Thierry, *Disputatio Catholicorum Adversus Dogmata Petri Abaelardi* (PL 180:322).

[8] Mews, 'The List of Heresies', pp.73-110. Mews notes elsewhere that Thierry of Chartres was reprimanded at Soissons in 1121 (where Abelard was first condemned over this issue) for linking the World Soul to the Holy Spirit. There is no evidence, however, that Thierry was following Peter Abelard in this line of thought. Mews, 'On Dating the Works of Peter Abelard', pp.100-01.

[9] William of Conches, *Philosophia Mundi*, 15 (PL 172:46).

Spirit is not made or created or born of God, but proceeds from Him".[10] Despite the lack of caution in William of Conches' teaching on this subject, William of St. Thierry only includes one minor reference to this teaching in his letter to Bernard,[11] although he does accuse William of Conches of changing the teaching of the faith in holding this view.

The most important point for William of St. Thierry in the issue of the Spirit being equated with the World Soul is the effect that this teaching had on the divinity of the Holy Spirit. Despite the fact that William's own writings on the Spirit are dominated by the experience which man has of God through the Holy Spirit, and thus concentrate on the temporary mission, William is at all times concerned to uphold the complete equality of the Spirit with the Father and Son in His divinity.

The Holy Spirit as the Goodness or Will of God

A second area where William of St. Thierry saw a need for correction was in the application of the names "Goodness" (by Abelard) and "Will" (by William of Conches) as particularly appropriate to the Holy Spirit. Both these terms were used alongside "Power" (for the Father) and "Wisdom" (for the Son) to create pictures of the Trinity. William argued against these terms because they were not used on the basis of Biblical or Patristic authority but because of reason. William of St. Thierry called the ideas "novam philosophiam" in teaching against William of Conches.[12]

The foundation for William's attack on these nomenclatures is Augustine's statement that "Quidquid ... in Deo est Deus est". To teach that one person in the godhead is particularly the goodness of God is therefore incorrect, as each of the three persons is equally goodness because each is fully God in himself. This point is expounded in the *Disputatio Adversus Petrum Abaelardum Ad Gaufridum Carnotensem et Bernardum*: "The Father is understood as being omnipotent, as is the Son and the Holy Spirit, yet no however three omnipotence being but one omnipotence, just as there is one wisdom; just as it is right to say that not only the Father is omniscient and all kind, but also the Son and the Holy Spirit".[13] William thus concentrates his teaching on the identical nature of the three persons as God.

The charge that is made against Peter Abelard on this point focuses on only one element of the teaching, that of power, as representative of this whole line of thought. The objection is that Abelard teaches that the Father has complete power, the Son some power, and the Holy Spirit no power.[14] This comes from

---

[10] William of Conches, *Glosae Super Platonem*, 1.74 (ed. E. Jeauneau. Paris: J. Vrin, 1965), pp.148-49.

[11] William of St. Thierry, *De Erroribus Guillelmi de Conchis ad Sanctum Bernardum* (PL 180:334).

[12] *Ibid.*, (PL 180:333).

[13] *Disputatio Adversus Petrum Abaelardum Ad Gaufridum Carnotensem et Bernardum* (PL 180:252).

[14] Mews, 'The List of Heresies', p.110.

Abelard's wider discussion of the nature and relationship of power, wisdom and goodness, but is an interpretation of what Abelard might mean, rather than a quote or direct reference. It represents what might be taught if this line of thinking on the attributes of the individual persons were taken to an extreme, but never occurs in Abelard's own writings.

William takes a similar exception to William of Conches' construct of power, wisdom, will. William of Conches makes a connection between the will of a person and the breath, and links this to Scriptural ideas that the Holy Spirit is breathed.[15] William of St. Thierry is on stronger ground in his opposition here because of the clear use of temporal things to apply to the Trinitarian persons without further support.[16] The major focus of his argument against William of Conches is on the identity of the three persons in their immanent state and their unity as one power, one goodness and one will;[17] this is the same attack that he made against Abelard.

The issue at stake for William here is the requirement of correct authority for any proposed teaching: Abelard introduces the power, wisdom, goodness trinity into his *Theologiae* without seeking either Biblical or Patristic support for his position. This is confirmed by the intriguing fact that neither William nor Bernard could be said to oppose the appropriation of the terms "goodness" and "will" to the person of the Holy Spirit on a reasonably fundamental level: both words are used repeatedly by William and Bernard in their works to refer specifically to the Holy Spirit in His eternal state and relations with the Father and the Son (as will be shown below). This fact takes away some of the argument, based on Augustine's thought that the characteristics of God are God, as William himself applies divine attributes to particular persons.

These two issues are informative for understanding William of St. Thierry's basic approach in writing about the Holy Spirit: the debate on the World Soul shows his determination to retain a unified perception of the Spirit, not in any way separating His immanent and economic states; the critique of Abelard's use of the term "goodness" displayed William's insistence that enquiry into the godhead should be ruled and regulated by what the church had traditionally taught. This chapter will now look at William and Bernard's specific teachings on the person of the Holy Spirit, before summarising the overall idea of the Spirit that they taught.

The Person of the Holy Spirit

This discussion of William and Bernard's views on the Holy Spirit will take a thematic approach, examining various terms that were applied to the third person and the reasons for their application. This will show that both writers, in their theological and mystical works, taught a definite, deep and developed person of the Holy Spirit in His eternal state that was crucial to their

---

[15] William of Conches, *Philosophia Mundi*, 1.9 (PL 172:45).

[16] William of Conches does not mention Augustine's use of the term will to refer to the Holy Spirit.

[17] William of St. Thierry, *De Erroribus Guillelmi de Conchis* (PL 180:335-36).

understandings of the relationship of the Spirit both within the godhead, and with mankind and the temporal world.

Unity

The concept of the Holy Spirit as unity in the Trinity is the foundation for much of the thought of William and Bernard. This idea is stated much more frequently and clearly in the writings of William, which will be the focus of this study, although it is also present in Bernard's work, as will be shown towards the end of this analysis.

It is important to study the concept of unity in William's work first in dealing with the person of the Holy Spirit, because the idea of drawing both Father and Son together in union with each other, and that of bringing mankind into the unity of the godhead, is the basis for the other terms which are applied to the Holy Spirit. Each of the subsequent attributes brings out some aspect of this uniting role that is central to William's thought. This is equally true whether William is considering the immanent or the economic roles of the Spirit. William bases all this teaching on concepts found in the Church Fathers, particularly Augustine and Origen.

The first way in which the Holy Spirit is seen as union is simply as commonality, or whatever unites the Father and the Son. This is stated most clearly in William's *Meditations*: The Father is in the Son and the Son is in the Father, and the Holy Spirit is the "uniting bond" of these two. William then writes that this unity is the cause of the Spirit's existence: "[the Holy Spirit] exists as such by the virtue of his unity of being with you both".[18] This seems to be extreme language concerned with processional teaching on the mode of the Spirit's procession, but William does not in this passage draw further conclusions on this point.

The idea of the Holy Spirit being a uniting bond between Father and Son is based on a belief that the Spirit is whatever is common to them both. In *The Enigma of Faith*, William sees the unity implied in the name of the Holy Spirit (as both Father and Son are holy and spirit), and concludes from this name that the Holy Spirit is whatever is common to Father and Son, listing here the terms divinity, love and sweetness.[19] This idea is important for understanding the relational position of the Holy Spirit to the Father and Son, whose own names are significant in their differentiation from each other. The same teaching is

---

[18] William of St. Thierry, *Meditativae Orationes*, 6.11-2, p.114 in *Oraisons Méditatives* (ed. J. Hourlier. Paris: Les Éditions du Cerg, 1985) and p.128 in *The Works of William of St. Thierry Volume 1: On Contemplating God; Prayer; Meditations* (tr. Sister Penelope. Kalamazoo: Cistercian Publications: 1977). References from William's works will be from both Latin and English versions, where available, with English edition page numbers in brackets.

[19] William of St. Thierry, *Enigma Fidei*, 97, pp.174-76 in *Deux Traités sur la Foi: Le Miroir de la Foi, L'Énigme de la Foi* (ed. M.-M. Davy. Paris: J. Vrin, 1959) and p.114 in *The Enigma of Faith* (tr. J.D. Anderson. Kalamazoo: Cistercian Publications, 1974).

contained in a more mystical work, his *Commentary on the Song of Songs*,[20] showing that it is not dependent on William's goal in writing the work. William is excellent at maintaining the same teaching whether he is concentrating more on theological or mystical ideas; this is also true in his reflections on both the eternal and temporal aspects of the godhead.

The second use of union to describe the Holy Spirit is in the context of the Spirit as the love and will of Father and Son.[21] In the tract *De Contemplando Deo*, William pictures the aspect of unity resulting from the strength of the love of Father and Son, and the unity itself showing the identical nature of the Trinity: "That love is so great that it is unity, and the unity is such that it is oneness of substance".[22] William does not imply in these words a progression from love through unity to substance, but is instead attempting to emphasise the strength of the love in connecting it to the idea of the Spirit as unity in the Trinity. Love is one aspect of the Spirit's immanent role of drawing the godhead together. The same connection of love and unity is found in the *Enigma of Faith*, though the implications of this link do not stretch as far.

Another reference to union comes in William's *Commentary on Romans*, in which William states that, "Divinity is the Holy Spirit, the divinity of the Father and the Son, who is understood to be their love and their goodness ... he is even the divinity common to both, and whatever is common to all three of them is certainly common to both".[23] This is an isolated reference in William's works to the Holy Spirit as "divinity", and therefore it is difficult to draw conclusions on this specific point. The passage does, however, emphasise the importance of unity as the central identity of the Spirit in William's thought. William is almost in danger of supporting Gilbert of Poitiers' statement that there is a divinity in God by which God is God, rather than God simply existing.[24] It is clear from the context that William does not wish to suggest this, but to write of one of the divine persons that they are the divinity of the others is misleading.

The final aspect of union in the eternal sphere that must be examined is found in the *Mirror of Faith* and concerns the mutual "recognition" of Father

---

[20] William of St. Thierry, *Commentary on the Song of Songs* 8.95, pp.220-22 in *Exposé sur le Cantique des Cantiques* (ed. J.-M. Déchanet. Paris: Les Éditions du Cerf, 1998) and p.78 in Exposition on the Song of Songs (tr. C. Hart. Shannon: Irish University Press, 1970) p.78.

[21] These themes will be developed themselves more fully below.

[22] William of St. Thierry, *De Contemplando Deo* 11, p.98 (p.54 in *The Works of William of St. Thierry Volume 1: On Contemplating God; Prayer; Meditations* (tr. Sister Penelope. Kalamazoo: Cistercian Publications: 1977)).

[23] William of St. Thierry, *Expositio Super Epistolam ad Romanos*, p.22 (in CCCM 86, ed. P. Verdeyen. Turnholt: Brepols, 1989) and in *Exposition on the Epistle to the Romans* p.38 (ed. J.H. Anderson. Kalamazoo: Cistercian Publications, 1980).

[24] Gilbert wrote that there was divinity by which God existed, as well as the God that existed. For a fuller discussion, see L. Nielson's *Theology and Philosophy in the Twelfth Century: A Study of Gilbert Porreta's Thinking and the Theological Expositions of the Doctrine of the Incarnation During the Period 1130-1180* (Leiden: E.J.Brill, 1982), pp.142-45.

and Son.[25] This concept is introduced by the statement that the recognition which is mutual to the Father and Son is their unity, which is the Holy Spirit. This would seem a surprising interpretation, but William is determined to complete this teaching, writing that the "recognition by which they recognise each other is nothing other than the substance by which they are what they are". William seeks to provide a basis for this by using language of knowledge: that the Father knows the Son and the Son the Father because of this mutual recognition; and that the Holy Spirit reveals this knowledge to people because He is the common knowing of both. This is an interesting conclusion to draw from the concept of unity, and is partially backed up by William's thought on the Spirit as love, will, goodness and sweetness of Father and Son, which indicates a relational side to the idea of the Spirit drawing the two together in unity. The question remains whether the Father and Son are able to recognise each other without the Holy Spirit, which would seem logically undeniable, and thus what exactly William's point is.

We have in this last section the first indications of what the doctrine of the Spirit as unity might mean for His temporal mission (in providing recognition and knowledge of Father and Son, in this case). The linking of this aspect of union in the Spirit's eternal nature to temporal matters occurs in two other works. The *De Contemplando Dei* applies this teaching to the spiritual union of people with God through prayer, stating that we are united with God through the Holy Spirit who is called unity.[26] The *Meditations* follow up this point, saying that it is the Holy Spirit "who creates and sets in order the unity that makes us one among ourselves and in you".[27] Renna summarises William's teaching on this point in writing: "As the Holy Spirit unites Father and Son, the Holy Spirit unites the holy soul with the other two persons of the Trinity".[28] These two mystical works show the interrelationship in William's thought between the perception of the immanent Spirit, and the experience of the Spirit in the life of the believer.

David Bell analyses the difference in William's writing on the Spirit in relation to the godhead and mankind. In God, the Holy Spirit is described as *unitas*, whereas in man He is *similitudo*, because of the imperfections of human nature.[29] Emero Stiegman is also helpful in his analysis of William on this issue, explaining that, for William, the Holy Spirit is the "very community" of the Trinity communicated to us in *unitas spiritus*: "As the persons of the Trinity are

---

[25] The following discussion comes from *Speculum Fidei*, 68, pp.80-82 in *Deux Traités sur la Foi: Le Miroir de la Foi, L'Énigme de la Foi* (ed. M.-M. Davy. Paris: J. Vrin, 1959) and pp.75-76 in *The Mirror of Faith* (tr. T. Davis. Kalamazoo: Cistercian Publications, 1979).

[26] William, *De Contemplando*, 11, pp.102-04 (p.57).

[27] William, *Meditativae*, 6.11-12, p.114 (p.128).

[28] Renna, 'Augustine and the Early Cistercians', pp.388-89. Renna also later remarks, "William perhaps gave the Holy Spirit a greater role in the realization of divine love in the soul than did Augustine" (p.391).

[29] Bell, *The Image and Likeness*, pp.134, 177.

subsistent relations and the Holy Spirit is the union of Father and Son, so our own union with the Trinity ... is the Holy Spirit, the reciprocal knowledge of Father and Son".[30] The work in man is an extension of the identity of the Spirit in God, but is necessarily less complete.

Bernard of Clairvaux does not provide any theological teaching as to why the Holy Spirit should be seen as union in the godhead,[31] but does use this idea to refer to the Holy Spirit, linked to the Spirit as the bond of love between Father and Son. The clearest reference in Bernard's works comes in his letter to the brothers at Chartreuse, in which he writes that the Holy Spirit, as *caritas*, holds and brings together the Trinity in the bond of peace.[32] In the same passage he declares, "What else maintains that supreme and unutterable unity in the highest and most blessed Trinity, if not charity?" Etienne Gilson shows how Bernard links this concept to the life of the believer in commenting on 1 John 4, as the Holy Spirit plays the part of the bond of union between God and the spiritual life.[33] The Holy Spirit is also described as unity in sermon eight on the *Song of Songs*, which focuses on the Spirit as the kiss of God.[34] Bernard extends this idea as William did to the experience that people have of God: "he manifests an awareness that such experience must necessarily be incomplete this side of eternity and so applies the phrase *unitas spiritus* to the future life ... In a completely different context, he applies the text to the life of the Holy Spirit within the Trinity".[35]

Understanding the teaching of William of St. Thierry on the Holy Spirit as the unity of Father and Son is crucial to grasping the overall picture of the Spirit in William's work. While in this initial discussion many of the concepts may appear unclear, they are clarified somewhat by his writings that will now be studied on the Holy Spirit as love, will, sweetness and goodness, which have greater support both from the Patristics and from contemporaries. The idea of the Spirit as the uniting force in the Trinity is important if these later concepts are accepted in this context of William's thought; the notion was also taught by Bernard, despite the fewer references that can be found in his works.

---

[30] Stiegman, 'Bernard of Clairvaux, William of St. Thierry, the Victorines', p.141.

[31] This is slightly surprising given that Bernard writes about unity in the godhead in sermon seventy-one on the Song of Songs. This sermon does not include any teaching on the Holy Spirit as union in the Trinity. Bernard of Clairvaux, *Opera*, Vol.2, pp.214-24 and pp.47-61 in *Sermon on the Song of Songs* (tr. I Edmonds. Kalamazoo: Cistercian Publications, 1980).

[32] Bernard of Clairvaux's letter on charity to the Holy Brethren of Chartreuse in *Opera*, Vol.3, p.149 and p.127 in *On Loving God* (tr. R. Walton. Washington, D.C.: Cistercian Publications, 1974).

[33] Gilson, *The Mystical Theology of St. Bernard*, pp.22-23.

[34] This will be studied more closely below.

[35] Casey, *Athirst for God: Spiritual Desire in Bernard of Clairvaux's Sermons on the Song of Songs* (Kalamazoo: Cistercian Publications, 1988), p.202. The context is sermon 5 of the Song of Songs.

Love

The concept of the Holy Spirit as love is very clear in the minds of these writers, and William states this very bluntly, as David Bell notes, in at least four of his works.[36] As with unity, Bernard's thought on the Holy Spirit as love in His immanent state is less detailed, and will be examined here first, before an analysis of William's more copious references is given. For both writers, love was the primary means by which they saw the Spirit drawing the Trinity together as one.

The most detailed reference to the Spirit as love in Bernard's works comes in his letter on charity to the Holy Brethren of Chartruse.[37] Although the Holy Spirit is not mentioned in person here, the discussion of the Holy Spirit as being both God and the gift of God shows that the third person is meant to be understood in the discussion. The linking of love to unity in this letter has already been noted above in the discussion on union. Bernard then goes on to stress that this charity that brings the Trinity together is no quality or accident in God, but is itself God. Bernard terms this love in God "substantial charity" which "produces the quality of charity. Where it signifies the giver, it takes the name of substance; where it means the gift, it is called a quality".[38] There is here a very definite picture of the Holy Spirit as love, not simply in an analogical way, but integral to His person and role within the eternal Trinity.

Bernard also refers to the Holy Spirit as love in his sermon on the Spirit as the kiss of God, in the series on the Song of Songs, and in his *Steps of Humility and Pride*, which links the Spirit's being love to the love in men. He states that the Spirit unites himself with the human will to create charity.[39] There is thus support in Bernard's work for this concept of the Holy Spirit as love in His immanent state, although Bernard's concentration on the experience of the Spirit means that there are not many references.

There are three important aspects of William's treatment of the Spirit as love that need mentioning. The first has already been discussed in the linking of love to unity in the role of the Spirit. The use of the accepted term love in this context strengthens William's ideas on the Spirit as unity. The connection of these two words often comes at the beginning of works to establish the person of the Spirit for later discussions. This is the case in his *Commentary on the Song of Songs*, the *De Contemplando Dei* and *The Enigma of Faith*. Bell shows how William unites these themes of union and love in man's experience of God: "Our love for God is our participation in the love which is God (which is God the Holy Spirit) or ... our love for God is our participation in God's loving

---

[36] Bell, *Image and Likeness*, p.134. The works quoted here are the *On Contemplating God*, the *Golden Epistle*, the *Sermons on the Song of Songs* and the *Exposition of the Epistle to the Romans*.

[37] Bernard, *Opera*, Vol.3, pp.148-54 (*On Loving God*, pp.125-32).

[38] *Ibid.*, p.149 (p.127).

[39] *Ibid.*, Vol.3, pp.31-32 and p.49 in *The Steps of Humility and Pride* (tr. M. Conway. Kalamazoo: Cistercian Publications, 1980).

himself, which is, in the last analysis, God's being himself".[40]

The second aspect relates to the passage quoted from Bernard, and is the Spirit as both the giver and the gift of love to mankind. In *The Enigma of Faith*, William explicitly states that "the Holy Spirit is not properly called the gift unless it is because of love", linking this to Romans 5 and the shedding of love abroad in the hearts of people.[41] There is also an indirect reference to 1 Corinthians 13 and the teaching that love is the basis of all of the gifts of the Holy Spirit. There is in this the tension between the Spirit as giver and gift, but William does not address it at this point. The relationship between the two roles of the Spirit is dealt with in the *Commentary on the Song of Songs*, and is seen as a result of the Spirit's identity as the commonality of Father and Son. The Spirit's dual identity as both union and love between Father and Son is seen as providing the two roles: "All this [commonness of Father and Son] is the Holy Spirit - God, Charity, at once Giver and Gift".[42]

The final writing on the Spirit as love which is significant is found in *The Mirror of Faith*. Chapter two of this work sets forth an analogy of the Trinity in Faith, Hope and Love. Faith is seen as a kind of power from which hope is born; love is then seen as proceeding from both faith and hope, "for one cannot help but love what he believes in and hopes for".[43] William claims extra strength for this analogy beyond the basic processional model because the attributes faith, hope and love are coeternal and consubstantial. This analogy is strong in its relational set-up, but the characteristics do not correspond to other understandings of the persons apart from that of the Holy Spirit, which may well have been the original inspiration for the analogy.

The teaching on the Holy Spirit as love in the godhead and in His mission to mankind was accepted in twelfth-century thought. William used this to strengthen his position on the Spirit as unity, and both he and Bernard connected the theme of love to that of gift, although this teaching is on a fairly basic level.

Sweetness, Embrace, Kiss

An idea extended from that of the Spirit as the mutual love of Father and Son is of the Spirit as the Embrace or Kiss of Father and Son, as well as being their sweetness. This concept is stronger in the work of Bernard of Clairvaux, forming the basis of his sermon on the person of the Holy Spirit in the *Commentary on the Song of Songs*, though it is also mentioned in the work of William. Bernard preached this message in sermon eight of his series: "Now, that mutual knowledge and love between him who begets and him who is begotten - what can it comprise if not a kiss that is utterly sweet, but utterly a

---

[40] Bell, *Image and Likeness*, p.234.

[41] William, *Enigma*, 99, p.176 (pp.115-16).

[42] William, *Exposition on the Song of Songs*, 8.95, pp.220-22 (p.78).

[43] William, *Speculum*, 4, p.28 (p.8).

mystery as well?"[44] This kiss is transferred beyond the Father and Son in the giving of the Holy Spirit to the disciples when Jesus breathed on them, "that favor, given to the newly-chosen Church, was indeed a kiss".[45]

William follows this teaching of Bernard in writing about the attributes of God in his own *Commentary on the Song of Songs*, relating this eternal picture of the Holy Spirit as kiss to His temporal mission, though noting also the different level of love that exists within the Trinity from that possible between people and God: "This embrace extends to man, but it surpasses man. For this embrace is the Holy Spirit. He is the Communion, the charity, the Friendship, the Embrace of the Father and of the Son of God; and he himself is all these things in the love of Bridegroom and Bride".[46] This development of the theme of love further supports the idea of the Spirit as the union of Father and Son. William and Bernard thus take the "mutual" part of the mutual love theory extremely seriously in their application of it to the Holy Spirit.

Gift

It is important to include a short section specifically on William's teaching about the Holy Spirit as a gift because of the value that this has both on his understanding of the Spirit's procession, and because this is an important contribution to the overall use of gift terminology in the twelfth century. Some references to this aspect of the Spirit's identity have already been mentioned in this chapter in connection with His role as love, which was the most common application of the fact that the Spirit was given to people.

The main contribution that William makes concerning the Holy Spirit as gift is his teaching about the Spirit's procession. William is clear in confronting the problems that are raised by this idea, which centre on the economic aspect of the term gift. The *Enigma of Faith* contains several references to this which teach that the Holy Spirit proceeds in His immanent person from both Father and Son as a gift.[47] The primacy in this procession is given to the Father, although William is quick to stress that there is no inequality between the givers, but rather concord of the two persons. William does not address at this point the fact that there is no object for the gift of the Spirit in His immanent state. There is some indication of his awareness of this issue in the *De Erroribus Guillelmi de Conchis*, in which William uses Augustine's word "giveable" to describe the immanent procession of the Holy Spirit, but the context of this does not lend itself to a major explanation of William's application of this term.

Later in the *Enigma*, William relates this idea to the economic procession of the Spirit, actually stating that it is because of His procession into the world that

---

[44] Bernard, *Opera*, Vol.1, p.36 (*Song of Songs*, p.45).
[45] *Ibid.*, Vol.1, p.37 (p.46).
[46] William, *Commentary on the Song of Songs*, 11.132, pp.282-84 (p.106).
[47] William, *Enigma*, 26, p.114 (p.55); 77, pp.158-59 (pp.98-99).

the Holy Spirit is called the gift of God.[48] This must be read both in the context of what has already been written in this work concerning the Holy Spirit as gift in His immanent state, and also in relation to William's teaching in his work about love that the Holy Spirit gives Himself when He is sent into the world. This clearly differentiates the two processions because there is no construct that allows the Spirit to proceed from himself in His immanent procession.

There is some valuable material in these brief references for understanding this aspect of the Spirit's character that can inform the overall discussion about how the Holy Spirit can be said to be the gift of God. However, William does not move far beyond Augustine's position in these sections, and it is slightly disappointing that he at no point seeks to tackle thoroughly the issue of potentiality when speaking of the immanent procession of the Holy Spirit as a gift.

Will

We come now to the first of two sections of great interest given the analysis of William and Bernard's opposition to Abelard and William of Conches. Having seen the rejection of the terms "will" and "goodness" as particularly attributable to the Holy Spirit because of a lack of authority for these assignations, we will now be shown that both words were used by both William and Bernard to refer to the Holy Spirit. This often takes place without Scriptural or Patristic backing, but seems acceptable because of the devotional, rather than philosophical, nature and intent of the passages.

The first of these terms, will, is readily acceptable to these more conservative writers because it forms part of one of Augustine's analogies of the Trinity: memory, understanding and will. Bernard does not advance much beyond this analogy, which he outlines in his *Sentences*, although he does link these attributes of God to people's relationship with God, writing that people "cling" to the three persons by memory, understanding and will.[49] In a separate section of the *Sentences*, Bernard relates the Spirit's identity as will to the irremissible sin against the Holy Spirit, stating that whoever is not "of good will" commits this sin.[50]

William makes clear his understanding of the relationship between the term will and the person of the Holy Spirit by stating that the Spirit is the "substantial will" of the Father and the Son, as Bernard had called the Spirit the "substantial charity". This phrase is used in two works: the *Commentary on the Song of Songs* and *The Mirror of Faith*.[51] This is an extremely strong term, and William is alone in the twelfth century in using it to describe the Holy Spirit. Once again, the position of the Spirit linking Father and Son is stressed in this.

---

[48] *Ibid.*, 99, p.176 (pp.115-16).
[49] Bernard, *Parables and Sentences*, 3.5 (tr. M. Casey. Kalamazoo: Cistercian Publications, 1989) pp.191-92.
[50] *Ibid.*, 3.59, pp.233-34.
[51] William, *Commentary on the Song of Songs*, 10.131, pp.276-80 (p.104); *Speculum*, 66, p.78 (pp.72-73).

William also relates this eternal characteristic to the mission of the Holy Spirit in the connection of a person's will to the will of God:

> The Holy Spirit, who is the substantial will of the Father and the Son, so attaches the will of a person to Himself that the soul, loving God and, by loving, sensing Him, will be unexpectedly and entirely transformed, not into the nature of divinity certainly, but into a kind of blessedness beyond the human form yet short of the divine, in the joy of illuminating grace and the sense of an enlightened conscience.[52]

William also joins the Spirit's mission as will to that of being Love in the *De Contemplando Dei*, in linking both the inspiration of the human will and love, as well as the concepts themselves: "For love is nothing other than a vehement, well-ordered will".[53]

Given William's criticism of William of Conches' teaching on the Spirit as will, it is surprising that it forms such a crucial and involved part of William of St. Thierry's own understanding of the person of the Spirit both eternally and in His temporal mission. However, William's own use does back up his concept of the Spirit being the uniting force within the Trinity.

Goodness

It is fascinating given the importance of the dispute between the mystics and Peter Abelard on the concept of goodness that both Bernard and William repeatedly refer to the Holy Spirit as the goodness of God. This idea is written of in similar ways to the passages on love and will, and the two writers seem to be satisfied with this concept that they had previously argued so strongly against.

Bernard of Clairvaux's main passages on the Holy Spirit as the goodness of God come in his *Sentences*, although there is one significant reference in the *Commentary on the Song of Songs*: "but where there is perfect knowledge of the Father and the Son, how can there be ignorance of the goodness of both, which is the Holy Spirit?"[54] This comes as part of the sermon in which Bernard expounds on the Holy Spirit as the kiss, peace, bond, unity and love of the Father and the Son.

On two occasions in his *Sentences*, Bernard explicitly states that the Father, Son and Holy Spirit are power, wisdom and goodness. The clearest reference is this: "In the Father God's power is denoted, in the Son his wisdom, and in the Holy Spirit his generosity".[55] Bernard further clarifies this passage by referring to sins against the persons, being weakness (against the Father), ignorance (against the Son) and malice (against the Holy Spirit). Although this slightly

---

[52] William, *Speculum*, 66, p.78 (pp.72-73).

[53] William, *De Contemplando*, 11, p.96 (p.54).

[54] Bernard, *Opera*, Vol.1, p.38 (*Song of Songs*, p.47).

[55] Bernard, *Sentences*, 3.68, p.238. 'Generosity' is translated from the Latin *benignitas*, which is synonymous with goodness.

alters what Bernard had earlier taught on this point,[56] it does solidify the overall teaching on the Holy Spirit as the goodness of God. This relation of the terms to the persons seems to belong to their eternal natures, given the references to sinning against them.

The second reference to power, wisdom and goodness concerns temporal things. Bernard writes that, "the Father's power creates and sustains; the Son's wisdom gives order and beauty to each creature; and the goodness of the Holy Spirit brings more and more benefits".[57] In this section, the goodness that is the Holy Spirit is linked through His procession to usefulness, which results from the power and wisdom of the first two persons.[58] In this way, goodness is linked from the temporal ideas back into the procession of the Holy Spirit. The significance of goodness in the procession of the Spirit is picked up again in the next part of Bernard's teaching, in which the Holy Spirit is described as a "fountain of goodness" pouring forth from the Father and the Son.[59] This is seen as supporting the difference between the mode of proceeding of the Son and the Spirit, because this language does not resonate with the concept of being born. Bernard thus taught that the Holy Spirit should be seen in some way as the goodness of God both in eternal and temporal things.

William of St. Thierry applies goodness in four separate ways to the person of the Holy Spirit. Three of these apply more to concepts of His eternal status, while one refers specifically to His temporal mission. This connection is between the Spirit's work in giving gifts and His nature as goodness, and is thus similar to Bernard's second point. The teaching is given in both *The Enigma of Faith* and the *Commentary on the Song of Songs*.[60] However, this line of thought is made truly influential only as a working out of William's idea of the eternal person of the Spirit.

The first application of goodness to the Holy Spirit is linked to the idea of love. In the *Commentary on Romans*, William states this point in the context of another interesting assertion - that "divinity is the Holy Spirit, the divinity of the Father and the Son, who is understood to be their love and their goodness".[61] The second linking of the terms love and goodness comes in the *De Contemplando Deo*, in which William moves from a contemplation of God as ultimate goodness (a point which generally refers to the whole godhead) to love and goodness as the person of the Holy Spirit: "But, O you who are the One supremely good and the ultimate Goodness, your love is your goodness, the Holy Spirit proceeding from the Father and the Son".[62] This use of goodness

---

[56] That the sin against the Holy Spirit was a bad will - although this does include a concept of goodness in its teaching.

[57] Bernard, *Sentences*, 3.61, p.234.

[58] *Ibid.*

[59] *Ibid.*, 3.62, p.235.

[60] William, *Enigma*, 79, pp.160-61 (p.100); *Song of Songs*, 8.95, pp.220-22 (p.78).

[61] William, *Expositio*, p.22 (p.38).

[62] William, *De Contemplando Deo*, 11, p.54.

is significant in its position in teachings both on the whole godhead and on love, which was recognised as referring particularly to the third person.

The second context in which goodness is applied to the Spirit is a passage on the relationship between the processional model of the Trinity and the work of the Holy Spirit in creation. In the introduction to this section, William stresses that the processional order "must also be observed most prudently in the operation of the divinity or the cooperation of the Trinity which seems to be intimately connected with the relation of the three persons".[63] In light of this, William's statement that all things are distributed from the Father, through the Word, and "in the Holy Spirit who is the goodness of the Father and the Son" is significant in establishing goodness as part of the Spirit's eternal relations in the Trinity.

The third way in which the Holy Spirit is referred to as goodness is in a meditation on God's eternal foreknowledge, irrespective of time ("ready for all from all eternity, even had nothing ever been created"[64]). William states outright that "God's foreknowledge is the same thing as his goodness, which he is eternally ready to bestow on all", and goes on to write, "this goodness is the Holy Spirit, coeternal with the Father and the Son".[65] This is an interesting association of terms, without sufficient continuing discussion for close study, but the strength of William's concept of the Spirit as goodness is well shown in these pronouncements.

Given the amount of debate on this teaching in the twelfth century, and William and Bernard's parts in that debate, the strength and diversity of William and Bernard's teaching on the Holy Spirit as the goodness of God is both surprising and important.[66] There is no suggestion here that the Father and Son are not goodness in themselves,[67] but there is developed support for the idea that the Spirit should be seen to be in some way the particular goodness of God, or that the term goodness is particularly relevant to the third person.

William and Bernard's Overall Understanding of the Holy Spirit

Given this analysis of the positions that William and Bernard held on the Holy Spirit, it is important to examine their cumulative significance in building up a balanced idea of the Spirit; and also to note weaknesses that may be raised about the overall picture that is created.

There are three outstanding features of Bernard and William's writings on the Holy Spirit: the first is their consistency in linking all features to the idea that the Spirit was the uniting force of Father and Son in their eternal state,

---

[63] William, *Enigma*, 78, p.160 (pp.99-100).

[64] William, *Meditativae*, 1.10, p.48 (p.92).

[65] *Ibid.*, 1.10, p.48 (p.92).

[66] Colish states that there was a movement in the middle of the twelfth century led by Lombard to 'banish' the analogy of power, wisdom and goodness, but fails in her work even to prove Lombard's part in this. Colish, *Peter Lombard*, p.119.

[67] As was noted in the discussion of the disputes with Abelard, there was no wish on the part of those seen to be radical supporters of the analogy to go this far.

drawing them together in one love, one will, one goodness; the second feature is their success in teaching one person of the Spirit in both His eternal state and temporal mission; the last point is their ability to present the same person in all of their works, whether mystical or theological. At no point does there appear to be a tension between their understandings of this dual procession. This unifying picture is far stronger than that achieved by any other writer in the twelfth century.

However, there are two reasons behind this success that prevent one from giving complete approval to their understanding of the Spirit. The first reason is the lack of substantial discussion of the role or status of the Holy Spirit as gift. This is one of the issues that scholars in the twelfth century most wrestled with because of the frequent references to the Spirit as gift in the Scriptures, and yet the seeming temporal nature of the term. William and Bernard restrict their discussions of the Holy Spirit as gift mostly to His temporal mission, and do not seek to solve the mystery of His eternal state as either gift or giveable. The absence of any attempt at resolution of this eternal-temporal dichotomy in the Spirit's identity weakens somewhat their success in providing a consistent picture of the Holy Spirit in His two processions.

The second reason for withholding complete support for this picture is the inconsistency in the teaching on the Spirit as will and goodness. Having rejected and condemned the views of William of Conches and Peter Abelard, it is surprising to see both terms given strong positions in both William of St. Thierry and Bernard's understandings of the person of the Holy Spirit. This is less of an issue, however, when the reasons for the opposition to William and Abelard are understood more as methodological than theological. Having allowed for this, part of the objection was that the Trinitarian persons should be understood as having all the attributes of divinity in themselves individually, and thus the particular ascription of love, will and goodness to the Holy Spirit by William and Bernard is slightly surprising.

Conclusion

William of St. Thierry must rank as one of the most important thinkers of the twelfth century both in the sheer volume of material that he wrote on the Holy Spirit, and in the varied and developed understandings that are displayed throughout his writings. He is supported in all his diverse opinions by his influential friend, Bernard of Clairvaux. In light of this, it is surprising that their work has not been analysed more closely on this point, being concentrated on more for "mystical" rather than "theological" significance.

The place of William and Bernard at the conservative extreme of twelfth-century thought is shown in their attacks on William of Conches and Peter Abelard's dialectical approach to Platonic thought and their analogies devised by reason rather than from authority; yet the strength of their own conception of the person of the Holy Spirit was in many ways more radical than any other proposed at this time. While they based their teachings consistently on ideas gleaned from the Scriptures and the Church Fathers, Bernard and, particularly, William preached a role of the Spirit both in the eternal relations of the godhead and in His temporal mission on earth as the uniting person drawing God together and mankind to God that exceeds in coherence and consistency anything that was written by their contemporaries. There may be minor objections to their methodology in reaching this position, but these may yet be met by a more complete analysis of the thought-world of which they were a part.

CHAPTER 5

Hugh and Richard of St. Victor

One of the most influential schools in the twelfth century was based at Saint Victor in Paris. Hugh and Richard were successive priors and masters of the school, and were thus important in the formation of theology based on both faith and reason that had begun with the work of Saint Anselm of Canterbury, at the end of the eleventh century.[1] Richard openly states that he will follow the method of using argumentation to delve into the truths of Christianity, writing that he is aware of these truths from the authority of the Fathers, but that he finds in the earlier writings no tests of the truths, and few arguments concerning them.[2] The *De Trinitate* must therefore be read from this perspective, searching out the truths of the Trinity from a non-Biblical basis. This is a different method from his predecessor, Hugh, who was more traditional in his theological teaching. Butler separates Richard's methodology from that of Bernard of Clairvaux and Cistercian mysticism, which he describes as "pre-scholastic". Richard's *De Trinitate* is described in comparison as a "scientific treatise of mystical theology".[3]

Richard's work will be the main focus of this chapter, as he wrote far more, and in much greater detail, on the person of the Holy Spirit, especially in his *De Trinitate*. Hugh's greatest thought on the members of the Trinity is found in the appendix to his *Didascalion*, which is a meditation on the invisible God.[4] Richard and his views have undergone a period of great popularity in recent times, to the extent that he is referenced in popular works on the Holy Spirit,

---

[1] Nico den Bok shows in his work on the *De Trinitate* how Richard follows Anselm's 'fides quaerens intellectum' methodology. Den Bok, *Communicating the Most High*, p.80.

[2] Richard of Saint Victor, *De Trinitate Libri Sex*, 1.4, p. (PL 196: 892-93). He explains in this title the *modus agendi* for his work, which will be "non tam auctoritates inducere, quam ratiocinationi insistere". It is slightly surprising that there is no mention of Anselm of Canterbury in this section, which may show that Richard was not familiar with his work.

[3] Butler, *Western Mysticism*, p.125.

[4] Although termed in its title an appendix, the length of this work is roughly the same as each of the books that comprise the *Didascalion*, with the result that Migne treated the appendix as book seven. As quotations from this source will be from the Migne edition, the footnotes will refer to this work as *Didascalion 7*.

such as Clark Pinnock's *Flame of Love*.[5] Nico den Bok has undertaken a major study on the concept of person in Richard's *De Trinitate*, but this work has the weakness that it focuses too heavily on personhood at the expense of developing the characteristics of the actual persons in Richard's understanding.[6]

Studies of Richard's writings have focused on his use of love within the Trinity, but this chapter will seek to show that this is merely one method that Richard uses to elucidate the theory of the Trinity (and the Spirit's place within the godhead) which is the overall goal of the *De Trinitate*.[7] One strong line running through Richard's thought is of the applicability of the terms power, wisdom and goodness to the Trinitarian persons. In this he followed his master, Hugh, who had taught this idea that had led to such controversy in the life of Peter Abelard. The Victorine theology did not match Abelard's directly, which may partly explain their absence from the debate that led to Abelard's condemnation on this point at the hands of William of St. Thierry and Bernard of Clairvaux.

Another strength of Richard's work is his use of giving and receiving terminology that had caused theologians so many problems since the time of Augustine. Richard is one of the most forthright writers on this aspect of the Holy Spirit. The *De Trinitate* uses all of these aspects of the Holy Spirit to build up a logic for His necessary inclusion in the godhead, and His identity within the godhead, from a rational basis. The style of Richard's writing in this work makes it seem more like a standard theological treatise on the Trinity than the exploration into the existence and nature of God which it in fact is.

Richard of Saint Victor's works show him to be first and foremost a mystical theologian and biblical exegete. It is therefore slightly strange to find in his corpus of works as logical and detailed a presentation of the godhead as exists in the *De Trinitate*. Few other mystics composed major systematic treatises of this kind.[8] It is perhaps unsurprising, therefore, that Richard's work is not as organised and straightforward in its thinking as, for instance, the work of Peter Abelard or Peter Lombard. Richard's mystical background and personality shine through the words and images. The work needs to be studied

---

[5] It is noticeable that although Pinnock uses Richard's theology of the Spirit, there is no indication that he has actually read Richard's work. Pinnock, *Flame of Love*, pp.33-34.

[6] Den Bok, *Communicating the Most High*. Richard of St. Victor's work does focus heavily on ideas of person, particularly in books one and four. However, as this chapter will show, there is also a great deal of material on the attributes of the individual persons that Den Bok does not devote much attention to in his work.

[7] One example of Richard's emphasis on his ideas on love, which comes only in book three of the *De Trinitate*, is Melone's mistaken comment that "Il III libro affronta il problema della pluralità in Dio". Melone states that the first two books concentrate on the unity and perfection of God, and thus implies that the power, wisdom, goodness triad outlined in these books is not meant to refer to the Trinitarian persons. M. Melone, 'Lo Spirito Santo nel *De Trinitate* di Riccardo di San Vittore: L'originalità di una proposta', *Antonianum* 71:1 (2002), pp.33-67, at p.38.

[8] Bernard of Clairvaux, for instance, despite writing a massive amount of work, produced no great systematic theological work.

within the context of the inherited theology of the Church Fathers towards which he was working and the theological environment within which Richard was writing. Seen from this view, the *De Trinitate* provides incredible depth of insight into many issues of Trinitarian thought while at the same time being presented in terms that are attractive and helpful to the reader.

Badcock seeks to place Richard of St. Victor in a separate tradition to Anselm and Peter Lombard in the following passage:

> There are only two significant Trinitarian traditions in Western medieval theology: the Augustinian, which is mediated by Anselm and Peter Lombard and which culminates in Thomas Aquinas, and that initiated by Richard of St. Victor, which continues in the Franciscan tradition in Alexander of Hales and Bonaventure.[9]

This book will show that, although Richard did have some novel ideas regarding the Holy Spirit, the overall thrust of his pneumatology complemented that being taught by his contemporaries. Indeed, Richard's stated methodology in the *De Trinitate* of using reason, rather than Scripture or the Fathers, to study the persons of the Trinity shows him to be a part of the burgeoning scholastic culture of his time.

Power, Wisdom, Goodness

The applicability of the terms power, wisdom and goodness to the individual persons of the Trinity was, as has already been seen, a cause of great debate in the twelfth century. Both Hugh and Richard of St. Victor wrote this model into their thoughts on the Trinitarian persons, and yet neither was heavily criticised; indeed, the only evidence of their involvement in the overall discussion that was taking place is a letter from Richard to Bernard of Clairvaux explaining why the power, wisdom, goodness triad should be accepted by the church. In the *De Trinitate*, Richard uses this model as the basis for his proof of the existence and procession of three persons in the godhead, above the concept of love with which he is most associated.

Hugh

Hugh is extremely careful in his use of the attributes power, wisdom and goodness, and their relationship to the individual persons of the godhead. This may be because he was writing during the time when Abelard's theology was being questioned. In the introduction to his work on the invisible God, Hugh writes: "There are three invisibles of God, power, wisdom, kindness", but does not refer to the persons of the godhead, nor does he specify in what way there are three, whether modal, personal or communal.[10] This passage comes right at the beginning of his meditation on the godhead, and is thus the basis for the following discussion. It is, in many ways, more bold than Abelard's opening

---

[9] Badcock, *Light of Truth*, pp.246-47.
[10] Hugh, *Didascalion*, 7.1 (PL 176:811).

statement on this point, as Hugh does not seek to elaborate at all on this Trinity, but launches immediately into a discussion of the works of the three in the world.

The fact that he is talking about the way that God can be seen in the visible world is one reason for his lack of specificity on the divine qualities at this stage. Hugh is thinking through Paul's teaching that "God's invisible qualities ... have been clearly seen, being understood from what has been made" (Romans 1:18). The application of the terms power, wisdom and goodness is therefore made at this stage in Hugh's work to the temporal world, which power creates, wisdom governs, and goodness conserves.[11] Hugh also stresses at this stage the ineffable oneness of these three characteristics in God, and their inseparability in operation. The phraseology that Hugh uses to show this unity of the three elements is worth noting for its applicability in studying the godhead: "Power creates wisely through kindness. Wisdom governs kindly through power. Kindness conserves powerfully through wisdom."[12] In this, Hugh continues to refrain from any direct application of the attributes to any divine persons, as the language connecting the three does not involve significant processional terms.[13]

The three attributes are further defined in their manifestation to creatures as immensity, beauty and utility. Utility, which expresses goodness and therefore the Holy Spirit (as shall be shown below), has four consistent roles in creation for the benefit of creatures: grace, which is what pleases; adaption, which makes things fitting and congenial; giving gifts, which are beneficial; and providing what is necessary, without which it would not be possible to exist.[14] We see in this explanation of the role of utility a connection between the attribute and the person of the Holy Spirit to whom this will later be linked, as all of these roles are traditionally ascribed to the Spirit. However, it is also clear that Hugh is providing firm foundations for himself before he is willing to clarify his thoughts on the applicability of the terms.

Hugh leaves the power, wisdom, goodness formula for much of the rest of his work, using instead Augustine's mind, wisdom, love analogy, which was accepted by the twelfth-century church, to introduce the Trinitarian persons into his meditation. Only once this discussion has taken place does he return to his earlier thoughts, in the section *De tribus diebus invisibilis lucis*. Here he explicitly states "Power pertains to the Father, wisdom to the Son and kindness

---

[11] "Potentia creat, sapientia gubernat, benignitas conservat". Hugh, *Didascalion*, 7.1 (PL 176:811).

[12] "Potentia per benignitatem sapienter creat. Sapientia per potentiam benigne gubernat. Benignitas per sapientiam potenter conservat", *Ibid.* 7.1 (PL 176:811).

[13] The idea of one element operating through another has vague echoes of the Greek idea of all things being done by the Father, through the Son, in the Holy Spirit, but the lack of 'by' and 'in' show that this is not what is being addressed by Hugh at this point.

[14] "Utilitas creaturarum constat in grato, et apto, et commodo, et necessario. Gratum est quod placet, aptum quod convenit, commodum quod prodest, necessarium sine quo quid esse non potest". *Ibid.*, 7.1 (PL 176:813).

to the Holy Spirit".[15] This is written in the context of the soul's perception of the light of God, which results in fear (power), truth (wisdom) and love (goodness). This passage, *De tribus diebus*, comes at the end of the overall meditation on the godhead, which is thus book-ended by the trinity of power, wisdom and goodness.

It is disappointing that Hugh did not seek to interweave this teaching with that on the Holy Spirit as love; there remains an element of temporality about the application of power, wisdom and goodness to the respective persons of the godhead because of the emphasis in this last section on the human soul's cognisance of the divinity, and the temporal application of the first section. The only occasion on which Hugh transfers these terms into the immanent godhead, the stress is laid more on the unity of the three persons in their possession of these qualities than on the application of the words to individual persons. It is thus left unclear by Hugh exactly how far he wishes to go in seeing the Father as power, the Son as wisdom, and especially the Holy Spirit as goodness.

Richard

Richard begins his *De Trinitate*, which seeks to examine God from the standpoint of reason, with the concept of God as ultimate power and wisdom. These two traits result for Richard from the fact that all things come from the divine essence, and are ordered according to that essence. Book one of the work is dedicated first to confirming that God is one, and second that the one God is both omnipotent and omniscient. There is as yet no necessity within this picture of God that he be good. It is only as the teaching about a binity of power and wisdom is explored through book two in relation to each other and creation that a need is created for a third person to complete the godhead.

It is not until chapter sixteen of book two that Richard moves on to write that within an omnipotent being there can be no fullness or perfection lacking, with the consequence that the omnipotence must be the highest good, and consequently must be its own good.[16] Richard goes on from this to state that there cannot be many goods, as this would create divisibility, which is not consistent with eternity. The ultimate goodness of God therefore demands simplicity, which in turn creates unity in the divine substance.[17] Goodness is given here an importance in the concept of God of equivalent weight with power and wisdom as an essential, coequal attribute. However, it is noticeable at this point that the concept of goodness is drawn only from that of power, rather than from both power and wisdom. This would seem to support the Greek, Monarchian view of the processional relations within the godhead.

In spite of this, Richard is confident enough in the power, wisdom, goodness

---

[15] *Ibid.*, 7.26 (PL 176:836).

[16] "Constat itaque de omnipotente quod ipse sit summum bonum, et quod consequens est, quod ipse sit suum bonum". Richard, *De Trinitate*, 2.16, p.123 (PL 196:910).

[17] Richard concludes, "Quidquid ergo in summo bono est, vere et summe unum est". *Ibid.*, 2.17, p.124 (PL 196:911). The themes of unity and concord in the Trinity will be further discussed later in the chapter.

depiction, that he uses it as his main argument in the processional model that he draws up for the three persons. He states first that power is rightly ascribed to the person who is of himself, without procession.[18] Richard then points out that it is possible to have power without wisdom, but not wisdom without power - there is some element of power in the ability to be wise. This creates the procession of wisdom from power as the second part of the godhead. The concept of goodness, and its procession from these first two, derives from the fact that there must be both ability for goodness, and the wisdom to choose between good and bad, for goodness to exist: "Power gives ability, wisdom gives knowledge; without these things, it would not be possible for goodness to exist".[19] Goodness is thus not possible within the divine without the existence of both power and wisdom from which it draws its perfect being. This is a clever transformation by Richard from his initial thoughts on the nature of God to a recognisable, Trinitarian processional model.

It is this model that Richard repeats in his letter to Bernard of Clairvaux, explaining why the terms power, wisdom and goodness should be attributed to the respective Trinitarian persons.[20] This letter is a fascinating document in the context of the debate that had taken place between Abelard and his opponents over this very issue, and shows the authority that the Victorine school had not only in early scholasticism, but also bridging the gap to the mystical thought of the monastics. The identical nature of Richard's teaching on this point would indicate that Bernard did not have a copy of the *De Trinitate*, as Richard does not expand on his original teaching.

It is noticeable that whereas Hugh, after his initial presentation of three things in the godhead, ultimately derives the concept of goodness from that of love in his writing on the third person, Richard does the opposite, approaching the concept of supreme love from that of supreme goodness. This is perhaps indicative of the shift in thinking in the time between the two writers, that Richard was able to use the term goodness to refer to the Spirit in His immanent state, whereas Hugh guardedly kept his references to goodness more to the temporal mission of the Spirit.

Richard does link the theme of goodness in the immanent state of the Holy Spirit to the temporal world in his tract *On Blaspheming the Holy Spirit*.[21] He takes here the power, wisdom, goodness model, and links it to sins against the godhead: the sin of inability is against the Father; the sin of ignorance is against the Son; the sin of evil is against the Holy Spirit. As this third sin is the most intentional against the character of God, it is this sin that cannot be forgiven.[22]

---

[18] Richard, *De Trinitate*, 1.12, pp.96-97 (PL 196:896-97).

[19] *Ibid.*, 6.15, pp.247-48 (PL 196:980).

[20] The epistle is entitled *De Tribus Appropriatis Personis in Trinitate, ad divum Bernardum abbatem Clarevallensem* (PL 196:991-94).

[21] Richard, *Tractatus de Spiritu Blasphemiae* (PL 196:1185-92).

[22] "Qui per solam malitiam peccantes in Spiritum Sancum delinquunt, nil ejusmodi remissionis accipiunt, et non remittitur eis in hoc saeculo, nec in futuro" in *Ibid.*, (PL 196:1187).

This is one example where it is possible to back up the more philosophical writing of the *De Trinitate* with references from another of Richard's works. It is also an interesting conclusion from the idea of the Holy Spirit as the goodness of God and shows the extent to which Richard attributed the term goodness to the Spirit.

Love

The concept of love was important for both Richard and Hugh in their ideas about the Holy Spirit. The use of love by each author, however, as has been suggested, was very different. For Hugh, the concept of the Holy Spirit as love, from Augustine, was foundational in his thinking of the Trinitarian persons, and it was primarily from this that he drew his thoughts on the Spirit as goodness. For Richard, choosing to work apart from the authority of the Fathers, love enters the argument both because it is an aspect of goodness and also because he sees in the concept of love a proof for the plurality of persons in the godhead. This is the aspect that is most accentuated in the study of Richard's works, and is a fascinating construct of intra-Trinitarian relationships.

Hugh

Hugh begins his thoughts on the persons of the invisible God by seeking to draw on visible examples. His main starting point, following the writings of Augustine, is on the concept of a rational mind, in which there can be seen a trinity of parts that resemble the processional model of the divine Trinity. Hugh reasons along similar lines to Augustine to find the concept of love within the mind, in a way which creates a trinity of attributes that can be readily applied to the Christian understanding of God.

The model that Hugh expounds upon consists of the mind, which simply exists; the intellect, which is generated by the mind; and love, which springs forth from both mind and intellect.[23] Hugh uses not only words for love in stating the relationship between mind and intellect. He writes that, on seeing the intellect and all its perfect attributes, the mind both "diligit eum, et complacet sibi in ipso".[24] The word "complaceo" is used in the Vulgate in the statement of the Father at Jesus' baptism, that he is "well pleased" with Him (Luke 3:22). The use of this term to refer to the Father's reaction to the eternal generation of the Son, which forms the basis for the returning love of the Son for the Father, and also implies the Father loving himself somehow in the Son, gives a more developed idea of the love that Hugh envisages in the godhead. The love between Father and Son in Augustine and Anselm was a natural reaction to the existence of an equal, perfect being. The word "complacet" is used in the context of the mind viewing the nature of the intellect generated from it, and involves a considered appreciation of the second person.

The concept of love as applied here to the Holy Spirit has the advantage that

---

[23] It is interesting that Hugh uses the word 'oritur' to describe the origin of the Spirit, which has more the meaning of to rise, or spring up, than the more standard 'proceed'.

[24] Hugh, *Didascalion*, 7.21 (PL 176:831).

it explains neatly the eternal, equal identity of the Spirit with the Father and the Son. If the mind is eternal, the intellect generated by it must be coeternal with that mind. If these two are perfect, and the result of their perfections is mutual love, that love must be both eternal with the first two persons, and equally perfect with them in every way. It also involves the third person with each of the first two both individually and in relation to each other which, although maintaining the sense of dependence on them for His existence, increases the status of the Holy Spirit by creating a four-fold procession.[25]

The nature of this third person, however, is open to some doubt due to the fact that it appears to be merely a force acting between two other persons. This is a problem when confronting the personhood of the Holy Spirit because the Western concepts of "person" are more easily adapted to the ideas of "Father" and "Son" than they are to "Spirit". Hugh attempts to show in his teaching on this point that, just as Father and Son are both spirit, so the Holy Spirit can fully enter into relationship with them as spirit, whilst remaining their love for each other.[26] Hofmeier writes that Hugh thus finds three persons in the godhead.[27]

Hugh does this by including the third person, the love itself, as part of the love relations within the godhead: "That the love of the Father and the Son loves himself, that the Father loves his love and that of the Son, that the Son loves his love and that of the Father".[28] The idea that love itself is loved and loves would seem to be strange, until it is realised that that love has equal status and attributes with the first two persons, which equal status is seen as the basis of their love for each other. This is reinforced at the end of this section of Hugh's work, with a significant, if slightly tautological, section on the object of the persons' loves. In this, each person is presenting as loving in himself what the other two persons love in him; and also what each person loves in himself, He also loves in the other two persons.[29] This emphasis on the equality of nature of the third person, and His involvement in love relations,[30] creates a greater concept of personhood than the simple mind analogy usually contains.

Hugh thus builds up a strong, solid picture of the Holy Spirit as especially

---

[25] From Father and Son as they love each other, and the self-love of each in their mutual perfection.

[26] Hugh, *Didascalion*, 7.23 (PL 176:833).

[27] Hofmeier, *Die Trinitätslehre des Hugo*, p.265.

[28] Hugh, *Didascalion*, 7.23 (PL 176:833).

[29] "Quod Pater diligit in Filio, hoc idem Filius diligit in seipso; et quod amor Patris et Filii diligit in Filio, hoc idem Filius diligit in seipso. Item quod Filius diligit in Patre, hoc Pater diligit in se; et quod amor Patris et Filii diligit in Patre, hoc Pater diligit in se. Item quod Pater et Filius diligunt in amore suo, hoc amor Patris et Filii diligit in seipso. Item quod Pater diligit in seipso, hoc diligit in Filio, et in amore suo. Et quod Filius diligit in seipso, hoc diligit in Patre et in amore suo. Et quod amor Patris et Filii diligit in se, hoc diligit in Filio et in Patre". Hugh, *Didascalion*, 7.23 (PL 176:833).

[30] As Hofmeier draws out from this teaching: "Was also der Vater im Sohn liebt, das liebt auch der Sohn in sich und das liebt auch die Liebe im Sohn". Hofmeier, *Die Trinitätslehre des Hugo*, p.265.

love within the godhead, without removing this quality from the Father and the Son. It is from this position that he is able to draw out the idea that the Holy Spirit can also be seen to be the goodness of God, particularly in His interactions with the world. Hugh inserted the significant term "complaceo" into his understanding of the inter-relations of the Trinitarian persons of the godhead, which aids comprehension both of the person of the Spirit, and the multiple relations that exist around the idea of love.

Richard

Richard of St. Victor was far more novel in his use of love terminology as regards both the Spirit and the whole Trinity. Richard used love in three ways in his discussions of the Trinity: he wrote an article expanding on the standard model of the Holy Spirit as the mutual love of Father and Son;[31] he used the concept of supreme love to create a proof of a trinity of persons in the godhead; and he developed his own processional model of love to draw conclusions concerning the temporal mission of the Spirit with ideas of giving and receiving connected to the immanent state of the Holy Spirit. In all this, Richard showed both the clarity and complexity of his mind as he drew out this detailed picture of the Holy Spirit as the love of God. Yves Congar brings out the depth of Richard's thought on this aspect: "The Spirit is, according to Richard, the particular and incommunicable mode of existence of the divine substance, which is Love ... [the Holy Spirit] consists in a manner of living and realising Love".[32] Badcock favourably compares Richard's teaching on love with that of Augustine: "Another important aspect of Richard's Trinitarian thought, which again distinguishes it sharply from Augustine's, is the fact that he successfully sustains a discussion of the persons as related in love, without immediate reference to the doctrine of the processions."[33]

THE HOLY SPIRIT AS MUTUAL LOVE

Richard wrote an article replying to an unnamed person explaining in what way Augustine could be correct in saying that the Father loves the Son by the Holy Spirit, and the Son loves the Father by that same Spirit.[34] The argument against this teaching is presented as a comparison between the ideas that the Holy Spirit is love and the Son is wisdom. Is the Father wise by the wisdom that He begets? If this were to be the case, then the Son would be the origin of the Father's wisdom. This cannot be true if He proceeds from the Father. The solution which Richard provides to this problem is that the Father teaches the Son, and the Son speaks the wisdom. In this way, the Son can be seen as embodying the wisdom of the Father.

Richard takes a similar, though not identical line, in supporting Augustine's

---

[31] His *Quomodo Spiritus Sanctus est Amor Patris et Filii* (PL 196:1011-12).

[32] Congar, *I Believe in the Holy Spirit 3*, p.105.

[33] Badcock, *Light of Truth*, p.249.

[34] Richard, *Quomodo Spiritus Sanctus est Amor Patris et Filii*, (PL 196:1011-12).

statement that the Holy Spirit is the love with which the Father loves the Son and vice-versa. Although the concept of the Holy Spirit as love comes from the analogy of the human mind (as was seen in Hugh's teaching), Richard seeks to distance himself slightly from this analogy in his explanation. The difference noted is that, whereas it is not thought that the human mind is love, but that love proceeds from the mind, God the Father (analogised as mind) is love in himself.[35] This removes the possibility that the Spirit could be said to be the origin of the Father's love, which would imply, as with wisdom, that the Father were not complete divinity in himself. The Holy Spirit is also the Father's love, and therefore the Father can be said both to love by himself, and also by His love.[36] This position is backed up from the fact that men love God by the Holy Spirit, which is said to be the same as their own love.[37] This is an interesting line to take as it equates human love for God with the Holy Spirit. However, as Richard has taken the dual approach connecting love to the Father both as His love and as the Holy Spirit, he is able to imply in this that the same duality exists in some way in the love of men for God. This is a necessary tension that arises from Richard's teaching on the Spirit as the love with which the Father loves the Son and vice-versa.

Richard uses this teaching on the Holy Spirit in addition to that on goodness in his *Tractatus de Spiritu Blasphemiae*. Having stated that sin against the Holy Spirit is the sin of evil (against God's goodness), he then changes tack and examines the Holy Spirit as the love of God. If the Holy Spirit is love, then sin against the Spirit must aspire to the hatred of God.[38] This hatred is not simply of one person in God, but is against that which binds the Trinity together in love, and thus encompasses all three persons of the godhead. The desire to oppose the love of God thus becomes the unforgivable sin. This teaching backs up the ideas on the Holy Spirit that Richard wrote about in the *libellus* on the Holy Spirit as mutual love. The *Tractatus* is more a meditation on the idea of the blasphemy against the Holy Spirit than a doctrinal text, but it does provide some insight into Richard's concept of the Holy Spirit as both goodness and love.

PROVING THE TRINITY FROM LOVE

Richard does not limit his idea of love in the Trinity to the traditional position given above. Indeed, in the *De Trinitate*, this teaching has only a minor part in Richard's greater section on the concept of ultimate love in the divine nature.

---

[35] Richard, *Quomodo Spiritus Sanctus est Amor Patris et Filii*, (PL 196:1012).

[36] "Pater vero amor est, et Spiritus sanctus ejus amor est, et ideo Pater diligit seipso, diligit Spiritu sancto. Diligit seipso amore, diligit suo amore". *Ibid.*, (PL 196:1012).

[37] "Similiter aequivoce dicerentur amor tuus et amor divinus, si Spiritus sanctus diceretur amor cordis tui, sicut Spiritus sanctus dicitur amor Patris et Filii. Quis, quaeso, posset negare te [the reader] Spiritu sancto (hoc est amore tuo) diligere? Si recte diligere diceris amore qui de te procedit, cur Pater et Filius non recte dicantur diligere amore qui ex ipsis procedit". *Ibid.*, (PL 196:1012).

[38] "Spiritus blasphemiae aspirat ad odium Dei" in *Tractatus de Spiritu* (PL 196:1188).

The more complete teaching is included at the beginning of book three of the work, and is presented as an essential and logical result of the previous teaching on ultimate goodness: "For where there is the fullness of total goodness, truly there must also be fullness of love".[39] Richard confirms this conclusion by stating that nothing is better, nothing is more perfect, than love. Love is thus included as a consequence of the presence of goodness in the Trinity, both of which are seen as corresponding to the person of the Holy Spirit.

Richard moves from this conclusion that there must be perfect love in the divine to a fascinating proof, unique to Richard, of the plurality in trinity of persons in the godhead. The first stage in this argument is that love must have an object which it loves.[40] This was an acceptable statement in twelfth-century thought as it followed the teaching of Gregory the Great that it is not possible to have love between less than two persons.[41] Richard is thus able to conclude that there must be a plurality of persons in God in order for Him to have the quality of love in Himself eternally. There are processional resonances here to the idea of wisdom, which must proceed from God eternally, and necessitates the existence of the second person. The idea of love is stronger in demanding the existence of more than one person in the godhead as an object is involved to whom love is communicated, whereas the wisdom that proceeds does not, immanently, have any object.

Richard notes a possible objection against the idea of love as a proof of multiple divine persons. If, he questions, love is part of the great goodness of God, would it not be possible for that love to be expressed towards creatures?[42] Love, in this case, would be a product of eternal goodness made manifest once there were creatures to love. Richard's reply focuses on the need for love in God to be supreme, for which there needs to be a coequal, supreme, perfect being for God to love. Love for creatures, in God, is love for that which is inferior in nature, and is therefore not able to be supreme. This argument shows the direct connection that Richard is drawing from goodness to love, as each is necessarily supreme in every way in the divine.

Richard is thus able to defend his theory that supreme love demands the existence of at least two persons. Richard explains from this that each of these persons between whom love exists must be equally powerful, wise, good, and everything else that pertains to divinity, continuing the idea that these persons are coequal in their divinity in every respect.[43] In this, Richard is also showing that, despite the fact that he sees power and wisdom as being primarily attributable to one of the divine persons in their origin or procession, each of

---

[39] Richard, *De Trinitate*, 3.2, pp.136-37 (PL 196:916).

[40] "Oportet itaque ut amor in alterum tendat, ut charitas esse queat". *Ibid.*, 3.2, pp.136-37 (PL 196:916).

[41] Peter Abelard was one of those who quoted this from Gregory: "Charitas autem, teste Gregorio, minus quam inter duos haberi non potest". Abelard, *Introductio*, 2.123 (Vol. 3, p.469). Gregory the Great, *Homiliae in Evangelica* (PL 76:1139).

[42] Richard, *De Trinitate*, 3.2, pp.136-37 (PL 196:916-17).

[43] *Ibid.*, 3.7, pp.141-42 (PL 196:919-20).

these persons is completely perfect. However, he remains, at this stage of his argument from love, limited to the necessity for two persons in the divinity.

Richard's argument for a trinity of persons in God has a fascinating teaching at its root. This teaching is that, for love to be at its maximum, there must be a desire that the person who is loved also loves, and is loved by, an equal third person.[44] Part of this need for a third is the passion (*fervente*) of the love between the first two persons that creates the need for a third.[45] Another element in this model is that love between only two persons lacks completeness. Richard's word for this completeness is *condilectio*.[46] *Dilectio*, delight in another, is possible between two persons who love each other. *Condilectio* is only possible once there is a third who loves and is loved by the person loved. This brings an element of sharing into love, of delight at seeing the beloved's joy in communal love with a third. There is something of selfless love in this concept of *condilectio*. Bligh notes that Richard sees the perfection of love when two wills are united in love of a third, meaning that *condilectio* is greater than *dilectio*.[47] The result of this complete love is *concordialis* and *consocialis* love,[48] emphasising the importance of this shared love for creating a bond between the persons of the godhead which, according to Richard, would not exist without the presence of a third person.[49] Mary Clark sums up Richard's teaching on this point in writing that "shared love, the characteristic of perfect love, is not present in the Trinity unless there is a third person".[50]

Richard uses the fact that highest goodness seeks the sharing of love with a third to develop the necessity for the procession of this third person. He states that knowledge of the condition for complete love means that both first two persons need to see the other complete in this *condilectus* love, or they would experience grief and pain;[51] he further states that it would be impossible for a divine person to see another person in need and not help as this would lead to

---

[44] "Praecipuum vero videtur in vera charitate alterum velle diligi ut ... nihil preclarius quam ut ab eo quem summe diligis, et a quo summe diligeris, alium aeque diligi velis." Richard, *De Trinitate*, 3.11, pp.146-47 (PL 196:922).

[45] Stanley Burgess writes that Richard of St. Victor's love procession implied reflection in human marriage, in the overflow of love to children. This is clearly mistaken, as Richard's main concentration throughout this proof is on the necessity of those involved in divine love being equal in every regard, which cannot be applied to the family model. Burgess, *The Holy Spirit: Medieval Roman Catholic and Reformation Traditions*, p.65.

[46] The discussion of the third person in the love model is in *De Trinitate* 3.11-13, pp.146-49 (PL 196:922-24).

[47] Bligh,, 'Richard of St. Victor's *De Trinitate*', pp.118-39.

[48] Richard, *De Trinitate*, 3.20, pp.143-45 (PL 196:928).

[49] Richard's use of 'concord' to describe the Holy Spirit will be discussed below.

[50] Clark, 'The Trinity in Latin Christianity', p.287.

[51] Richard, *De Trinitate*, 3.12, pp.147-48 (PL 196:923).

ashamedness because of their unwillingness or inability.[52] It is not in the nature of the supreme being to experience grief or pain, or to be unwilling or unable to help, and so the third person must proceed from the first two. Richard thus reasons from his principle of shared love and the nature of the divine persons to insist on this procession of a third person. The implication is that both the godhead itself, and each of the divine persons individually, would be incomplete were the third person not to exist. This does not mean that God chooses to be three, but that the procession of a third person is a necessary consequence of the nature of the first two persons.

It is interesting to note that, in this proof of the Trinity from a relational model of love, there is no indication that the Holy Spirit has in himself the particular quality of love in the godhead that is suggested in the mind analogy that Richard himself supports. The third person that results from the *condilectus* love of the first two is not given any particular quality, except that it must have the fullness of divinity for the love of the first two persons to be complete. However, although this proof does not define the nature of the third person, the love image does support Richard's teaching on the Trinity that love in the Father and the Son is both their love and that the love that proceeds from them is somehow connected to the Holy Spirit. The redefinition of the Holy Spirit's role as providing *condilectio* and completeness in the love relationships is a helpful approach to the seeming paradox between God as love and the Holy Spirit as love in particular.

GIVING AND RECEIVING LOVE: THE PROCESSION AND MISSION OF THE HOLY SPIRIT

Richard also uses love to conclude his processional teaching on the Trinity, and links this to the mission of the Holy Spirit.[53] Having proved the existence of three persons in the Trinity from both the power, wisdom, goodness teaching, and also his discussion of love in the godhead, Richard turns his attention to the mode of proceeding of the second and third persons, and states that their procession must either be immediate (from one person) or mediate (from one person through another). This combines the dual procession model provided by Richard's initial discussion on the third person as goodness and the idea of love providing a third person in the Trinity, and clarifies the nature of the Spirit as a result of this integration.

Richard states that there must be binity before there can be Trinity.[54] The second person must therefore come immediately from the first. The reason for the existence of the second person is given as the perfection of the first: "The

---

[52] *Ibid.*, 3.13, pp.148-49 (PL 196:923-24). Both these last two points are drawn out by Den Bok in his work on this section of the *De Trinitate*. Den Bok, *Communicating the Most High*, pp.306-09.

[53] This discussion is based on book five of *De Trinitate*, pp.194-225 (PL 196:947-68).

[54] "Naturaliter autem prior est dualitas quam trinitas". Richard, *De Trinitate*, 5.7, pp.202-03 (PL 196:953). This is acceptable in the Western model, but against the Eastern idea that Son and Spirit both proceed eternally only from the Father.

perfection of one person is the cause of the existence of the other".⁵⁵ This is based on the fact that the first, because of the perfect love innate in him, would will the existence of a second person of equal dignity. As equal dignity is seen as part of the nature of the second person, mutual delight (*condilectum*) results, which is the cause of the third person, resulting from the mutual perfection of the first two persons: "Just as the perfection of one is the cause of the other, so clearly the perfection of both is the cause of the third of the Trinitarian persons. Just as the perfection of one required co-worth, so certainly the perfection of the other leads to mutual love."⁵⁶ Because the third person proceeds equally from the perfection of first and second persons, His procession must be seen as both mediate and immediate: immediate from the first person; and mediate from the second person, who owes His existence to the first.

This processional teaching informs Richard's earlier writing on *condilectum* and shows that it is partially a result of the existence of two persons *condignum*. It should also be noted that, whereas in the proof of plurality in God from love the uncertainty concerned the nature of procession of the third person, here there is a lack of clarity about the second person, who is merely said to proceed as *condignum*. There is thus a need in reading the *De Trinitate* to cross-reference Richard's teachings on the origins and processions of the persons to gain insight into the various ways in which he attributes qualities to each of the persons in his different models, which back each other up in the overall picture.

This theory of Richard's that perfection in the godhead is the cause of the second and third persons does pose a problem. The third person that is produced is equally perfect with the first two, and Richard's argument would seem to imply that, perfect as He is with no lack of creative power, a fourth person should proceed in some way from the third. Richard himself notes this, which is an interesting point.⁵⁷ It would seem from the nature of the first two persons that one aspect of divinity is to have a divine person proceeding from that essence. The mutual interaction of divine persons seems to necessitate further processions because of their common perfection and delight.

Richard's first reply to this is simply that there must be one person in the divinity from whom no other person proceeds. This initial reply is based on the fact that there is no new method of procession left, either immediate or mediate, that would completely distinguish the fourth person from the other three.⁵⁸ This is an important point because it develops the classical Western position on procession to show not only the existence, but the necessity of three persons in the godhead. The Eastern, monarchical, model leaves open room for more processions from the Father. It is also interesting that this point focuses completely on the relational model of the persons, without reference to any attributes connected to their origin or procession.

---

⁵⁵ *Ibid.*, 5.7, pp.202-03 (PL 196:954).
⁵⁶ Richard, *De Trinitate*, 5.8, pp.203-05 (PL 196:955).
⁵⁷ *Ibid.*, 5.15, pp.213-14 (PL 196:960-61).
⁵⁸ *Ibid.*, 5.11-12, pp.208-10 (PL 196:957-59).

The second reply states that there can be no fourth person in the divinity, and this is based on concepts of giving and receiving. Richard writes that one person must have giving as His only role; one person should only receive; and one person should both give and receive. There is in this formulation no place for a fourth person.[59] This is related to the previous point, and reinforces the need for a unique position for each of the persons in relation to the other two. It shows that the three persons are not modes of one being, but have distinguishing traits that separate the three within one divinity.

This language of giving and receiving is linked to the idea of love in the Trinity. The Father is thus said to be completely owed love; the Holy Spirit to completely owe love; and the Son to both owe and be owed love. Richard returns to this theme when dealing with the mission of the Holy Spirit as the gift of God to His creatures. Richard sums up the mission of the Spirit as "debiti amoris infusio".[60] He states that this creation of a debt of love to God is one reason why it is the Holy Spirit, and not the Father or the Son, who was the divine person placed in human hearts to shed the love of God abroad. It is slightly strange to use language of "owing" in relation to the Trinitarian persons, as this conjures up ideas of incompleteness in some form. Richard's point is not that the persons are incomplete in any way, but that they have their existence from another. Mary Melone comes to the conclusion from her study of Richard's teaching on the owing of love, *condilectio* and gift terminology that, "L'uso dell'espressione *Amor debitus* si rivela in realtà centrale per la riflessione pneumatologica del *De Trinitate*".[61]

The idea of the Holy Spirit being the person who completely owes love, which is then transformed into His mission, is a new side to the traditional idea of the Spirit as the love of God. Richard does not seek to tie this concept into the picture of the Spirit as the mutual love of Father and Son, and it is not clear how the Holy Spirit can be both love in the godhead, and yet also somehow be that which completely owes love to the other two persons. Perhaps Richard would see these two elements as complimentary, rounding out the person of the Spirit as not only the love between the first two persons, but also as the source of His own love of those persons because of the manner of His procession. It is disappointing that Richard did not attempt to make any connection on this level.

Union

This last section, on the Holy Spirit as union in the Trinity, is taken only from the writings of Richard of St. Victor (not from Hugh), and from only a small part of his works. It is significant, however, both because of its context (in the letter to Bernard in which Richard also talks about power, wisdom and

---

[59] Richard, *De Trinitate*, 5.15-20, pp.213-19 (PL 196:960-64). There are reminiscences in this of St. Anselm's relational models of the Trinity that explain the persons in their similarities and differences to the other two persons.

[60] *Ibid.*, 6.14, pp.245-46 (PL 196:978).

[61] Melone, 'Lo Spirito Santo', p.49.

goodness), and also because of the overall significance for his understanding of the person of the Spirit in the immanent Trinity beyond, but including, the ideas of goodness and love. It is interesting to see how this teaching, in a separate document, draws together ideas about the Holy Spirit that are contained in the *De Trinitate*.

The letter to Bernard begins by stating that Bernard had asked Richard to explain what he thought was meant by Augustine in attributing unity to the Father, equality to the Son, and the union (*concordias*) of both to the Holy Spirit.[62] It is only after the discussion of these terms that Richard goes on to explain his theory of power, wisdom and goodness. Richard writes that the Father is described as unity (*unitas*) because He is the principle of the entire godhead, and the others have their existence from him; the Son is equality as the image of the Father; while the Holy Spirit is not an image because He does not have the origin of a divine person in himself.[63]

The Holy Spirit is given the term union because in the Holy Spirit is the completion of the Trinity: "in Spiritu sancto completio Trinitatis".[64] In addition to this, Richard states that it is this fullness of union that makes the whole Trinity have the same desires, which union is the love of Father and Son.[65] There are a number of terms linked together here in Richard's ideas, all of which have their root in Augustine's thought, but which are brought together here to support each other. The three terms that are interlinked are union, will (desire) and love, and all three are seen as results of the presence of the Holy Spirit in the Trinity. The basis of this line of thought is the necessary presence of the Holy Spirit not only proceeding from Father and Son, but binding them together in, and because of, this procession. This is a helpful passage for a deeper understanding of Richard's meaning in the *De Trinitate* on the nature of the third person in the teaching on love, which has similar implications, as Mary Clark has noted: "The love of two persons is not merely mutual but unites into one love, a common love for another that establishes them in the deepest possible union".[66]

This concept of the Holy Spirit as the union of God thus has implications far beyond the ideas of goodness and love as applicable terms. Richard seems to be implying that, without the Spirit binding them together, there would be no necessity for the Father and Son to act in unity of purpose and spirit, although it should be noted that there is no possibility in Richard's thought for the non-existence of the Spirit. The concept of goodness is not included in the passage on union because Richard sees love as being one element of the goodness that

---

[62] This teaching is found in the *De Doctrina Christiana*, 1.5 (ed. R. Green. Oxford: OUP, 1995) pp.16-17.

[63] This has similarities to the teaching on the *De Trinitate* about why there cannot be a fourth person in the Trinity.

[64] Richard, *De Tribus* (PL 196:992).

[65] "Addamus et illud, quia plenitudinem concordiae facit idem velle, et idem nolle, recte itaque duorum concordia dicitur, qui est amor utriusque" in *Ibid.*, (PL 196:992-93).

[66] Clark, 'The Trinity in Latin Christianity', p.287.

must proceed from the existence of ultimate power and wisdom; it is from the love idea that the teaching on union is based.

Conclusion

The Victorines' contribution to twelfth-century thought on the Holy Spirit was thus both broad and deep. Firstly, they supported the traditional ideas that had been received from Augustine, using his terminology to describe the immanent person of the Spirit; secondly, they developed these ideas by relating them to each other to identify further the place of the Spirit in the Trinity; and thirdly, they provided new analyses of the Trinity, and the Spirit's place within the godhead, particularly in Richard's use of the concept of love.

Both Hugh and Richard saw the concept that the Holy Spirit was the mutual love of both Father and Son as an important part in the identity of the Spirit. Both also supported the idea that this was an extension of the Spirit as the goodness of God (although Hugh was careful about his use of the term goodness in its application to the Spirit until he had first clarified his ideas on love). Richard then took the further step, implied in the processional writing of the *De Trinitate* and more explicitly stated in a letter to Bernard of Clairvaux, of writing about the Holy Spirit as union within the Trinity, drawing the entire godhead together in one love and one will. The different analyses that Richard, in particular, uses regarding the origin, procession and relations of the third person of the Trinity create a complex, yet complimentary, picture of the immanent person of the Holy Spirit.

CHAPTER 6

Peter Lombard

Peter Lombard was Italian by birth, but undertook his education in Paris, at the school of St. Victor, and at the time when Abelard was teaching. There was thus a range of influences on his thought, and Lombard's major work, the *Sentences*, does not betray reliance on any one school or thinker of his time, but is instead a masterful analysis of the whole field of dogmatic theology. As such this work was to become the standard textbook for theological study for the rest of the medieval period, being the basis for numerous commentaries. Lombard provides a balance in this book, showing his reliance on established authorities as well as his use of reason.

A large amount of the first book of the *Sentences*, that on the doctrine of God, concentrates on the person of the Holy Spirit. Philipp Rosemann notes in his new study of Lombard that there is an "exceptionally long and rich pneumatology" covering thirty-eight chapters of the *Sentences*.[1] Given this length and richness, Lombard's writings on the Holy Spirit have received very little treatment in the two most recent and comprehensive works on Peter Lombard: six pages in Rosemann's work, and only ten pages specifically on this teaching in Marcia Colish's two volume work.[2] It is not clear why a topic that was clearly of such interest to Peter Lombard himself should receive so little attention from modern commentators on his writings.

This chapter will begin by outlining Lombard's presentation of the procession of the Spirit from both Father and Son. This will include an examination of the differences between the eternal and temporal states of the Spirit, which is an important issue for Lombard. Peter Lombard's discussion on the person of the Holy Spirit focuses on the term "love", although there is also

---

[1] Rosemann, *Peter Lombard*, p.73. The concentration on the Holy Spirit also comes very early on in the *Sentences*, beginning at Distinction 10. Even the brief article in the *Dictionnaire de Théologie Catholique* notes that the theology of the Holy Spirit is "tres developpée dans le *Livre des Sentences*" (J. de Ghellinck, 'Peter Lombard' in *DTC* 12(2), column 1993).

[2] Rosemann, *Peter Lombard*, pp.85-90; Colish, *Peter Lombard: Volume 1*, pp.253-63. Much of Colish's writing even in these pages concerns a comparison of Lombard with Peter Abelard. Colish does include some references to the teaching on the Holy Spirit in her section on *The Problem of Theological Language* as part of her treatment of terms used to refer to the whole Trinity. To provide a comparison, Colish devotes twenty-two pages to Lombard's discussion of predestination and foreknowledge, which takes up far less space in the *Sentences* (Colish, *Peter Lombard 1*, pp.268-89).

some significant teaching on "gift" terminology regarding the Spirit. The second part of the chapter will examine how Lombard uses these names to describe the person of the Holy Spirit, tying in his ideas here to those he had stated on the procession of the Holy Spirit. Finally, the chapter will consider Peter Lombard's views and impact on the debate over the terms power, wisdom and goodness, and their applicability to the divine persons in light of Marcia Colish's claim that he rejected this doctrine.

Lombard begins his *Sentences* with a discussion of the eternal nature of God, including the procession of the second and third persons. Tied into this discussion is a stress on the simplicity of the divine essence (which discussion will be addressed below in the section on power, wisdom and goodness). Although Lombard then begins his discussion of the Holy Spirit by noting the name love, it is appropriate to start this assessment of the *Sentences* with the processional model of the Holy Spirit in light of the eternal nature of God.

The Procession of the Holy Spirit

Peter Lombard's first objective in explaining the procession of the Holy Spirit is to confirm the dual procession from both Father and Son. This is slightly surprising given the fact that Lombard was writing some time after the major controversy between the Greek and Latin churches, and the fact that most other writers spent more time developing the persons of the Trinity before moving onto the question of procession. For example, Anselm of Canterbury, writing at the height of the debate, began both his *Monologion* and *Proslogion* with discussions of the nature of the third person in relation to the first two before dealing with the mode of procession.[3] Peter Abelard and Richard of St. Victor also concentrated first on the persons themselves before moving on to discuss the procession.[4] Lombard chose to establish his relational model of the Trinity, from which he then draws out the attributes that pertain to each of the persons. The advantage of this approach is that Lombard starts with material that is more clearly taught in scripture and which forms the core of teaching on the Holy Spirit in the creedal statements.

Lombard's first *Distinctio* on the Holy Spirit is a short rebuttal of the Greek position. Using the scriptures and the writings of the Greek Fathers Athanasius, Didymus, Cyril and Chrysostom, Lombard shows that the Latin position of dual

---

[3] This was partially affected by Anselm's decision to begin from the standpoint of no knowledge of the Trinity.

[4] The Cistercian writers were less systematic in their presentation of the their theologies, but the concentration which William and Bernard gave to the experience of the Spirit meant that they also taught more on the natures of the persons than on any processional model.

procession has roots in authorities that would be accepted by both sides.⁵ This is similar to the arguments that Abelard put forward from the same sources, but is given a primary place in the *Sentences* whereas Abelard had included this much later in each of his *Theologiae*.⁶

Having confirmed that, in his view, the basic concept of dual procession of the Spirit is in line with the teaching of the church, Lombard moves on to discuss the status of the Holy Spirit in comparison to the other two members of the Trinity. His purpose here is to establish that the Holy Spirit is coequal and consubstantial with the Father and Son in every way, despite His procession from two other members of the godhead. This follows his initial concern up to this point in the *Sentences* which has been to outline his views on the eternal nature of God. This discussion has two major factors: the primacy of procession (*Distinctio* 12); and the mode of procession (*Distinctio* 13).

Primacy in Procession

The issue of primacy in procession arises from the teaching of Augustine, who suggested in his *De Trinitate* that the Holy Spirit proceeded primarily from the Father, but also from the Son.⁷ The basis for this teaching was that the Father was the root of the whole Trinity, and it was only as He received His being from the Father that the Son had the capacity to have the Spirit proceed from him. This was one area under question in the twelfth century, although the writers do not seem to have engaged with each other directly on this issue.

Peter Lombard teaches equality in procession of the Spirit, not granting primacy to the Father. He notes first of all that Augustine wrote about eternal procession, which means that the Holy Spirit cannot have proceeded from the Father first in time: "For who is able to understand the eternal generation of the Son from the Father may also understand the eternal procession of the Holy Spirit from both".⁸ This is a necessary truth if the divinity of all three persons is to be upheld. Having defended Augustine from being seen to introduce time into the eternal relations of the Trinity, Lombard now turns to the question of

---

⁵ Lombard, *Sentences*, 1.11.2.2-5, pp.116-17 (in *Sententiae in IV Libris Distinctae Vols. 1-2* (3rd Edition). Grottaferrata: Collegii S. Bonaventurae ad Claras Aquas, 1971, 1981), and PL 192:552-53, 1.11.5. References from the *Sentences* will be from both the modern and (in brackets) Migne versions. The two editions have different divisions within the sections of the *Sentences* (as here 1.11.2.2-5 against 1.11.5). The footnotes will thus refer both to page/column numbers, and to the relevant section number in each edition.

⁶ Every, writing in an article that concentrates on the modern debate about the *filioque*, notes a difference between Lombard and Richard of St. Victor on the dual procession of the Holy Spirit. Lombard is said to teach that the Spirit proceeds from both Father and Son as from the same substance, while Richard is said to deny this. The relevant section of the *De* Trinitate does not focus on the procession of the Holy Spirit, and Richard provides many different processional models and ideas that are in accord with Lombard. It is hard, therefore, to agree with Every on this issue. G. Every, 'Peter Lombard and II Lyons', *Eastern Churches Review* 9 (1977), pp.85-90, at p.86.

⁷ Augustine, *De Trinitate*, 15.17, pp.503-04 (p.419).

⁸ Lombard, *Sentences*, 1.12.1.3, p.118 (PL 192:553, 1.12.2).

whether the Spirit could be said to proceed more fully (*plenius*) or more greatly (*magis*) from the Father.

Lombard's own answer to this is that the Spirit proceeded equally in all ways from the Father and the Son: "He does not proceed in any greater way from the Father than from the Son".[9] Peter realises that, because this teaching differs from that found in the writings of Augustine, his readers may become worried about the reliability of either Augustine or Lombard himself: "Sed ne te hoc turbaret".[10] In seeking to respond to this, Lombard explains Augustine's teaching in light of his own on equality in procession by looking back to the procession of the Son. It was possible for Augustine to say that the Holy Spirit proceeded primarily from the Father because the Son himself receives from the Father the power to have the Spirit proceeding from Him.[11] Lombard differs from Augustine in focusing on the Holy Spirit in His own procession in the context of the eternal Trinity rather than as a secondary part of the formation of the godhead. While Lombard notes Augustine's position, the major teaching at this point of the *Sentences* is on equality in procession from both persons.

However, Lombard does not leave the issue with the clarity of this passage. He returns to the question of primacy in the next *Distinctio* that deals with the mode of the Spirit's procession. In considering whether the Spirit should be termed "ingenitus", and seeking to show that the Spirit differs from the Father, to whom the term "ingenitus" is correctly applied, and from the Son (who is "genitus"), Lombard quotes from Augustine that the Spirit is "The faith certainly declares that He is neither born nor unborn".[12] The explanation given for this by Augustine, which Peter Lombard also notes, is that "The Holy Spirit proceeds from the Father principally and communally from both".[13] It is surprising that Lombard refers to Augustine's teaching in such a straightforward manner given what he had taught in the previous *Distinctio*, with Peter's emphasis here on procession primarily from the Father. This clouds the reader's understanding of precisely what Lombard wants to say on this point.

Mode of Procession

Having dealt with the issue of primacy in procession, Lombard moves on to the mode of the Spirit's procession, asking the question: why was this procession as a Spirit and not as a Son? The initial treatment of this is simple, and is taken from the writings of Augustine. It would be most absurd (*absurdissimum*) for the third person to be the Son of the first two, as this would involve there being

---

[9] Lombard, *Sentences*, 1.12.2.1, p.119 (PL 192:553, 1.12.3).

[10] *Ibid.*, 1.12.2.3, p.119 (PL 192:553, 1.12.3). This short phrase shows the authority that Augustinian theology held over those writing in the twelfth century.

[11] "Ecce exposuit ipsemet quomodo Spiritus Sanctus principaliter procedat a Patre: non quia prius vel magis procedat a Patre quam a Filio, sed quia cum procedat a Filio, hoc ipsum habet Filius a Patre." *Ibid.*, 1.12.2.3, p.119 (PL 192:554, 1.12.3).

[12] *Ibid.*, 1.13.4.2, p.124 (PL 192:556, 1.13.5).

[13] *Ibid.*, 1.13.4.2, p.124 (PL 192:556, 1.13.5).

a father and a mother. This would be ridiculous given their own relations as Father and Son.[14] This is an important point to address, as dual procession does raise the question of the form in which a third person can come from a Father and a Son.

The next stage in Lombard's argument is fascinating, as he asks why the Holy Spirit is not said to be born when the Son is said to proceed: "If the Holy Spirit is not said to be born, why is the Son said to proceed?"[15] The evidence for the procession of the Son is taken from John 16, when Jesus said "I came from the Father and entered the world" (John 16:28). Lombard notes that "came" could come from two Latin words, *exivi* and *processi*.[16] There must therefore be two different (*dissimiliter*) processions from the Father. The concept of the procession of the Son is notable because most writers differentiate between the Son and the Spirit because one is born and the other proceeds, making procession a mark of the Spirit. Given the dismissal of the procession of the Spirit as a son, this formulation would seem to add confusion to the issue, as it reduces the distinction between the processions of the second and third persons.

The situation is not helped by the next stage in the argument of the *Sentences*. Peter Lombard clarifies the procession of the Spirit as "Not so much born, but in some way given or a gift", whereas the Son proceeds "Being born, he proceeds as one born".[17] The concept of the Spirit as the gift of God will be expanded on below. At this point, however, it must be noticed that Lombard uses terms that are tied to the temporal procession of the Spirit (he will later state in the *Sentences* that the Spirit proceeds eternally as "giveable"). It remains unclear why Peter Lombard chooses to differentiate the procession of the Holy Spirit with gift language. This is accentuated when one considers that there is a procession of the Son in which He is said to be "given", in His temporal mission. This comparison of the two processions does not therefore seem to help to understand the difference between the two.

Having sought, in this unsatisfactory way, to clarify the two processions of the Son and the Holy Spirit, Lombard then immediately titles his next section, "That is it not possible for us to distinguish between the generation of the Son and the procession of the Holy Spirit."[18] Whilst this is in line with one aspect of traditional teaching on the ultimate mystery of knowing the divine persons, it is out of context in light of Lombard's present discussion. If this sentiment is to be included in a treatise on the procession of persons in the godhead, its place must surely be at the beginning, to provide perspective for the reader in assessing what will be presented.

Another aspect of the procession of the Holy Spirit that was important for Lombard was the two-fold (*gemina*) nature of the procession, both eternal and

---

[14] It is not noted in this that the Son is begotten without a maternal parent, which would seem to go against this teaching of Lombard's about sonship.

[15] Lombard, *Sentences*, 1.13.2, p.122 (PL 192:555, 1.13.2).

[16] *Ibid.*

[17] *Ibid.*

[18] *Ibid.*, 1.13.3.1, p.122 (PL 192:555, 1.13.3).

temporal. So far, we have been looking at the eternal aspect of this issue, but must now turn to the temporal. Lombard notes that some say that the Holy Spirit himself is not given temporally, but only His gifts, which are not the Spirit: "His gifts, which are not that Spirit".[19] Lombard quotes Augustine to refute these people, writing that, "Augustine clearly says that the Holy Spirit, who is God and the third Trinitarian person, is given".[20] Lombard wants to be clear in this refutation of the idea that the Spirit only gives gifts.

He thus sees that it is the Holy Spirit himself, in His divinity, who is given to work in the temporal creation. This is a logical necessity when it is considered that the Holy Spirit cannot be seen as a "gift" in His immanent state, as traditional models of procession within the Trinity do not use giving language to communicate the relations of Father and Son to the Spirit and to each other. If the Holy Spirit is to be seen as a gift, therefore, it must be as He is given to creation, and to mankind in particular. This line of thinking goes against Marcia Colish's assessment of Lombard's views, which are that the Holy Spirit "gives the gift of divine grace; He does not communicate Himself or the divine essence as such to the believers."[21]

The other major issue for Lombard in discussing the temporal procession of the Spirit is whether the Spirit could be said to have given Himself. This question shows that there is a distinct difference between the economic and immanent processions of the Spirit, and Lombard supports the idea that the Holy Spirit gave Himself temporally. The reason that he gives is that this procession is the same as the mission of the Spirit, which is the same as the operation of God: "The temporal procession or mission of the Holy Spirit, which is the gift of the spirit, is also the operation of God".[22] As the Holy Spirit is Himself God, He must therefore have given Himself. This follows Augustine's theory that all three persons of the Trinity were involved in one operation of God. In this case, as God gave the Holy Spirit, so the Holy Spirit as part of God must have been involved in the giving. This does not rule out particularly appropriate roles within the Trinity, but is intended to affirm the unity of the godhead in all its activities. It is only the Holy Spirit who is given, but He is given, as Anselm of Canterbury would put it, "from the unity of the divine nature".

This radical separation of the two missions of the Holy Spirit, so that one would not seem to mirror the other, would seem to question the eternal identity of the Spirit. The question is raised, to what extent is it possible for a divine person to proceed differently in His economic state to His immanent procession and not change in His divinity? Related to this is the possibility and extent to which God can change. One of the effects of this will be noted below in the section on the Holy Spirit as gift.

---

[19] Lombard, *Sentences*, 1.14.2.1, p.127 (PL 192:557, 1.14.3).

[20] *Ibid.*, 1.14.2.2, p.127 (PL 192:557, 1.14.3).

[21] Colish, *Peter Lombard* 1, p.261. This issue will be returned to below in the section on love.

[22] Lombard, *Sentences*, 1.15.1.3, p.131 (PL 192:559, 1.15.1).

Peter Lombard seems to confuse unnecessarily the issue of the procession of the Holy Spirit. Having clarified initially the dual procession against the Greek position, Lombard complicates his own views on the possible primacy of procession from the Father; and then proceeds to provide a confusing comparison of the "processions" of Son and Spirit, using temporal language to refer to eternal relations, and weakening the impact of his initial discussion by claiming that it is impossible to discern the differences between the two processions. The use of "gift" language does nothing to help the reader understand Lombard's position. This discussion casts doubt upon Marcia Colish's assertion that, "in tackling the recalcitrant problem of theological language, and in clarifying his terms and using them with rigor and consistency, he goes farther toward the development of a practicable vocabulary than was achieved by any European thinker prior to the reception of Aristotle."[23]

Love

The prime term which Lombard uses to describe the Holy Spirit is love. Indeed, as has been noted, this idea is introduced before the discussion of the nature of the Spirit's procession (in *Distinctio* 10). It is not clear why Lombard feels the necessity to introduce the name love before dealing with the Spirit, as there is no mention of the Son as wisdom, word, or any other term in the introduction to the second person. The initial discussion of the Spirit as love is not linked into the next part on the procession of the Spirit, and even involves some material on the temporal mission of the Spirit, which is out of place in the overall presentation of the *Sentences*. The idea of the Holy Spirit as love is mentioned again in discussion of the Holy Spirit's mission (*Distinctio* 16-18), and is then returned to in *Distinctio* 32, where it is considered whether it is possible that the Father and Son love through the Holy Spirit. The argument thus moves from the eternal to the temporal, and then back to the eternal. Given the importance of this term for Lombard in his theology of the Holy Spirit, it is surprising that the teaching is not more connected and logical.

Lombard begins his teaching on the Holy Spirit as love by associating three Latin words for love with the person of the Holy Spirit: "The Holy Spirit is the love or the charity or the delight of the Father and the Son".[24] These three terms are all used in the Vulgate to describe the love of God.[25] Peter Lombard thus begins his teaching on the Spirit with this very strong and clear link to a complete concept of love, which will be one of the main bases for his overall theology of the Holy Spirit. Having made this initial statement, Lombard then goes on to a major problem with this, which is that the whole Trinity, and each of the persons that make up the Trinity, are able to be called love; and yet in spite of this the Holy Spirit is seen in a special way as the love of God.

---

[23] Colish, *Peter Lombard*, p.92.

[24] Lombard, *Sentences*, 1.10.1.2, p.110 (PL 192:549, 1.10.1).

[25] As noted above in the chapter on Abelard. Rosemann writes that Lombard "seems to regard *amor*, *caritas*, and *dilectio* as synonymous". Rosemann, *Peter Lombard*, p.85.

Lombard seeks to support his statement about the Holy Spirit by turning to the person of the Son, and notes that the Son is said to be the wisdom of God, yet all of God is wisdom.[26] This is not very well organised by Lombard, because there has as yet been no discussion of the Son as wisdom, which subject is treated briefly, and without authoritative support, as part of this section on the Holy Spirit. Although wisdom was a recognised term to be applied to the Son, both from Biblical teachings and from the writing of Augustine, to base the idea that the Holy Spirit should be especially thought of as love on a point that Lombard has not yet established, and that is open to similar questioning, does not seem to strengthen his teaching.

Slightly more convincing in arguing for the dual applicability of love, to both the Trinity as a whole and the Holy Spirit in particular, is the comparison with the law, which Lombard notes can be used to refer both to the whole Old Testament, and also that part of the Old Testament which was given through Moses.[27] Although linguistically this has merit in showing how words can be used for two separate designations, Lombard's case in defending his use of the word love for the Holy Spirit is not greatly helped because the problems here are more theological than semantic.

Peter Lombard does note that the description of the Holy Spirit as love is not as clear in scripture as that of the Son as wisdom. Because love is described as coming from God (*ex deo*), Lombard concludes that is must be from the Son or the Spirit as both of these are God from God.[28] There is an assumption in this that the love that comes from God is in some way equal to God. Love is attributed to the Holy Spirit rather than to the Son because love remains in us, as the Spirit does. This line of reasoning from the temporal world is slightly out of place in the overall argument of the *Sentences*, but does back up the main position on the Holy Spirit as love.

Having provided two examples (wisdom and the law) of how a name can refer to both a collection and an individual within that collection, Lombard moves back to his main argument at this stage of the *Sentences*, that the Holy Spirit is the love with which Father and Son love each other.[29] Lombard is on more solid ground with this, as he is able to back it up by appealing to the Bible and to the Church Fathers, than he was in his theoretical attempts to show that it might be possible for an attribute of the divinity to apply to one of the persons within the Trinity particularly.

His main support for the Holy Spirit as love in this section is the description of the Holy Spirit by Augustine as that which draws the Father and Son together in unity. This idea has not yet been considered by Lombard, but is included as a major basis for accepting the Holy Spirit as the love of God: "That communion is consubstantial and coeternal. For what is able to be said

---

[26] Lombard, *Sentences*, 1.10.1.4, pp.110-11 (PL 192:550, 1.10.3).

[27] *Ibid.*, 1.10.2.1-3, pp.111-12 (PL 192:550, 1.10.4-5).

[28] *Ibid.*, 1.10.2.3, p.112 (PL 192:550, 1.10.5).

[29] *Ibid.*, 1.10.2.4-5, pp.112-13 (PL 192:551, 1.10.6).

well about friendship, it is more apt to be said of love".[30] Schupp notes this in his work on grace in Lombard's thought, stating that Lombard saw the Holy Spirit as "die konsubstanziale Einheit, Verbindung und Liebe" in the Trinity.[31] Lombard goes on to state that there are three in the Trinity: one who loves that which comes from him; one who loves what He is from; and love itself, which must be a person equal to the first two for God to exist fully.[32] Lombard is probing here into the heart of divine relations within the Trinity to discover more about the person of the Holy Spirit.

The eternal aspect of this discussion is left for much of the rest of book one of the *Sentences*, despite the fact that it is included in the account of the temporal mission (as will be mentioned shortly). When Lombard finally returns to this point, he begins by enquiring whether the Father and Son can be said to love through the Holy Spirit, when love is part of what God is.[33] This is one of the crucial questions about the Holy Spirit's identity as love in the godhead, and yet Lombard's poor organisation leaves its treatment until the end of book one of the *Sentences*. Given that this is part of his opening passage about the person of the Holy Spirit, and concerns the eternal identity of the Spirit, it is remarkable that this discussion is not included earlier in the work.

Again, the question of whether the Holy Spirit is love in the godhead is linked to that of the Son being wisdom. Much of this *Distinctio* does not progress Lombard's argument beyond that of his opening account of the Holy Spirit. However, there is a significant admission here. Lombard asks the question whether God is wise by the wisdom that He produces (the Son) as He loves with the love proceeding from Him.[34] This position is rejected, as the wisdom that the Son is in His procession from the Father is not a relational quality as is the case with love and the Holy Spirit. The first procession from the Father is connected to His self-expression that does not have an object. There is thus a difference between the Son as wisdom and the Holy Spirit as love that undermines Lombard's decision to use the wisdom-Son example as a basis for his theology of the Holy Spirit as love. The only escape for Lombard from his dilemma here is to say that the difference between wisdom and love in the godhead is inexplicable.[35]

There is one additional problem that Lombard notes, which is that, if the Father and Son are said to love by the Holy Spirit, it would appear more

---

[30] Lombard, *Sentences*, 1.10.2.5, p.113 (PL 192:558, 1.10.7).

[31] Schupp, *Die Gnadenlehre des Petrus Lombardus*, p.216.

[32] "Tria ergo sunt, et non amplius: unus diligens eum qui de illo est, et unus diligens eum de quo est, et ipsa dilectio, quae si nihil est, quomodo Deus substantia est?" Lombard, *Sentences*, 1.10.2.5, p.113 (PL 192:558, 1.10.7).

[33] *Ibid.*, 1.32.1.1, pp.232-33 (PL 192:607, 1.32.1).

[34] *Ibid.*, 1.32.2, pp.234-36 (PL 192:607-10, 1.32.3-7).

[35] *Ibid.*, 1.32.6.1, pp.238-39 (PL 192:609-610, 1.32.8). David Luscombe traces Lombard's association of the terms power, wisdom and love back to Hugh of St. Victor, from whom Peter also took the idea that the Holy Spirit is *proprie* the love of the Father and Son. Luscombe, *School of Peter Abelard*, p.263.

suitable to say that they are from the Spirit than vice-versa as it is the same in the godhead to love as to be: "It does not sem that the Holy Spirit is from the Father and the Son, but the Father and Son from the Holy Spirit, since it is the same thing in the godhead to love as to be".[36] This is an interesting philosophical point, although there are no grounds from Scripture why it should be held. Peter Lombard does not go into any explanations why it is the Holy Spirit who proceeds and not vice-versa, but merely appeals to the authority of Augustine. It is unclear why Lombard should introduce this point and not explore it further.

In between these two sections on the Spirit as love eternally is the part on the missions of the Holy Spirit, in which Lombard examines the love which is in people's hearts and their love for God, to see how these things relate to the Holy Spirit.[37] The question Lombard is addressing is whether there is a difference between God's love for man and man's love for God and his fellow man, and the place of the Holy Spirit in this relationship.

Lombard begins by stating his belief that it is the same Holy Spirit, the love of Father and Son, by which we love God and our neighbour: "That said Holy Spirit is the love or charity by which we love God and our neighbour", which Schupp calls Lombard's "berühmte Sonderlehre".[38] This is clarified as a love which "makes us love God and our neighbour".[39] He backs up this position by quoting from Augustine and the scriptures. Lombard's initial statements on this thus point towards an identical love that men have for God as that which God has for men, which is the Holy Spirit.

This is an interesting position to hold as it could seem either to remove the responsibility for love from people or to give them some control over the Holy Spirit, as it is the Spirit by which men are able to love God. Peter Lombard himself notes this problem, quoting "many people" who deny that it is the same love by which God loves us and by which we love God.[40] These people claim that the scriptures and Augustine show a clear difference between the two loves, which if both were applied to the Holy Spirit would be absurd. The basic text for these people is Romans 5:5, which teaches that "God has poured out his love into our hearts by the Holy Spirit". This love they place as one of the gifts of the Spirit alongside justification, faith and salvation, which are not themselves said to be the Holy Spirit. The claim is made that the Holy Spirit spreads love abroad which makes people love God, but is not that love with

---

[36] Lombard, *Sentences*, 1.32.6.1, p.239 (PL 192:610, 1.32.8).

[37] *Ibid.*, 1.17, pp.141-52 (PL 192:564-69, 1.17).

[38] *Ibid.*, 1.16.1.2, p.142 (PL 192:564, 1.17.2). Schupp, *Gnadenlehre*, p.216. Saarinen agrees that Lombard sees the love that people have for God and their neighbour as being the Holy Spirit. Saarinen, 'Ipsa Dilectio Deus Est' p.185.

[39] "Quae charitas cum ita est in nobis, ut nos faciat diligere Deum et proximum". Lombard, *Sentences*, 1.16.1.2, p.142 (PL 192:564, 1.17.2).

[40] "Quod autem ipse idem sit charitas qua diligimus Deum et proximum, a plerisque negatur". *Ibid.*, 1.17.6.1, p.149 (PL 192:567, 1.17.11). Lombard does not clarify who the 'pleris' are.

which people love God.

Peter Lombard accepts the phraseology of God making people love by His love, but denies that this causes any division between the love with which God loves us and that with which we love him: "The love by which God loves us is not possible to be divided nor shown to be different by these words from that by which we love".[41] In Lombard's understanding, all of the love that exists between God and man is caused by the work of the divine person that is love working to draw people into relationship with the Father and the Son, from whom He proceeds as love.

The important difference between this position on love and "the others' teaching" on the gifts of the Spirit is the fact that the Holy Spirit is love, whereas He is not justification, faith or salvation, which his opponents claim correspond equally to love in the gifts of God. They state that love cannot be both from God and be God; Lombard replies that the Holy Spirit is both giver (temporally) and gift, and that love is therefore given by God, and yet is God: "In this sense, it is said that the love of him is in us, yet however it is the Holy Spirit".[42] This is a well-reasoned argument against those who would doubt this view, as any objector would need to deny that the Holy Spirit proceeds in some sense from the Father and Son as love.

The final objection to this idea noted by Lombard is that love is an affection of the mind (*charitas affectio mentis est*) whereas the Holy Spirit as a divine person cannot be said to be this.[43] The reply given is that love does indeed affect the mind, but the love that is the Holy Spirit is not an affection of the mind. Instead, the Holy Spirit moves in each person according to His will, giving His gifts and helping each person to love God. The mind is moved by the Holy Spirit towards God and our neighbour, but the love that proceeds is no affection of the mind, but is the Holy Spirit drawing the person into relationship with God.

Lombard confirms this teaching of his regarding the Spirit and love in book three of the *Sentences*, when he returns for a short passage to the concept of love in God and in men:

> Clearly it is the same love by which God us loved and our neighbour, which is the Holy Spirit, as was said above, because God is love. There is one love and two precepts; one Spirit and two givers; because there is no other love for a neighbour, unless it is that which loves God. Therefore, by the love that we love our neighbour we also love God.[44]

Marcia Colish misunderstands Lombard in this theology of the Holy Spirit as love. Taking *Distinctio* 14 as the basis for her thought, Colish concentrates on the Holy Spirit giving divine grace, and the effects of this grace. *Distinctio*

---

[41] Lombard, *Sentences*, 1.17.6.4, pp.149-50 (PL 192:568, 1.17.12).
[42] *Ibid.*, 1.17.6.5, p.150 (PL 192:568, 1.17.15).
[43] *Ibid.*, 1.17.6.6-9, pp.150-52 (PL 192:568-69, 1.17.16-9).
[44] *Ibid.*, 3.27.3, Vol.2, p.163 (PL 192:812, 3.27.3).

17, used for the discussion above, is surprisingly not included in Colish's appraisal of Lombard's views on the Spirit as love. As a result, the conclusion reached is that "in speaking of the Holy Spirit as the love bonding believers to each other, and to God, therefore, Peter means, strictly, the effects of the Holy Spirit, which assist man in developing the virtue of charity and other virtues".[45] This implies that the Holy Spirit is not that love himself, which Lombard himself declares in *Distinctio* 17, and elsewhere in the *Sentences*.[46] Kaufman believes that Lombard was clear on the concept of *gratia inhabitans*: "Peter described it as the presence of the Holy Spirit itself and identified it with the love of God and neighbour".[47] He further clarifies this thought:

> Other theologians objected that *gratia inhabitans* referred to the gifts of the Spirit but not to the Spirit's presence and direct activity, and variations of this qualification came to obscure Peter's strict identification of *gratia inhabitans* with the Holy Spirit and of both with love.[48]

One more comment needs to be made on the Holy Spirit as love, which is the connection that Lombard makes between this idea and that of the Holy Spirit as the concord of the Trinity, also taken from Augustine. The idea is that the Spirit is the unifying bond of the Trinitarian persons. Lombard does not comment greatly on this issue, but accepts the designation without great question, and links it to the idea of love, first confirming the idea of love with that of concord;[49] and then, in his brief discussion of the trinity of unity, equality and concord, supporting this view of the Holy Spirit by referring to authorities that speak of the Spirit as love.[50] Schupp notes the range of terms for union and love that Lombard uses to speak of the Holy Spirit: "The connection, concord, union, communion, community, love, charity and embrace of both".[51] It is disappointing that Lombard did not further develop these ideas in a more connected manner to show the relationship that he saw between the Spirit's identity as love and union.

---

[45] Colish, *Peter Lombard 1*, p.261.

[46] Philipp Rosemann does show that Peter Lombard taught that the Holy Spirit is Himself the love with which people love ("the charity that makes us love"). The fact of this line of thought does cause Rosemann some uncertainty, as he raises the question whether, if the Holy Spirit is love, people can be said to love at all? The only response that he finds from the *Sentences* is that Lombard focuses on spiritual teachings rather than logic. Rosemann, *Peter Lombard*, pp.85-89.

[47] P. Kaufman, '*Caritas non est nisi a Spiritu Sancto*. Augustine and Peter Lombard on Grace and Personal Righteousness', *Augustiniana* 30 (1980), pp.209-20, at p.209.

[48] *Ibid.*

[49] Lombard, *Sentences*, 1.10.2.5, p.113 (PL 192:551, 1.10.7).

[50] *Ibid.*, 1.31.6, p.232 (PL 192:607, 1.31.11).

[51] Schupp, *Gnadenlehre*, p.216.

Gift

Some of Lombard's gift terminology has already been noted in the discussions on love and procession. However, this part of the identity of the Spirit is important in itself both as part of the ongoing debate about Augustinian terminology in the twelfth century, and as it affects the overall picture of the Spirit in Lombard's work, and therefore deserves a separate, thorough account of the use that Peter Lombard made of the fact that the Holy Spirit is said to be the gift of God.

The great problem already seen with stating that the Holy Spirit is a "gift" is that this can only refer to Him in His temporal mission, as He is not a gift between Father and Son. Lombard himself has been shown to be vulnerable to the problems of this issue when he distinguished between the eternal processions of Son and Spirit by stating that the Son proceeded eternally as a Son, while the Spirit proceeded eternally as a gift.[52] Lombard used the term "gift" in this section without any discussion of the temporal significance of the word, which is essential for understanding his meaning in relating this procession of the Spirit to the procession of the Son.

The main discussion of gift terminology in the *Sentences* begins in the passage on the temporal mission of the Spirit. Lombard is on safe ground here, and the only significant debate that Lombard involves himself in is whether the Spirit can be said to be given by himself. The conclusion to this is that, as the Holy Spirit is God, and the Holy Spirit was given by God, that He was in fact given by himself.[53] This point does not affect the immanent person of the Spirit beyond confirming that He is God in His nature. Lombard does not seek at this point to relate this teaching to the overall procession of the Spirit.

Having dealt with the Holy Spirit's temporal role as love, Lombard then returns (somewhat belatedly, perhaps) to the Spirit's identity as either a gift (*donum*) or as given (*datum sive donatum*),[54] thus moving the discussion back to the immanent person of the Spirit. Lombard addresses the major problem of this pneumatology at the outset of this passage, stating that He is called a gift because He is given, and yet He is only given temporally, which would seem to mean that He cannot be eternally given.[55] This would rule out the concept of "being given" from the Spirit's eternal nature.

Having established this, Lombard then goes on to state that the Holy Spirit is eternally a gift. His reasoning for this is questionable in two main ways: firstly, Lombard simply states that to proceed from the Father and the Son means to proceed as a gift; and secondly this is backed up by comparison with the procession of the Son from the Father as one born (*genitus*),[56] which picks up on his earlier contrast between the two processions. Neither of the arguments

---

[52] Lombard, *Sentences* 1.13.2, p.122 (PL 192:555, 1.13.2).

[53] *Ibid.*, 1.15.1.1, p.131 (PL 192:559, 1.15.1).

[54] *Ibid.*, 1.18, pp.152-59 (PL 192:569-72, 1.18).

[55] *Ibid.*, 1.18.2.2, p.153 (PL 192:570, 1.18.2-3).

[56] *Ibid.*, 1.18.2.4, pp.153-54 (PL 192:570, 1.18.4).

given here is satisfactory. There is no evidence that Lombard can provide why procession from Father and Son should be seen in terms of a gift; it is simply stated as a logical progression without any attempt to show philosophically or theologically why it should be accepted. The rationale for this statement comes solely from quoting Augustine, but is otherwise absent.

The return to the comparison with the Son is confusing in many ways in the context of Lombard's overall work. He has stated previously that it is not possible for us to distinguish between the processions of Son and Spirit, having sought once to make a distinction between the two. Here he retreats to the idea that the Son is begotten, and somehow seeks to confirm the identity of the Spirit as a gift by differentiating between the Spirit and the Son as the Spirit is not begotten of the Father, but proceeds. This is not submissible as an argument in light of his earlier reasoning that the Son proceeds.

The conclusion that Lombard thus comes to is that it is possible for the Holy Spirit to be eternally a gift without being eternally given, which is logically questionable. The point is emphasised by noting that neither Father nor Son give the Spirit to each other eternally, although He is the Spirit of both of them. The final point in this part of the discussion finally introduces the term "giveable" (*donabilis*) as part of the Spirit's eternal nature as a gift.[57] This word has some uses for solving Lombard's problems, but his argument to this point has become so convoluted, and at times almost contradictory, that the reader is not helped to understand Lombard's ideas by the mere introduction of the word.

What is more, it has been noted above,[58] that Lombard noted a difference between the eternal and temporal processions of the Holy Spirit, as the Spirit gave himself temporally. If there is this change in the temporal procession, the link between His eternal nature as "giveable" and "gift" from the Father and Son is confused when He is finally "given" not only by these two, but also by himself. This shows that the introduction of "giveable" has not provided a solution for Lombard to the web of theories that he has given on the Spirit as gift.

If there were not enough confusion yet in this discussion, Lombard now introduces even more by entering into a comparison between the Holy Spirit as Lombard sees Him and the Son, who is said in Isaiah 9 to be "given" to mankind.[59] There are thus two divine persons who proceed in some way as a gift. The question is raised whether, if the Son is a gift, He is also this eternally, as the Spirit is. The reply given is that the Son proceeds eternally from the Father not so much as giveable (*donabilis*), but as one born who is also able to be given.[60] The clarity is not helped by the fact that this is followed immediately by the statement that the Son proceeds both as born and giveable. The Holy Spirit is contrasted as an eternal gift both because He is giveable, and because

---

[57] Lombard, *Sentences*, 1.18.2.6-7, pp.154-55 (PL 192:570, 1.18.4).

[58] In the section on the temporal procession of the Holy Spirit.

[59] Lombard, *Sentences*, 1.18.2.7, p.155 (PL 192:570, 1.18.5).

[60] "Et Filius vere datus est nobis, et ab aeterno processit a Patre non ut donabilis tantum, sed ut genitus qui et donari posset". *Ibid.*, 1.18.2.7, p.155 (PL 192:570, 1.18.5).

He proceeds from the Father and the Son, the point previously made without any logical reasoning.

In his adherence to the work of Augustine on the status of the Holy Spirit as gift, Peter Lombard presents a confusing picture that is not helped by the fact that each new section of teaching that he provides on this point seems to raise further questions about what he had already written. Perhaps most unhelpful are his comparisons in this between the processions of Son and Holy Spirit, both eternally from God the Father, and temporally as gifts when they are in the world. Lombard's only real help to discussion on this point is to show the immense complexity that surrounds consideration of the Biblical picture of the Holy Spirit as in some way the gift of God.

Goodness

One of the major issues in twelfth-century theology was whether the terms power, wisdom and goodness could be applied to the Trinitarian persons, or whether these were all attributes of the divinity and therefore equally applicable to each member of the godhead. The greatest debate, as has been shown in the chapter on Peter Abelard, was about the assignation of goodness to the person of the Holy Spirit. Peter Lombard's position on this point in his *Sentences* is important for understanding the overall position, which will be studied in the chapter on "Goodness" in the second half of this book.

Marcia Colish seeks to provide a summary in her book on Peter Lombard of the debate up until the time of Peter's writing. However, there are weaknesses in this presentation as a context for the views of Lombard, as there is a complete absence of material on Richard of St. Victor, a contemporary of Lombard, who was important in his position on this question; and very little on the writings of William of St. Thierry and Bernard of Clairvaux, who were crucial to the overall debate in the twelfth century. From this inadequate background, Colish concludes that Lombard joined with others "in seeking a means of banishing the Abelardian power, wisdom, goodness argument from theological discussion",[61] and that he "went farther than anyone else at the time to expose the inadequacies" of this idea.[62]

It is unclear, when reading the *Sentences*, where Colish gets these conclusions from. It is true that Lombard focuses at times on the unity of the divine essence meaning that the three persons are equal in all attributes,[63] but this point was not under great discussion, and is shown to be limited in its scope by Lombard's repeated use of the terms wisdom and love as particular to the Son and the Spirit. Lombard also writes against the idea that, if the Father is power, the Son and Spirit have little or no power, an idea that Abelard defended himself against any association with,[64] as has been noted above.[65] These seem to

---

[61] Colish, *Peter Lombard 1*, p.119.
[62] *Ibid.*, p.131.
[63] This point is made in *Sentences*, 1.33, pp.240-46 (PL 192: 610-13, 1.33).
[64] Abelard's response is in *Responsio Petri Abaelardi*, (PL 180:330). Lombard's comment comes in *Sentences*, 1.42.3.5-6, pp.297-98 (PL 192:637, 1.42.8).

be the teachings from which Colish bases her theory that Lombard opposed the idea that goodness was an appropriate name for the Holy Spirit.

However, the actual references to the idea of the Holy Spirit as goodness are rare and inconclusive.[66] Indeed the first reference, in the discussion of the appearance of the Trinity in created things, quotes Augustine, who wrote that everything seeks to "remain in the Good itself; which goodness is understood (to be) the Holy Spirit, who is the Gift of the Father and the Son."[67] This point clearly supports the idea that the Holy Spirit can be considered goodness within the Trinity in a special sense, although the link to the Spirit as gift could be argued to imply a temporal meaning to this quotation.

The main section on the power, wisdom, goodness model receives only 370 words, and three short sections. It begins with the declaration that there is only one power, one wisdom and one goodness, and that each of the persons is the same power, wisdom and goodness.[68] However, after this, Lombard admits that scripture does attribute these names to the respective persons "However, it is a common frequency in the Holy Scriptures for these names to be referred distinctly to the persons, so that power is attributed to the Father, wisdom to the Son and goodness to the Holy Spirit",[69] and, while stressing that none of the persons is exclusively power, wisdom or goodness, does not completely refute the use of the terms for the persons.[70] In the discussion on the Father as power, Lombard notes that this does not involve priority in time to the Father over the Son or the Spirit. The section on the Son as wisdom is short as Lombard has already strongly linked the term to the Son.[71] Lombard does not enter into a discussion at this point of the connection between the Spirit and goodness, noting only that Scripture says that the Spirit is good. The concentration overall in this passage is on the equality of all three persons in their divinity, rather than any particular teaching on the power, wisdom, goodness debate.

Furthermore, Lombard does provide teaching that supports the power, wisdom, goodness trinity in book two of the *Sentences* regarding the sin against the Holy Spirit. There are two elements of the Spirit's person that are used at the basis of this discussion: His identity as love; and His being the goodness

---

[65] In the section on 'Goodness' in the chapter on Abelard.

[66] The word 'goodness' in reference to the Holy Spirit appears only 18 times in the *Sentences*, 10 of which are in the short discussion on the model of power, wisdom and goodness.

[67] Lombard, *Sentences*, 1.3.1.8, p.71 (PL 192:530, 1.3.6).

[68] *Ibid.*, 1.34.3, pp.251-52 (PL 192:616, 1.34.6). "Una est ergo potentia, sapientia, bonitas Patris, et Filii, et Spiritus sancti; et hi tres eadem potentia, eadem sapientia, eadem bonitas".

[69] *Ibid.*, 1.34.3, pp.251-52 (PL 192:616, 1.34.6).

[70] Marcia Colish does pick up on this part of Lombard's thought, writing that one reason Peter was unhappy with the power, wisdom, goodness formula was because he did not consider that these attributes were unique to any one of the three persons. Colish, *Peter Lombard* 1, p.119.

[71] In *Distinctio* 10, for example (Lombard, *Sentences*, 1.10 pp.110-14, PL 192:549-51).

that proceeds from power and wisdom.[72] The concentration of the teaching about the blasphemy, however, is against the Holy Spirit's identity as goodness.

Despite Colish's statements, therefore, Lombard has remarkably little to say on this issue, and what he does say is by no means definitive. Given the importance of the issue to many writers of this time, and considering the attention that it earned in the writing of Richard of St. Victor, who wrote at the same time as Peter Lombard, the paucity of references is surprising, but little can be concluded from this comparative silence.

Conclusion

The amount of material in the *Sentences* that Peter Lombard devoted to considering the person and procession of the Holy Spirit shows that this issue was of great importance to him. Lombard was attempting to be clear in his outline of the three persons in their origin and relation to each other and the way in which their immanent states were reflected in their involvement in the things of this world. In this, Lombard sought to be ruled both by the Bible and by the teachings of the Church Fathers, most notably Augustine.

Lombard was most successful when he wrote about the Holy Spirit as the love of God, of Father and Son for each other, and as the love bond between the godhead and people. Although he has been misinterpreted on this point by Marcia Colish, Lombard clearly taught that it was the Holy Spirit, the love of Father and Son, who himself was the love shed abroad in men's hearts, and was the love by which men love both God and their neighbour.

However, when Lombard sought to define in what way the Holy Spirit should be understood to be the gift of God, he began on shaky ground in comparing the procession to that of the Son, and then seems to have been unaware that each new point he taught further confused the issue. On the other hand, he wrote tantalisingly little on the concept of the Spirit as union and goodness, which is surprising given the former's link to the idea of love, and the latter's importance in twelfth-century thought.

---

[72] Lombard, *Sentences*, 2.43.1-2, pp.572-73 (PL 192:754, 2.43.1).

CHAPTER 7

Love

Love was the most commonly-used attribute to describe the person of the Holy Spirit in the immanent Trinity in the twelfth century. The concept was taken from the writings of Augustine, who had used love both in his relational model of the Spirit in the Trinity, and in his analogies of the Trinity. Both Mary Clark and John Burnaby believe this was one of Augustine's greatest legacies: "[the] naming of the Spirit as love is one of the most important and original aspects of his Trinitarian theology".[1] However, Augustine was not entirely convincing in his use of love terminology, as David Coffey puts it: "Augustine has not even succeeded in showing from Scripture that the Holy Spirit is the divine love in some special way, let alone mutual love".[2] The twelfth-century writers created a clearer picture of the Holy Spirit as love in His procession and relations, backing this up in their analogies. Not only did they give more persuasive arguments for this basic position, these writers also worked with the concept of love to provide new insights into how this identity of the Spirit affected the relations of the Trinitarian persons. In addition, the economic role of the Spirit as love was consistently tied into the ideas concerning His immanent person, supporting this overall position on the Holy Spirit. In short, the diverse writers studied in this book presented a unified, clear, developed teaching that love should be considered as a fundamental part of the identity of the immanent person of the Holy Spirit.

Augustine

Augustine did teach that the Holy Spirit is love in the godhead,[3] but his

---

[1] Clark, *Augustine*, p.67. Burnaby writes that the "connection of love and the Holy Spirit was one of most important and lasting contributions of Augustine". Burnaby, *Amor Dei*, p.173.
[2] Coffey, 'The Holy Spirit as the Mutual Love of the Father and the Son', p.201.
[3] Many writers have examined the teaching of Augustine on the Holy Spirit as the mutual love of Father and Son. David Coffey has done a lot of work on this topic from a variety of angles, two of the best of these are his book, *Grace: The Gift of the Holy Spirit*, and his article, 'The Holy Spirit as the Mutual Love of the Father and the Son'. Bourassa and Ouellet are also helpful in their discussions (F. Bourassa, '"Dans la communion de l'Esprit Saint": étude théologique', *Science et Esprit* (1982) pp.31-56, 135-49, 239-68; M. Ouellet, 'The Spirit in the Life of the Trinity', *Communio* 25 (1998), pp.199-213). Two other works need mentioning in this context: Colin Gunton argues

strongest work on this came in the analogies that he sought for the Trinity. The use of analogy must be to back up a point that is being made, rather than as a major method of teaching doctrine, and Augustine's underlying weakness on the Holy Spirit as love means that the analogies have less force. However, Augustine's writing on this point was one of the bases for the twelfth-century writers, and it thus deserves a brief summary.

Augustine wrote on the subject of love in the godhead in both the *De Trinitate* and the *De Doctrina Christiana*. It is interesting that the treatment of love in the *De Doctrina* does not discuss the idea that the Holy Spirit is Himself love. The *De Trinitate* divides into two sections: the first examines the nature of God and the persons within the godhead; the second seeks to find analogies for these teachings to help the reader understand Augustine's thought.[4]

The main teaching on the Holy Spirit as love in the first section comes in book six, after teaching on the Son as the power and wisdom of God. The Spirit is pictured providing unity in the Trinity, and the best word that Augustine finds to describe this is *charitas*.[5] Studer also shows how Augustine works with 1 John 4:16 to apply love to the person of the Holy Spirit:

> Auf diese Ebene nun kann man sich fragen, ob der Vater oder der Sohn oder der Geist oder die ganze Trinität als "die Liebe" zu bezeichnen ist. Augustinus antwortet darauf, dass jede der drei Personen als "die Liebe" betrachtet werden kann, so gut wie jede "die Weisheit" genannt wird. Wie jedoch nur der Sohn der Wort ist, so ist auch nur der Geist im eigentlichen Sinn die Gabe Gottes. Selbst wenn die Liebe von Gott substantiell ausgesagt wird, wird also dennoch im eigentlichen Sinn nur der Heilige Geist die Liebe genannt.[6]

This brief section in book six is all that the concept receives in the first half of the *De Trinitate*. Augustine returns to the idea after his analogies, in book fifteen. Here he includes two reasons why the Holy Spirit can be considered as love: the Spirit is love because He is the Spirit of both Father and Son; and He is love because of His mission as a gift to mankind, to spread the love of God abroad in their hearts.[7] Burnaby writes on this second point: "He whom we have loved has given us himself: he has given us that from which our love derives; for the presence in us of the Holy Spirit means that we love God 'through God'".[8] Both of these arguments are limited in their force: the first has no logical reasoning behind it; and the second is tied to the economy of the Spirit.

---

against Augustine's teaching on the Holy Spirit as love in the godhead in his *The Promise of Trinitarian Theology* (Edinburgh: T & T Clark, 1991, pp.48-55); while Arendt's study of Augustine's view of love does not bring out the concept of the Holy Spirit as the love of God (Arendt, *Love and Saint Augustine*).

[4] Although, as will be seen below, there is teaching on the persons in the second half as Augustine clarifies his ideas in light of the analogies he presents.

[5] Augustine, *De Trinitate*, 6.5, p.235 (p.209).

[6] Studer, 'Zur Pneumatologie des Augustinus von Hippo', pp.569-70.

[7] Augustine, *De Trinitate*, 15.17, pp.501-07 (p.421).

[8] Burnaby, *Amor Dei*, p.176.

This short analysis shows the unconvincing nature of Augustine's main teaching on the Holy Spirit as love.

Augustine is stronger in identifying the Spirit as love in the analogies for the Trinity that he creates. Two of these in particular were influential for the writers of the twelfth century: lover, beloved, love; and mind, knowledge, love.[9] Both of these analogies express well a processional model of the Holy Spirit from both Father and Son, and show the Spirit drawing these persons together in the bond of love. The first of these analogies reflects the relations of the Trinitarian persons; the second is a construct intended to see the Trinity in the human mind, and is thus less effective as an expression of the godhead.

Augustine was very influential in establishing the western position on the Holy Spirit as the love of God, and yet his own teaching is not very persuasive on this point. This chapter will now show how the twelfth-century writers took these basic ideas from Augustine and formed them, with some insights of their own, into a convincing case for this doctrine.

The Holy Spirit as the Mutual Love of the Father and Son

At the basis of thought on the Holy Spirit as love is the concept that the Spirit is the love with which the Father loves the Son and the Son loves the Father. As such the Holy Spirit draws the Trinity together in love as He is the uniting bond. This root idea is taught by many writers in the twelfth century, and is the starting point from which many broaden and develop their thoughts on this aspect of the identity of the Spirit. All three of the Latin terms for love mentioned so far in this book, *amor*, *caritas* and *dilectio* are used to describe the role of the Spirit as the mutual love of Father and Son.

The most direct teaching on this issue is given by Richard of St. Victor in his article *Quomodo Spiritus Sanctus est amor Patris et Filii*.[10] In this, Richard begins with the fact that Augustine had written about mutual love, but immediately notes the difficulty that is presented in the comparison of this to the concept that the Son is the wisdom of God. Richard is very clear in the presentation of his understanding, starting with the question whether, if the Father loves by the Holy Spirit, the Spirit is necessarily the love itself with which the Father loves? Richard concentrates on the Father as the principle of the Trinity, containing the fullness of divinity in Himself. This means that the Father must be the source of the love that is the Holy Spirit. The conclusion that Richard reaches is that the Father does love by the Holy Spirit, while the relation of the Son to this love is not clearly defined.[11] Mary Melone also finds the idea of mutual love in Richard's *De Trinitate*: "Lo Spirito Santo non è nella sua persona *l'amor mutuus* del Padre e del Figlio, il legame o l'unità che si crea

---

[9] Augustine, *De Trinitate*, 8-9, pp.268-310 (pp.241-55, 270-82).

[10] Richard, *Quomodo Spiritus Sanctus* (PL 196:1011-12).

[11] "Pater vero amor est, et Spiritus sanctus ejus amor est, et ideo Pater diligit seipso, diligit Spiritu sancto". Richard, *Quomodo Spiritus Sanctus*, (PL 196:1012). This will be discussed more fully concerning the manner in which the Father loves by the Holy Spirit later in this chapter.

tra le due prime persone".[12]

Abelard does not develop the concept of mutual love to the extent that Richard does, but he does use this idea to reinforce the principle of dual procession in response to Greek objections. Abelard not only states that the Holy Spirit is mutual love, he also shows that there is wider patristic support for this beyond the writing of Augustine, citing Chrysostom and Jerome as supporters of this position.[13] It is interesting that Abelard uses these sources in referring to the attribute of love and the person of the Spirit, whereas Anselm of Havelberg had quoted widely from the Church Fathers to support dual procession without focusing in this on the attributes that he had ascribed to the Spirit.

William of St. Thierry uses the mutual love idea in writing of his basic position on the procession of the Spirit in the *De Contemplando Deo*. Having stated that "Your love is your goodness, the Holy Spirit proceeding from the Father and the Son," William goes on to declare that "You love yourself in yourself, when the Holy Spirit ... proceeds from the Father and the Son."[14] The phraseology of 'loving yourself in yourself' is an excellent way of describing how the concept of mutual love can exist between separate persons in one godhead. In this, the persons are shown to be one, and yet able to relate to each other.

Richard of St. Victor used three terms to develop the idea of the Holy Spirit as mutual love. The first two of these are *felicitas*, implying happiness, and *jucundus*, meaning pleasant or delightful. Richard states that any love in the godhead must have these two qualities, which would not be possible if the love were not mutual.[15] A third term, *condilectum*, is used later in the *De Trinitate* as part of Richard's processional teaching on the Holy Spirit.[16] It is this "mutual delight" in each other that is the reason for the procession of the Spirit as love from the Father and Son.

A related teaching to that on mutual love is the idea put forward by Clarembald of Arras and Thierry of Chartres that the Holy Spirit, as love, connects the Father and Son. This is taken from Augustine's teaching that the Father is unity, the Son equality and the Holy Spirit union.[17] Clarembald brings the love that is the Holy Spirit into this discussion, saying that "The unity loves equality and equality loves unity and these are connected by the love".[18] Thierry uses the same language of the Spirit joining Father and Son by love, and goes on from this to the processional model of the Spirit. He writes that love is not

---

[12] Melone, 'Lo Spirito Santo', p.60.

[13] Abelard, *Theologia Christiana*, 4.130, 132 (Vol. 2, pp.330-31).

[14] William, *De Contemplando*, 11, p.98 (p.54).

[15] Richard, *De Trinitate*, 3.3, pp.137-38 (PL 196:917).

[16] *Ibid.*, 3.15, pp.150-51 (PL 196:925).

[17] Augustine, *De Doctrina*, p.12.

[18] Clarembald of Arras, *Tractatus Super Librum Boetii* De Trinitate, 2.39, in N. Häring, *Life and Works of Clarembald of Arras: A Twelfth-Century Master of the School of Chartres* (Toronto: Pontifical Institute of Medieval Studies, 1965), p.122.

born or unborn, "But it proceeds from the unity and from the equality of unity".[19]

This element of teaching on the person of the Holy Spirit as the mutual love of Father and Son is held in common by all the writers studied in this book. From this common basis, there were many developments of the idea of the Spirit as love beyond that which had been received from Augustine, which complement each other and provide deeper insight into the person of the Holy Spirit.

Expansion of the Idea of Love
Sweetness, Embrace, Kiss

One way in which the person of the Holy Spirit as love was extended was with the use of words such as sweetness, embrace and kiss, often taken in readings from the Song of Songs. Unsurprisingly, the more mystical William of St. Thierry and Bernard of Clairvaux were the most prominent proponents of this line of thought, both of whom wrote major series on the Song of Songs. Augustine had briefly mentioned the words sweetness and embrace in connection with the Spirit, but did not leave any organised thought on these points.[20]

Bernard of Clairvaux wrote one of his sermons specifically on the Holy Spirit as the kiss of God, in which he elaborated on this role of the Spirit in the godhead, showing the passionate love which exists within the Trinity.[21] William wrote about the Spirit as kiss not only in his work on the Song of Songs, but also in his *Liber Seu Tractatus de charitate* and the *Mirror of Faith*. This again shows the consistency of William across the range of his works, including this concept in a commentary, a meditation and a theological treatise. Another work, his *Commentary on the Book of Romans* contains teaching on the Holy Spirit as the embrace of the Father and Son as a major part of His role as love: "That unspeakable embrace of the Father and the Image is not without fruition, charity and joy. In the Trinity the Holy Spirit is that love, delight, happiness or beatitude".[22]

Sweetness is the term that is most used in this period as an extension of the Spirit being love in the Trinity: Bernard mentions this in his *Sentences*, linked

---

[19] Thierry of Chartres, *Commentum Super Boethii Librum De Trinitate*, 2.37-38 (in N. Häring ed., *Commentaries on Boethius by Thierry of Chartres and his School*. Toronto: Pontifical Institute of Medieval Studies, 1971) p.80. Maurer and Evans both show that the main teaching about the Holy Spirit as love in the Chartrain School concerned His economic state as love sharing God's perfection and giving guidance. A. Maurer, *Medieval Philosophy* (Toronto: Pontifical Institute of Medieval Studies, 1982), p.72; G. Evans, *Old Arts and New Theology: The Beginnings of Theology as an Academic Discipline* (Oxford: OUP, 1980), p.185.

[20] Augustine, *De Trinitate*, 6.10, p.242 (p.213).

[21] Bernard, *Opera*, Vol.1, p.37 (*Song of Songs*, p.46).

[22] William, *Expositio*, p.162 (p.224).

to the sanctifying work of the Spirit in believers;[23] and William writes of the Spirit as sweetness in both of his major theological works, the *Mirror of Faith* and the *Enigma of Faith*.[24] This idea is also found outside these writers though, being mentioned by both Richard of St. Victor and Peter Lombard. Richard uses the language of sweetness in one of his more mystical works, *Benjamin Major*, in reference to the work of the Spirit in the lives of people;[25] Peter Lombard's reference comes in the midst of discussion about the equality of the divine persons and is compared to the procession of the Son from the Father: "The Holy Spirit is not born, but is the sweetness of begetter and begotten".[26] It is important that Lombard makes clear this link between these extended ideas of the Spirit as love and His immanent personhood because the other references are more focused on the economy of the Spirit. However, all these teachings are consistent with the authors' views not only of the Spirit's work, but of who He is in His immanent state.

Complaceo and Condilectio

Two terms that needs to be added to this discussion are *complaceo* and *condilectio*. *Complaceo* was used by Hugh of St. Victor in his meditation on the divine.[27] Although this section is initially entitled, "From the rational mind it is possible to show the divine Trinity", the discussion quickly moves past Augustine's mind, wisdom, love analogy to discussion of the relations of the divine persons: Father, Son and Love (the Holy Spirit is not mentioned, but merely understood to be the love between Father and Son). The main word for love used by Hugh in this passage is *dilectio*, which is that used for love of conscious preference. Hugh writes of the pleasure that the Father takes in the perfection of His *sapientia* and the love that the Son has because of the perfection from which He proceeds. This *dilectio* extends to the perfect love that proceeds from each, and from each person to Himself: "[the Father] mox diligit eum, et complacet sibi in ipso".[28] The great benefit of Hugh's analysis here is that it includes the Holy Spirit in the love relations of the godhead, and helps to clarify how each person can be love and yet the Holy Spirit particularly seen as love in God. The concept of mutual love is extended here so that the Holy Spirit is part of the relationship of love that exists in the Trinity.

Condilectio was the word used by Richard in his *De Trinitate* to express the perfection of love that is created by the existence of a third person in the Trinitarian relations. This term does not involve the Holy Spirit in the love relations in the same way that *complaceo* does because the concentration in Richard's work remains on the love of the first two persons, which is

---

[23] Bernard, *Sentences*, 3.97, p.313.
[24] William, *Enigma*, 97, pp.174-76 (p.114); *Speculum*, 46, p.64 (pp.54-55).
[25] Richard, *Benjamin Major*, 3.24 (PL 196:134).
[26] Lombard, *Sentences*, 1.31.2.2, p.226 (PL 192:605, 1.31.4).
[27] Hugh, *Didascalion*, 7.21-23 (PL 176:831-33).
[28] *Ibid.*, 7.21 (PL 176:831).

completed by *condilectio*. This is shown by the use of *condilectum* in book six of the *De Trinitate* to explain how the Holy Spirit proceeds, as the mutual and reciprocal love of Father and Son.[29] Both of these terms deepen our understanding of writers' views on love in the immanent Trinity.

Equality of the Spirit with the Father and the Son

One conclusion that some of the writers drew from the teaching on mutual love was the equality of the person of the Spirit with the Father and the Son. The third person in the processional model, who receives His being from the first two, could be seen as inferior, and had been viewed as such in the history of the Church by groups such as the Pneumatomachi.

Anselm of Canterbury argued from his views on the Spirit as love that He must therefore be equal in every way with the Father and the Son, in both his *Proslogion* and *Monologion*. In the *Proslogion*, Anselm begins this point with the concept of the Father and Son being the supreme good that the divine had been declared to be. The Son is said to have the fullness of the Father dwelling in Him, because "there cannot be born of You any other than what You are".[30] This product is said to be the love common to Father and Son, which is the Holy Spirit. Anselm concludes from this that the Spirit must be equal to the Father and Son because "Your love for Yourself and Him, and His love for You and Himself, are as great as You and He are".[31] The discussion in the *Monologion* follows the same lines, but is more extensive because it is more in line with the overall flow of the work, which expands on Augustine's mind, knowledge, love analogy.[32] Anselm works with the extent of love in the Supreme, stating that, "[love is] as great as the supreme spirit. But the only thing that can be equal to the supreme spirit is the supreme spirit. This love, then, is the supreme spirit".[33]

Two other writers also show the equality of the Spirit to the Father and Son on the basis of His identity as love. Richard of St. Victor brings love into his discussion of God on the basis of the need for supreme goodness. This results in a love that is also supreme, which in turn implies the equality of all three persons: "sicut charitas vera exigit personarum pluralitatem, sic charitas summa exigit personarum aequalitatem".[34] It is interesting to note that it is at this point that Richard brings the concept of *dilectio* love into his work which will ultimately be used as the root of his *condilectum* teaching on the equal, mutual love between all three persons.

Peter Lombard supports the equality of the Spirit as love as part of his

---

[29] Richard, *De Trinitate*, 6.17, p.252 (PL 196:981-82).

[30] Anselm C, *Proslogion*, 23, Vol.1, p.117 (p.100).

[31] *Ibid.*, 23, Vol.1, p.117 (p.100).

[32] The *Monologion* reasoning occupies four chapters. Anselm C, *Monologion*, 50-53, Vol.1, pp.65-66 (pp.61-62).

[33] *Ibid.*, 53, Vol.1, p.66 (p.62).

[34] Richard, *De Trinitate*, 3.7, pp.141-42 (PL 196:919).

discussion of gift terminology. Following Augustine's thought that there is nothing greater in the gift of God than love, and that the Holy Spirit is the greatest gift of God, Peter Lombard writes, "What follows more than that it is that love, which is said to be both God and from God?"[35] This establishes the identity and status of the immanent person of the Holy Spirit at the outset of a discussion of the economic role of the Spirit. There is thus strong teaching in the twelfth century that the concept that the Spirit is love in the godhead is a solid support for the equality of the Spirit with the Father and Son as God.

On Whether Mutual Love implies that there are Two Spirits

One of the major objections of the Greek Church to the dual procession of the Spirit from Father and Son is that this would seem to imply the existence of two Spirits, one proceeding from the Father and one from the Son. This issue was directly addressed by Anselm of Canterbury by using the concept of love; and both Peter Lombard and the Victorines also taught that the procession of the Spirit from the Father and Son as love did not imply two separate Spirits, but the one Holy Spirit who is their mutual love.

Anselm of Canterbury wrote about the love proceeding from the Father and the Son in the *Monologion*. The context for this point was the equality of the Spirit with the Father and Son examined above. On the basis of his thought on the procession of the Spirit as love, Anselm wrote:

> Love does not proceed from the Father ane Son being two separate things. Rather it proceeds from their being one ... in virtue of their being (their essence, which cannot be multiple ... from the Father, as an individual, floods forth the supreme spirit's whole love. From the Son, as an individual, floods forth the supreme Spirit's whole love. But from Father and Son together, floods forth not two whole loves, but one and the same love.[36]

Given this clear teaching on the procession of the Spirit from two sources as one person, it is surprising that this idea was not used in the *De Processione* when that work addresses the Greek objection that dual procession implies two Spirits. Having said this, it is noteworthy that Anselm of Havelberg does not use love language to answer the Greek charge of two Spirits, focusing instead on the one essence of Father and Son at this point in the debate.

Peter Lombard hints at this aspect of the Spirit as love in *Distinctio* 10, which defends the idea that God is love and that the Holy Spirit is in particular the love of God.[37] However, direct application of the love identity of the Spirit to the idea of two Spirits is left until *Distinctio* 32, where Lombard clarifies that there is only one love in the Trinity, despite the dual procession of the Spirit and the fact that both Father and Son are love, and that that love is the one Holy

---

[35] Lombard, *Sentences*, 1.17.2, pp.143-44 (PL 192:565, 1.17.4).
[36] Anselm C, *Monologion*, 54, Vol.1, p.66 (p.62).
[37] Lombard, *Sentences*, 1.10.1.4-2.1, p.111 (PL 192:550, 1.10.3-4).

Spirit.[38] It is after this that Lombard gives the strange idea that it would seem more correct to say that the Father and Son proceed from the Holy Spirit than vice-versa, because in God it is the same thing to love as to be.[39]

The Victorines' teaching on the Holy Spirit as *complaceo* and *condilectio*, studied above, is also relevant to this point, although Hugh and Richard themselves do not directly apply their thoughts to the idea that there might be two Spirits. However, these two terms are based on the idea that it is the mutual perfection of the first two persons that is the cause of their love for each other. As that perfection is the result of their common essence as God, so the love that flows from each is the same Holy Spirit.

Anselm of Havelberg's account of his debate with Nechites would seem to indicate that this issue of two Spirits was one of the major stumbling blocks to Greek acceptance of the dual procession of the Holy Spirit. Western thinkers were clearly aware of this, and one way in which they addressed the problem was by expounding on the Holy Spirit's identity as the love of Father and Son to show that the love of each was the one Holy Spirit.

Owing Love

It is important to add to this discussion the concept put forward by Richard of St. Victor that the Holy Spirit could be said to owe love to the Father and Son. This idea comes as part of the relational model of the Trinity in book five of the *De Trinitate*, immediately after Richard dismisses the notion that there could be a fourth person in the divine nature.

The relations that Richard outlines here are that there is one person who only gives (the Father); one who only receives (the Holy Spirit); and one who both gives and receives (the Son). This is drawn from the procession of the three persons. Richard then moves to the concept of love and begins to talk of love that owes, and love that is gratuitous: "in uno ex tribus est amor summus et gratuitus. In altero vero sic summus, ut sit solum debitus".[40] The Father has no need to love either of the other persons because He does not receive anything from them, whereas both Son and Holy Spirit have their existence in different ways from the Father.

On the basis of this, Richard introduces a new set of relations, of one who is owed love completely (Father); one who both owes and is owed love (Son); and one who owes love completely (the Holy Spirit).[41] Richard claims that everything about love is thus contained in the three Trinitarian persons. The idea that the Holy Spirit owes love is an interesting concept to hold alongside Richard's earlier teaching on the Spirit as the love of God.

The interaction of these ideas is not addressed until book six of the *De Trinitate*, when Richard is discussing the Holy Spirit's economic role as the gift

---

[38] *Ibid.*, 1.32.5, p.238 (PL 192:609, 1.32.7).
[39] "Idem est ibi diligere quod esse". *Ibid.*, 1.32.6.1, pp.238-39 (PL 192:610, 1.32.8).
[40] Richard, *De Trinitate*, 5.19, p.217 (PL.196:963).
[41] Richard, *De Trinitate*, 5.19, p.217 (PL.196:963).

of God. This is linked to the Holy Spirit's identity as the love of God, and this in turn is related to the thought that the Spirit is said to owe love completely. Richard states that it is because of this overall picture of the Spirit that it is the proper mission of the Spirit to "infuse in men the debt of love".[42]

The relation between the Spirit's identity as love and the notion that He owes love thus seems to strengthen Richard's concept of the procession of the Spirit as a person rather than a mere energy or emotion. Just as the Son proceeds in some sense as the wisdom of God, but still with the capacity to relate to the Father from whom He proceeds, so the Spirit is able to proceed as love, yet still as fully divine and able to interrelate with the Father and the Son. The use of love relations in this instance therefore strengthens the overall concept of the identity of the Holy Spirit as love.

On Whether Father and Son Love with the Love that Proceeds from Them
Several authors comment on this issue of the Holy Spirit's procession from the Father and Son as love, comparing this with the Son's identity as the wisdom begotten of the Father. The question centres on the relationship between the Father and the two processions, whether the Father is wise by the wisdom born from him, and whether He loves by the love that proceeds from Him. Augustine had commented only on the former, stating that the Father must have His own wisdom or He would rely on the Son for part of His nature.[43]

All of the writers studied in this book who dealt with this problem, taught the traditional, Augustinian position on the Son as wisdom: Peter Abelard noted Augustine's thought that "It is the same to be wise as to be", implying that wisdom must be part of the Father's being;[44] the author of the *Summa Sententiarum* believed that it was not possible for the Father to be wise by the wisdom that He produces as this would mean that He has something from His Son;[45] and William of St. Thierry taught that wisdom is part of the Father's essence, and so the Son must receive this part of His existence from the Father.[46] Of these three writers, both Abelard and William wrote that this connection extended to the Father's relationship to the love that is the Holy

---

[42] *Ibid.*, 6.14, pp.245-46 (PL 196:978).

[43] Augustine, *De Trinitate*, 6.1, pp.228-29 (p.206).

[44] Abelard, *Theologia Christiana*, 4.115 (Vol. 2, p.322).

[45] *Summa Sententiarum*, 1.11 (PL 176:60). Opinion on the authorship of the *Summa Sententiarum* is divided. While Migne attributes the work to Hugh of St. Victor and, while it is thought to come from the school of St. Victor, Hugh is now not generally accepted as the author. Courtney states that the most probable author was Otho of Lucca, with which Fortman agreees. F. Courtney, 'Cardinal Robert Pullen: An English Theologian of the Twelfth Century', *Analecta Gregoriana LXIV* (Rome: Apud Aedes Universitatis Gregorianae, 1954), pp.24-25. Fortman, *The Triune God*, p.190. Gillian Evans does attribute the work to Hugh however in her article 'Anselm of Canterbury and Anselm of Havelberg: the controversy with the Greeks', *AP* 53 (1977), pp.158-75, at p.163, n.24.

[46] William, *Enigma*, 57, p.142 (p.82).

Spirit, so that the Father has love in Himself, and does not love by the Spirit, although the Spirit is the love proceeding from the Father.[47]

Richard of St. Victor deals with this issue in his *Tractatus* on the Spirit as mutual love. In this work, Richard writes that the Father teaches the Son the wisdom with which He is wise. This is a helpful insight into his views on the relations between the first and second persons. However, Richard seeks to extend this to the Father's love in the Spirit, stating, "Therefore, just as the Father teaches by the Son, yet it does not follow that he is from the Son, so he loves by the Spirit, but this does not mean that he is from the Spirit".[48] At this point, it is unclear exactly what Richard is saying about the love that is in the Father and that which is the Holy Spirit. Fortunately, Richard clarifies his point in many ways: first, although the Father loves by the Holy Spirit, it does not follow that the love is the Holy Spirit; second, the Father is the love by which the Son loves and the Holy Spirit breathes love; third, the Father loves by the Holy Spirit, not as having love from the Holy Spirit, but showing love through Him; and finally the Father is love, and the Holy Spirit is His love, and for that reason the Father loves both by Himself and by the Spirit.[49] Richard thus gives many different ways of explaining his basic point that both the Father and the Holy Spirit are love in the Trinity; however, there is no clear picture of the exact relationship between the two persons in love.

Peter Lombard is consistent in his presentation both of the Son as wisdom and in his views on the Holy Spirit. In *Distinctio* 5 of the *Sentences*, Lombard follows Augustine's line that the Father is not wise with the wisdom begotten from Him.[50] He returns to this issue in *Distinctio* 32, the main teaching of which is that both Father and Son do love by the love that proceeds from them, the Holy Spirit. Lombard writes that there are not two loves in the Trinity, as the Holy Spirit is the love which the Trinity is.[51] He goes on to say that the two do not love each other by something that is of them (*non est aliquis eorum*), but by the Holy Spirit.[52] Lombard thus seems to disagree with his contemporaries on this point. In the same *Distinctio*, Lombard deals thoroughly with the idea that the Father might be wise by the wisdom that is the Son, and clarifies his original position that there is a difference between the Son being begotten as wisdom and the procession of the Spirit as love, which is beyond human knowledge.[53]

The writings on this issue show the difficulties that were presented by the idea that the Holy Spirit is the love of Father and Son within the context of a

---

[47] The author of the *Summa* does not deal with the relationship between Father and Spirit on this issue.

[48] Richard, *Quomodo Spiritus Sanctus* (PL 196:1011).

[49] *Ibid.* (PL 196:1012).

[50] Lombard, *Sentences*, 1.5.1.4, pp.81-82 (PL 192:535, 1.5.3).

[51] Lombard, *Sentences*, 1.32.5, p.238 (PL 192:609, 1.32.7).

[52] *Ibid.*, 1.32.6.1, pp.238-39 (PL 192:610, 1.32.8).

[53] *Ibid.*, 1.32.2.1-3, 1.32.6.1, pp.234-35, 238-39 (PL 192:607-08, 610, 1.32.3,8).

divine nature that itself is supreme love. While Richard of St. Victor's discussion is most helpful in understanding how this problem might be resolved, Peter Lombard's statement that the difference between Son and Spirit in this is beyond human knowledge is perhaps the most convincing conclusion.

Analogies Involving the Holy Spirit as Love

Numerous analogies were used by twelfth-century authors involving the Holy Spirit as love supporting this position, or using the Spirit as love to illustrate the Trinitarian relationships. Of Augustine's analogies that have been mentioned containing this concept, it was the mind, knowledge, love trinity that was most regularly appealed to in the twelfth century. However, in this period this triad was only used analogously by the author of the *Summa Sententiarum* to show how the Trinitarian processions could be seen as mirrored in the human person.[54]

Other writers in the twelfth century used the mind, knowledge, love triad o describe the persons of the godhead in their immanent state. Anselm of Canterbury's *Monologion*, Peter Lombard's *Sentences* and Hugh of St. Victor's meditation on the essence of the divine all adopted this approach.[55] Anselm uses these three attributes as the results of logical deduction that any person might achieve when meditating on the divine; Lombard does make a comparison with the human mind, but notes that whereas a person has these attributes, the divine persons are these same qualities; while Hugh begins his discussion by stating that he wants to provide a proof of God from the rational mind.

William of St. Thierry provides a fascinating analogy for the Trinity in his *Mirror of Faith*. The trinity he uses here is that of faith, hope and love. William states that, like the eternal Trinity, faith, hope and love are so joined and united to each other and among themselves that each is in all and all are each.[56] Faith is linked to power (representing the Father), which "begets" hope; love is said to proceed from faith and hope because one must love what one hopes for and believes in. William supports this analogy by noting that these three attributes need not come before or after one another in time, mirroring the coeternal nature of the Trinitarian persons. The joining of love to the person of the Holy Spirit is the most convincing part of this analogy, but the whole cannot be seen as a convincing analogy of intra-Trinitarian relationships because of the necessary outward focus of faith, hope and love beyond themselves.

Peter Abelard could be said to be providing an analogy for the Holy Spirit in his teaching on the World Soul, given a correct understanding of his use of the term *involucrum*. In the discussion on the World Soul in the *Theologia Summi Boni*, Abelard notes that the *caritas* that is one element of the World Soul could be said to be the Holy Spirit, working in creation.[57] In the *Introductio ad*

---

[54] *Summa Sententiarum*, 1.6 (PL 176:50-52).
[55] Anselm C, *Monologion*, 50-54, Vol.1, pp.65-66 (pp.61-62); Lombard, *Sentences*, 1.3.2.1-3, pp.71-72 (PL 192:530-1, 1.3.7); Hugh, *Didascalion*, 7.21 (PL 176:820).
[56] William, *Speculum*, 5, p.28 (p.9).
[57] Abelard, *Theologia Summi Boni*, 1.6, p.40.

Theologiam, Abelard notes that the Bible analogises the love that is the Holy Spirit as heat or fire in His work in the hearts of men: "Truly the Holy Spirit, who is called the love of God, is rightly seen to be understood through heat, when that love in us, through which our hearts are warmed, is frequently called warmth or fire".[58]

Blasphemy Against the Holy Spirit

Three writers studied in this book back up their view of the immanent person of the Spirit as love by writing that one interpretation of the blasphemy against the Holy Spirit is the sin of evil or hatred against God. When the sin against the Holy Spirit is discussed, as will later be shown, it is generally part of a model of the Trinitarian persons - either power, wisdom, goodness, or mind, knowledge, will. Hugh of St. Victor used a trinity of mind, knowledge and love in his *De Amore Sponsi ad Sponsam* to indicate that blaspheming the Holy Spirit was an act of hatred, offending the Holy Spirit as love.[59] However, both Peter Lombard and Richard of St. Victor wrote about sin against the Holy Spirit as love in a separate section to emphasise this aspect of the Spirit's identity.

Peter Lombard does not include this idea as part of his major teaching on the godhead in book one of the *Sentences*, but includes an entire *Distinctio* on the sin against the Holy Spirit in book two. The section dealing with the Holy Spirit as love is drawn from Cain's statement in Genesis 4 that his sin is so great that it deserves death. Lombard comments on this statement, "Truly it is said to be a sin against the Holy Spirit, because the Holy Spirit is the love of the Father and the Son, and the kindness by which they in turn love each other and us".[60] Lombard is alleging that Cain's action of hate against his brother was a sin against the identity of the Spirit as love.

Richard of St. Victor wrote a tract about the blasphemy against the Holy Spirit, the second half of which focuses on sin against the love that is the Holy Spirit. Richard writes that the sin against the Holy Spirit is an affection and desire to curse God.[61] He also states that, because love is the greatest thing in God, this is the cause of the eternal punishment.[62] He concludes that the sin is that of hatred, which is the opposite of love.

The connection between the blasphemy against the Holy Spirit and His identity as love is important because it shows the extent to which the writers held that love was part of the Spirit's immanent personhood, and was not merely one of the particular roles of His temporal procession.

The Economic Role of the Holy Spirit as Love

Although this book is focusing on the immanent person of the Holy Spirit, it is

---

[58] Abelard, *Introductio*, 2.118 (Vol. 3, p.466).

[59] Hugh of St. Victor, *De Amore Sponsi ad Sponsam* in *The Divine Love* (tr. A Religious of C.S.M.V.. London: A.R. Mowbray, 1956), p.28.

[60] Lombard, *Sentences*, 2.43.1-2, pp.572-73 (PL 192:754, 2.43.1).

[61] Richard, *Tractatus de Spiritu Blasphemiae* (PL 196:1188).

[62] *Ibid.* (PL 196:1190).

important to look at the thoughts of twelfth-century writers on the economy of the Spirit when this affects their overall views of the third person. The concept that the Holy Spirit is the love of the godhead was important for many writers in this period in their understanding of the work of the Holy Spirit in creation, and particularly in the hearts of men in their relationships with each other and, more importantly, with God. There is some debate about Augustine's view on this point. David Bell believes that Augustine's position on this is that people do not love by the Spirit, but are one with God (*communio*) in the Holy Spirit.[63] Canning argues against this, stating that, "When a person is said, as in the eighth Book, to love the brother "from love" (*de dilectione*), then the Holy Spirit, who is consubstantial with the Father and the Son, and who is indeed *donum dei*, is at least implicitly understood as the living source of such love, a source which is present in the love itself".[64]

It is not surprising that William of St. Thierry and Bernard of Clairvaux, with their emphasis on the experience of God, most tied the element of love in the immanent person of the Spirit into their thoughts on the work of the Spirit. The main focus of their teaching was that it is only possible for man to love God and his neighbour as he is moved by the Holy Spirit, the love of God. This idea is contained in many of William's works. In the *De Contemplando*, William writes, "This is how you love yourself in us. We love you through you. This union of us with God through the Holy Spirit called unity - that they may be one in us. The Holy Spirit himself is the love by which we reach out to you".[65] The same thought is contained in the *Enigma of Faith* and the *Mirror of Faith*: "When given to man, the Holy Spirit kindles love for God and one's neighbour ... the Holy Spirit is that love because God is love";[66] "the Holy Spirit is the Spirit of life. By the Holy Spirit anyone loves who loves what truly ought to be loved ... the Love of God is to our love, to our natural affection, what our soul is to its body".[67] Bernard supports William's position, writing in his *Steps of Humility and Pride* that "charity is a gift of the Holy Spirit" which is "poured out into our hearts"; "The union of the Holy Spirit with the human will give birth to charity".[68]

Peter Lombard was another writer who wrote a large volume of material on this point. The main teaching comes in *Distinctio* 17 of the *Sentences*, which concerns the invisible mission of the Spirit. The point which is drawn out is that, as the Holy Spirit is the love of the Father and the Son, so He is the *caritas* love by which we love God and our neighbour.[69] Lombard treats several objections that might be raised against this teaching in the *Distinctio* - such as the creation of two different loves (ours and Gods) and a comparison with our

---

[63] Bell, *Image and Likeness*, p.59.
[64] Canning, *The Unity of Love for God and Neighbor*, p.307.
[65] William, *De Contemplando*, 11, p.98 (p.55).
[66] William, *Enigma*, 99, p.176 (pp.115-16).
[67] William, *Speculum*, 65, p.78 (pp.71-72).
[68] Bernard, *Opera*, Vol.3, pp.31-32 (*Steps*, pp.48-49).
[69] Lombard, *Sentences*, 1.17.1.2, p.142 (PL 192:564, 1.17.2).

faith which is a gift of the Holy Spirit rather than the Spirit Himself - but solidly defends his initial teaching, often backing this up by references to Augustine. He makes his point clear in passages such as this: "The love of God is poured into our hearts, not with which he loves, but which makes us able to love. This does not divide love of God for us from that by which we love. Rather it shows it to be one love, and that love to be God".[70] Peter Lombard returns to the same issue in book three of the *Sentences*, writing that "Clearly it is the same love by which God is loved and a neighbour, which is the Holy Spirit, as said above, who is the love of God".[71]

Two other writers use the Spirit's immanent identity as love in their presentations of His economic role. Richard of St. Victor's use of "owing" language in the immanent Trinity has been studied above. One of the conclusions that Richard drew from this is the role of the Holy Spirit in infusing into men the debt of love. This is why the Holy Spirit is called divine fire, because love is like fire, which inflames men's cold hearts into warm love.[72] This is a similar teaching to that found in the work of William of St. Thierry and Peter Lombard.

Peter Abelard draws out two parts of the Spirit's work in creation from His identity as love: the first is the care which the Spirit has for creation; and the second is the infusion of the Holy Spirit into men's hearts through the gift of faith, which enables them to do good works, which idea mirrors the work of the Spirit outlined by the other writers.[73]

Although this book does not focus on the economy of the Holy Spirit, it is clear from these writings that this element of the Spirit was closely tied into the authors' thought on His immanent personhood. This is important because it rules out the possibility that love was used analogically to help clarify divine relations without being directly attributed to the third person.

Conclusion

The writers of the twelfth century, taken together, had an extremely developed concept of the Holy Spirit as the love of God. Although they took the basic concept from Augustine, there is little left of his weak, analogically-based teaching, which was buried under the strong, sure ideas that were put forward.

The central premise was the that the Spirit is the mutual love of Father and Son, but this was heavily built on by thoughts drawn from the Scriptures, from the mutual love theory itself, and from other notions connected to love. The Holy Spirit's identity as love was taught in both His immanent and economic states, and was crucial to many writers' presentation of His procession.

In addition, new analogies were given which included this description of the Spirit, and some authors wrote concerning the blasphemy against the Holy Spirit as being directed at His identity as love in the godhead. The variety and

---

[70] *Ibid.*, 1.17.6.4, pp.149-50 (PL 192:568, 1.17.12).

[71] *Ibid.*, 3.27.3, Vol.2, p.163 (PL 192:812, 3.27.3).

[72] Richard, *De Trinitate*, 6.14, pp.245-46 (PL 196:978).

[73] Abelard, *Introductio*, 1.65-6, 170 (Vol. 3, pp.344, 388).

depth of notions connected with this idea in the twelfth century produced an impressive and convincing case for acceptance of this aspect of pneumatology.

CHAPTER 8

Goodness

The application of the term goodness to the person of the Holy Spirit was one of the most controversial issues in pneumatology in the twelfth century. One of the main reasons for this was the lack of authoritative support for this position in the writings of the Church Fathers. Augustine occasionally mentions the term goodness in his discussion of the godhead, but does not apply this word specifically to the Holy Spirit. The greatest debate concerned a model for the Trinity in which the Father was power, the Son wisdom and the Holy Spirit goodness. Peter Abelard was the foremost proponent of this idea, which received some support, but also serious criticism in this period. However, all of the major writers studied in this book applied the word goodness to describe the person of the Holy Spirit, not only in his work in the created world, but also as part of His immanent personhood. Peter Abelard and Richard of St. Victor used goodness as their primary term for the Spirit, but the suitability of this concept was reinforced by its use in processional teaching, passages on the blasphemy against the Holy Spirit and in connection with many other terms associated with the third person. Two Latin terms, "bonitas" and "benignitas" were used, often interchangeably, to describe this element of the person of the Spirit.[1] Goodness was thus one of the primary attributes that were used to describe the Holy Spirit in the twelfth century.

The Power, Wisdom, Goodness Debate

The most significant analysis of this issue in recent scholarship is that by Marcia Colish in her two-volume work on Peter Lombard.[2] As has already been shown in this book, Colish argues that there was a major reaction to Peter Abelard's use of power, wisdom and goodness to refer to the divine persons.

However, while there was some concern to correct a possible conclusion from the power, wisdom, goodness formula (that this might exclude two attributes from each of the persons), it is a mistake to understand this issue as being solely over Abelard's construct, or to conclude that these terms were discarded from theology after the time of Peter Lombard. The best illustration of this weakness in Colish's approach is the use of the term wisdom to refer to the Son. This appropriation was not in doubt in the twelfth-century, as Scripture

---

[1] 'Benignitas' is literally translated 'kindness' rather than goodness, but the two terms seem to have been equivalent in the understanding of twelfth-century writers.

[2] This was part of the study in the chapter on Lombard.

refers to Christ as the wisdom of God (1 Corinthians 1:30), and this is backed up by the concept that the Son is the word of God. This was not seen to imply that the Father and Spirit are not wise (and many writers clarified this), but asserted that the Son could be understood to be particularly the wisdom of God. This idea was often also tied into the procession of the Son from the Father. There was thus little debate about this part of the model.[3]

The issue revolved around two main points: firstly, did the Abelardian formula seek to deny some or all power to the Son and Holy Spirit (and likewise wisdom and goodness to the respective persons)? And secondly, how appropriate were the actual terms in their application? This second point most concerned goodness and the Holy Spirit, since the Father, being the person from whom the other two have their existence, could be seen to be power in the godhead and the Son's clear relationship to wisdom has been noted above. This initial section of the chapter will deal with the first question about the power, wisdom, goodness model; the applicability of goodness to the Holy Spirit will be dealt with in the rest of the chapter.

Abelard was charged in his trial at Soissons that he taught "That the Father is full power, the Son certain power and the Holy Spirit no power".[4] This is a fundamental question for any understanding of the divine persons: can any divine attribute be said to apply particularly to any one person? None of the major writers studied in this book would object to this approach as they all, for example, used the word love to describe the Holy Spirit. This did not mean, as was shown in the previous chapter, that the Father and Son are devoid of love. The power, wisdom, goodness trinity seemed to threaten the persons' divine status more seriously, and it is this which was questioned.

However, neither Abelard nor any other writer in this period, taught that the applicability of a term to one of the divine persons implied that that quality was lacking in either of the other persons. The only word which came close to this was love, studied above, which was sometimes applied to the Holy Spirit so strongly that Father and Son were said to love by the Holy Spirit, as if He were not their love. The greater understanding of love terminology meant that objections were not raised to this kind of teaching.[5]

The most forthright writers against the power, wisdom, goodness paradigm were Walter of Mortagne and Clarembald of Arras, both of whom objected on the grounds that whatever the Father is, the Son and Holy Spirit also are.[6] Both are shown to be inconsistent on this point, because both assert, in the same works that they teach this initial thought, that the Holy Spirit is the love of God proceeding from the Father and the Son. If the term love, which is one aspect of

---

[3] Objections were raised by writers such as Gilbert of Poitiers who were unwilling to find any difference between the divine persons beyond the method of their procession.

[4] Mews, 'The List of Heresies' p.110.

[5] Gilbert of Poitiers would have been unhappy with this because of his extreme position that the divine persons were inseparable except in their procession.

[6] Walter of Mortagne, *De Trinitate*, 13 (PL 209:589-90); Clarembald of Arras, *Life and Works of Clarembald of Arras*, p.101.

divinity, can be applied particularly to the Holy Spirit, the fact that goodness is a divine attribute cannot be used to refute Abelard's model of the Trinity. No writer in the twelfth century wrote that any of the divine persons were lacking in any element of divinity.

It would seem from the charges brought against Abelard by Bernard of Clairvaux and William of St. Thierry that these writers were also concerned by the effects that this model would have on the overall divinity of the persons. Neither Bernard nor William objected to the idea that goodness pertains to the person of the Spirit, as will be shown later in the chapter, but both were unhappy with the prominence that was given to the power, wisdom, goodness formula in Abelard's works. Abelard defended himself against these charges by making it clear that he did not see that his application of any term to one person implied a lack of full divinity in any other person.[7] In his *Apologia* to Bernard, Abelard confirmed this stance and accused Bernard of concluding from the power, wisdom, goodness model that "his [God's] charity or love has no power" if Abelard is denying power to the Holy Spirit.[8]

Despite Bernard's forceful opposition to Abelard on this point, it appears that he continued to be open to discussion. Although Bernard's letter to Richard no longer exists, we have a reply in which Richard explains why the power, wisdom, goodness model should be accepted.[9] In this letter, Richard appears to be clarifying his position rather than defending himself, which implies that Bernard was not hostile in his inquiries, but rather interested in Richard's point of view.

The application of power, wisdom, goodness to the Trinity was not only considered appropriate by Peter Abelard: Hugh of St. Victor taught this, although he concentrated on these attributes in the economies of the persons, and only implied their transference to the immanent states;[10] William of Conches used power, wisdom, goodness as part of his processional model of the persons in his *De Philosophia Mundi*;[11] and Peter Lombard included this idea as part of his teaching on the blasphemy against the Holy Spirit.[12] This shows the strength that was perceived in the formula in the completeness that the three terms represent, and in the processional similarities to western ideas on the Trinity.

It is important to understand correctly the debate that took place in the twelfth century over the power, wisdom, goodness model. There were questions raised, primarily by the major place that it occupied in Abelard's *Theologiae*,

---

[7] Abelard, *Responsio Petri Abaelardi* (PL 180:330).

[8] Abelard, *Apologia*, 8 (CCCM 11, p.363). Abelard linked the concept of goodness in the Holy Spirit to that of love.

[9] Richard, *De Tribus Appropriatis* (PL 196:991-94).

[10] Hugh, *Didascalion*, 7.1 (PL 176:811-12). This was covered in detail in the chapter on the Victorines above.

[11] William of Conches, *De Philosophia Mundi*, (PL 172:45).

[12] Lombard, *Sentences*, 2.43, pp.572-77 (PL 192:754-56, 2.43). This will be examined as part of the discussion on goodness and blasphemy against the Spirit later in this chapter.

but those who taught this formula did not seek to limit any divinity in the persons of the godhead; instead they used these attributes in a manner that was consistent with other terms that were applied to the Trinitarian persons in this period. The rest of this chapter will analyse how the various writers sought to use goodness to describe the immanent person of the Holy Spirit.

Goodness as the Primary Concept of the Holy Spirit

Two writers used goodness as the main attribute that they applied to the Holy Spirit in the presentation of their thoughts on the Trinity: Peter Abelard and Richard of St. Victor. The two writers used goodness in very different ways. Peter Abelard concentrated on goodness as the most appropriate term that he could find to describe one who does the work of the Spirit set out in Scripture, and then linked this to His immanent state in connection with the Father as power and the Son as wisdom. Richard began his *De Trinitate* with a search apart from Scripture for God, and then the persons that would make up the godhead. He thus worked his way methodically from the concepts of power and wisdom to that of goodness.

Abelard's use of goodness to describe the Holy Spirit in his power, wisdom, goodness model was explained by looking at the work of the Holy Spirit, and seeking the best term to apply to this person. One of the main connections that Abelard gave was that between goodness and the operation of the Holy Spirit in giving grace and charity to the world.[13] The natural effect of the work of the Holy Spirit is goodness in all creation and in people, illuminated here by the words grace and love.

This concept of the effects of the divine in creation was linked by Abelard to the concept of the World Soul in Plato, whose divine mind was active in creation through the World Soul. This activity and its effects were the Spirit according to Abelard, coming about through the goodness of the creator, which is the Holy Spirit. The Christian ascribes this work to the Spirit as it is the "natural effect of eternal goodness".

Abelard also twice points to creation to back-up his concept that goodness is the primary identity of the Spirit. Firstly, in looking at the creation account, Abelard states that the "good" that God saw in His creation was the Holy Spirit: "In this also we see what was written: And God saw that it was good. The goodness of God, which we say is the Holy Spirit, is insinuated here".[14] Secondly, Abelard writes of the work of the Trinity in creation, and states that the establishing of the work of the Father and Son is done by goodness, which is the Holy Spirit: "But the work of the three persons is indivisible, just as they are spoken of communally, so that whatever the power work, that also wisdom moderates and goodness flavours".[15]

It is only later in the *Theologiae* that Abelard fully extends the power,

---

[13] Abelard, *Introductio*, 1.12 (Vol 3, p.324).

[14] *Ibid.*, 1.13 (Vol. 3, p.325). This is part of a passage in which Abelard declares that the creation account is evidence of an understanding of the Trinity in the Old Testament.

[15] *Ibid.*, 1.10 (Vol. 3, p.323).

wisdom, goodness model to the immanent persons of the Trinity, inserting the standard terminology of the godhead, that power begets wisdom, while the Holy Spirit is the goodness that proceeds from these two.[16] Abelard thus draws strongly on the Scriptures for his initial application of goodness to the Spirit; he also links this concept into his interpretation of the philosophers' understanding of God; and finally seeks to show how goodness can be understood in the eternal procession of the Holy Spirit from Father and Son.

Richard of St. Victor also has goodness as his primary term for the Holy Spirit, but teaches this in a very different way from Peter Abelard. Richard begins his *De Trinitate* with a search for God from the perspective of one who does not have the Scriptures. In this, he begins with concepts of power and wisdom, and towards the end of book two, introduces the idea that the supreme being must have supreme goodness as the natural product of supreme power and wisdom.[17]

This processional model is examined in greater depth in book six of the *De Trinitate*, which questions why power is said to be unborn, wisdom to be born, and goodness to be the Holy Spirit.[18] Richard writes that it is possible to have many kinds of power without any kind of wisdom, but not possible to have wisdom without power. He then looks at the devil, who has both power and wisdom, but no goodness. Goodness needs both the power to act and the wisdom to choose between good and bad, and so is said to proceed. It is this teaching that Richard repeats in his letter to Bernard of Clairvaux, explaining why the power, wisdom, goodness model should be accepted as valid in its application to the Trinity. Richard's analysis is helpful as an extension of the point that Abelard briefly mentioned in his *Theologiae*.

Richard also puts great emphasis on the link between goodness and love as part of the identity of the Holy Spirit. This has led some readers of his work to focus on his teaching on love to the exclusion of that on goodness. At each major stage in Richard's teaching on goodness, in books two, three and six, this idea is linked to that of love as one of the primary manifestations of the identity of the Holy Spirit in both His immanent and economic states.

It is noteworthy that two such major and different writers of the twelfth century should use goodness as the main, overarching term that they apply to the person of the Holy Spirit. Both interact this concept with other words that can apply to the Spirit, and yet see that, particularly in relation to ideas that the Father is power and the Son wisdom, goodness is the most helpful understanding of the Spirit in these Trinitarian relations.

Goodness and the Procession of the Holy Spirit

One important aspect of any term's relevance to the person of the Holy Spirit is how writers build the concept into their processional model of the Trinity,

---

[16] Abelard, *Theologia Christiana*, 4.101 (Vol. 2, p.319).
[17] Richard, *De Trinitate*, 2.16, p.123 (PL 196:910).
[18] *Ibid.*, 6.15, pp.247-48 (PL 196:979-80).

looking at the Spirit in His relations with the Father and Son. This element has already been discussed in the analysis of Peter Abelard and Richard of St. Victor in relating goodness to power and wisdom. This section will deal with two more authors who taught concerning the procession of the Holy Spirit as goodness: Bernard of Clairvaux and Robert Melun.

Bernard twice pictures the goodness that is the Holy Spirit proceeding from the Father and the Son, both in his *Sentences*. The first of these, interestingly, is in the context of the Father as power and the Son as wisdom, thus relating to a model that he was unhappy with in the work of Peter Abelard. Bernard wrote regarding the creation that it was created by the Father's power, ordered by the Son's wisdom, and "given benefits" by the Spirit's goodness.[19] He moved on from this linking goodness to the concept of utility and uses language similar to that used by Richard: "Usefulness is found both in power and in wisdom, because the Spirit proceeds from both the Father and the Son".[20]

The second reference comes in the very next part of Bernard's *Sentences*, which analyses why the Holy Spirit is not said to be born but to proceed. In discussing this aspect of the Spirit's immanent identity, Bernard uses language which extends to the work of the Spirit: "The Holy Spirit, however, is believed not to be born but to proceed, for he flows out always and everywhere ... just like a perpetual, unceasing fountain of goodness. For this reason he is called the goodness of God".[21] This picture of the Spirit as a fountain pouring out goodness relates the immanent procession of the Spirit to His economic state; and this link to the effects of the Holy Spirit wherever He goes is a parallel to Peter Abelard's ideas on why the Spirit should be termed the goodness of God.

Robert Melun's processional teaching on the Holy Spirit in this context comes in his *Questiones de Epistolis Pauli*, looking at the teaching of Paul in the letter to the Romans. In discussing Romans 1:20 and the concept that God can be perceived through creation, Robert brings in the concept of the Holy Spirit as utility, with the Father as greatness and the Son beauty. This is then linked to goodness, as "In usefulness is the divine kindness, which is the Holy Spirit".[22] Robert moves on from this idea to the procession of the Holy Spirit as goodness: "The Holy Spirit is indeed divine kindness proceeding from both".[23]

There was thus teaching on the procession of the Spirit as goodness from the Father and the Son that originated both from the immanent and economic views of writers on the person of the Holy Spirit. This is important as it links this term into the core identity of the Spirit.

Goodness and the Blasphemy Against the Holy Spirit

As was noted in the chapter on love, another means of establishing an attribute

---

[19] Bernard, *Sentences*, 3.61, p.235.
[20] *Ibid.*
[21] *Ibid.*, 3.62, p.234.
[22] Robert Melun, *De Epistola ad Romanos*, 1.20, in R.M. Martin, *Oeuvres de Robert de Melun Tomes 1-4* (Louvain: Spicilegium Sacrum Lovaniense, 1932, 38, 47), Vol.1, p.25.
[23] *Ibid.*, 1.20, Vol.1, pp.27-28.

as a significant understanding of the immanent person of the Holy Spirit was to teach about the blasphemy against the Holy Spirit in the context of that terminology. Three writers used the Spirit's identity as goodness in the godhead to describe this sin: Peter Lombard, Richard of St. Victor and Robert Melun. Again, there is a diversity in background of the various writers, yet an agreement on this aspect of the Holy Spirit.

Given Marcia Colish's contention that Peter Lombard was one of the foremost opponents of the power, wisdom, goodness model, it is interesting that in his *Distinctio* on the sin against the Holy Spirit, Lombard makes use of this very formula in his description of the divine persons. Initially, Lombard focuses merely on the Spirit as goodness, against which are the sins of desperation and obstinacy: "Obstinatio est induratae mentis in malitia pertinacia, per quam homo fit impoenitens. Desperatio est, qua quis diffidit penitus de bonitate Dei, aestimans suam malitiam divinae bonitatis magnitudinem excedere".[24] Both of these sins are thus seen as being against goodness, and are sins of malice.

At the end of this *Distinctio*, Lombard brings in the relation of these ideas on the sin against the Holy Spirit to sins against the Father and the Son, which are sins of infirmity and ignorance: "For the sin against the Father is understood to come from weakness, because the Scriptures frequently attribute power to the Father; the sin against the Son is through ignorance, because wisdom is attributed to the Son".[25] In this latter section, the sin against the Holy Spirit is against Him as the power, goodness and grace of God, but the conclusion reached about the divine persons only mentions the Holy Spirit as the goodness of God. Lombard does discuss other theories about the blasphemy against the Holy Spirit, but this is book-ended by focusing on the Spirit as goodness.

Richard of St. Victor's *Tractatus de Spiritu Blasphemiae* has been mentioned in the chapter on love. Half of this work focuses on the Spirit as love, and the other half on the Spirit as the goodness of God.[26] Richard also features goodness here as part of the power, wisdom, goodness model for the Trinity, which he had clarified in his *De Trinitate* as well as his letter to Bernard. Having stated this picture of the persons, Richard then teaches that the sin against the Father is one of inability, that against the Son is ignorance, and that against the Holy Spirit is evil.[27] This last is explained as the affection and desire to curse God. Richard thus uses this element of Biblical teaching on the Holy Spirit to back up his main picture of the Trinitarian persons.

The third writer who uses goodness language in terms of the sin against the Spirit was Robert Melun, in his work on the Scriptures. It is interesting that Melun only refers to sins against the Son and the Holy Spirit in this passage, and states that whoever sins against either Son or Spirit also sins against the

---

[24] Lombard, *Sentences*, 2.43.2, pp.573 (PL 192:754, 2.43.1).

[25] *Ibid.*, 2.43.11, p.577 (PL 192:756, 2.43.4). This is in the context of some teaching from Augustine.

[26] Richard, *Tractatus de Spiritu Blasphemiae*, (PL 196:1188).

[27] *Ibid.*, (PL 196:1188).

other. This would seem to detract from the exclusivity of the curse attendant on the sin against the Spirit. The sin against the Son is said to be against the excellence of human nature. That against the Spirit is against the goodness of God and the good things made by God: "To sin against the holy Spirit is to knowingly disparage divine goodness and to speak with a bad spirit against that which is know to be made by goodness".[28] This teaching does not focus on the power, wisdom, goodness model, but on the economic roles of Son and Spirit, which explains the omission of the Father from Robert's thought.

It may seem surprising that the same writers can teach two separate thoughts on the blasphemy against the Spirit (indeed Richard includes ideas of goodness and love in one small *tractatus*). However, this shows that twelfth-century writers were not using these terms exclusively either in their attachment to the Holy Spirit, or in the Spirit's own identity. Rather, they were building up a more complete picture of the Spirit in relation to the Father and Son in both His immanent and economic states. The Spirit, as has already been shown, was thought to be both goodness and love, and these were not seen as being in any way contradictory to each other.

Goodness Linked to Other Concepts About the Holy Spirit

Although Richard of St. Victor and Peter Abelard were comfortable enough in their understanding of goodness to use this concept as the basis for their interpretation of the person of the Holy Spirit, both they and other writers often used goodness in association with other terms to clarify their insight into this aspect of the Spirit. Some of these related ideas refer more to the immanent person of the Spirit, which will be looked at first, and others to the economic.

In terms of goodness and the immanent person of the Holy Spirit, the related words that were used were almost exclusively those that are being studied in this second half of the book: love, will, unity and gift. The one other term to which goodness is connected is "foreknowledge", which is one aspect of omniscience, and therefore part of the divine essence, and yet necessarily has impact outside of Trinitarian relationships. This association is made by William of St. Thierry in his *Meditations*, in which he writes that foreknowledge is the same as goodness, which in turn corresponds to the person of the Holy Spirit.[29] From the context in his meditations, William is clearly drawing lessons about the work of the Holy Spirit, but as always is careful to root this in the Spirit's eternal identity.

Both Abelard and Richard, in their appropriation of the term goodness to the Holy Spirit, emphasised the importance of the connection between goodness and love. While goodness was the best word they could find to complete the image of the Trinity, given the Father's identity as power and the Son's as wisdom, this did not discount the Spirit being love, but sought to encompass this element of the Spirit in a broader term that better fitted their overall thought on the Trinity. This is shown in Richard's immediate transference of

---

[28] Robert Melun, *Questiones de Divina Pagina*, 1.17, Vol.1, p.12.

[29] William, *Meditativae*, 1.10, p.48 (p.92).

the concept of goodness to love at the beginning of book three of the *De Trinitate*, after the establishment of his basic Trinitarian model; and in his equating goodness with love (*caritas*) at the outset of his defence of the power, wisdom, goodness formula that is found both in book six of the *De Trinitate* and in his letter to Bernard.[30] Abelard also made the connection early on in each of his *Theologiae*, repeating his belief that goodness was the best word for the Holy Spirit in his role of giving grace and love to the world.[31]

Another writer who made a clear link between love and goodness was William of St. Thierry. William's concept of the Holy Spirit and his meditative style of writing enabled him to interchange words describing the Spirit to enhance the points that he was making. The two occasions on which he utilised goodness and love to achieve this came in his *De Contemplando Deo* and his commentary on the book of Romans. The first of these works is very direct in associating the two ideas: "Your love is your goodness, the Holy Spirit proceeding from the Father and the Son".[32] This passage goes on to develop the person of the Spirit from being love to will and unity. The section from his commentary on Romans draws both love and goodness from the Spirit being the "divinity" of Father and Son.[33] The sense that comes out of this passage is that William is exploring the unifying power of the Spirit in the Trinity, and the outworking of this to creation. There is thus William's characteristic consistency in providing a unified picture of the Spirit in both His immanent and economic states.

Both of these passages in William's works also connect goodness to the Spirit's identity as unity in the Trinity. Richard of St. Victor also does this, at the beginning of his thought on goodness in book two of *De Trinitate*, before he moves onto the concept of love. Richard provides one of his typically neat pieces of logic in introducing goodness: "in highest goodness exists unity and supreme simplicity ... In supreme greatness of anything, there cannot be complexity ... Where there is supreme simplicity, there is also supreme unity".[34] This reasoning shows the platonic environment in which Richard was working, but also reveals Richard working within this to bring the clarity of what he believes through to his readers.

Two writers from the school of St. Victor used the term goodness in association with will in relation to the person of the Spirit: the author of the *Summa Sententiarum* and Richard of St. Victor.[35] The links, despite the fact that the context of each is a defence of the power, wisdom, goodness model, are slightly different. The author of the *Summa* questions whether there should be

---

[30] Richard, *De Trinitate*, 6.15, pp.247-48 (PL 196:979-80); *De Tribus Appropriatis* (PL 196:991-92).

[31] For example, Abelard, *Summi Boni*, 1.2, p.4.

[32] William, *De Contemplando*, 11, p.96 (p.54).

[33] William, *Expositio*, p.22 (p.38).

[34] Richard, *De Trinitate*, 2.17, p.124 (PL 196:910-11).

[35] This discussion will necessarily be brief as 'will' will be analysed more closely in the next chapter.

more than three persons in the Trinity with characteristics such as justice or mercy. The answer given is that everything in the divine is contained in the original three, and nothing is separate from the ability to be able (Father), to know (Son) and to will (Holy Spirit).[36] Will is thus substituted as the action associated with goodness. Richard's discussion of power, wisdom, goodness states that it is possible to have power and wisdom without goodness (as the devil does). Goodness is then described as "good will, the will to do good".[37] The approaches of the two writers are thus different, and yet both conclude that there is a link in the person of the Spirit between goodness and will.

Peter Lombard describes the Spirit as goodness alongside gift terminology at the beginning of his *Sentences*. This is part of his initial statement of the Trinitarian persons and is thus focusing on their immanent states, and yet Lombard uses the idea that the Spirit is a gift to explain this. He writes that goodness is understood to be the Holy Spirit, the gift of Father and Son, and this is shown in the ministry of the Spirit in men's hearts.[38] Those connections already studied have all shown the writers integrating elements of the Spirit's work into their understanding of His immanent person, but Lombard is here clearly combining the two parts of the Spirit's identity.

Goodness and the Economic Role of the Holy Spirit

Much of what has been written so far in this chapter has shown the link that writers have made between the economic and immanent person of the Holy Spirit when considering goodness as an accurate attribute. These points will not be repeated here, but there is additional teaching on this issue that has not linked into what has been considered that needs to be included to complete the picture that was drawn of the Spirit as goodness. Abelard uses a great deal of goodness language in his presentation of why the World Soul should be understood to be the Holy Spirit. He writes that Plato gives to the World Soul the concord of all things "in the goodness of divine grace" which phraseology is reminiscent of his definition of the Spirit as goodness.[39] In discussing the concept in Plato of the divine mind going out into effect through activity, Abelard states that the effects have reference to the Spirit because they are said to come about through the goodness of the creator, which is the Holy Spirit.[40] Abelard also refers to Pythagorus, who talks of the nature and goodness of God being diffused through the whole world, and being that from which all things are born and live.[41]

Three other writers make use of the idea of "utility" to explain the work of

---

[36] *Summa Sententiarum*, 1.10 (PL 176:57-58).

[37] Richard, *De Trinitate*, 6.15, pp.247-48 (PL 196:979-80).

[38] Lombard, *Sentences*, 1.3.1.8, p.71 (PL 192:530, 1.3.6). The understanding of 'gift' in this section will be more fully examined below in chapter ten.

[39] Quote taken from McCallum's translation of Abelard's *Theologia Christiana*, 1 (p.53).

[40] McCallum, *Theologia Christiana*, 4 (p.88).

[41] Abelard, *Introductio*, 1.18 (Vol. 3, p.326).

the Holy Spirit as the goodness of God. Bernard of Clairvaux links goodness to utility in his *Sentences* as part of the work of the Spirit, that "all things are turned to the good".[42] He then links this back to a power, wisdom, goodness procession of the Spirit, as "usefulness is found both in power and in wisdom, because the Spirit proceeds from both the Father and the Son".[43] Robert Melun sees a distinction of the Trinity in the world in greatness (Father), beauty (Son) and utility (Holy Spirit). Hugh of St. Victor also using this terminology, stating that goodness not only conserves all things, but even "shows to creatures the utility of all things".[44]

The Chartrain school, which did not concentrate on attributes ascribed to the divine persons, also taught about the Holy Spirit as goodness in His economic role. Looking at their work regarding creation, Maurer writes that the Father was seen as the "efficient" cause, the Son as the "formal" cause, and the Holy Spirit as the "final" cause. This final cause, or purpose, of creation is described as divine goodness, linking this term to the person of the Holy Spirit.[45]

Robert Melun taught about the divine persons from Romans 11:36 in his commentary on that book. The operation of the Trinity in creation described there is that all things come from the Father, through the Son, in the Holy Spirit.[46] In this, Robert wrote that the Father is the principle of all things, who fashions everything through His wisdom, the Son, and creates and sustains creation by His goodness, the Holy Spirit: "But through the saying, 'In whom all things', the Holy Spirit is understood. For in the kindness of God all things were made and these things are conserved. But the kindness of God is the Holy Spirit".[47]

William of St. Thierry uses the same Trinitarian language in describing the incarnation of the second person of the Trinity and temporal procession of the Holy Spirit in his *Enigma of Faith*. In talking of these two missions, William wrote that everything was distributed among the persons as being "from the Father, through the Son, in the Holy Spirit, who is the goodness of the Father and the Son".[48] William also taught about the Holy Spirit in relation to creation, that "the Spirit of the Lord fills the earth with the goodness of God's omnipotence".[49] It has been shown as part of the power, wisdom, goodness debate that both Peter Abelard and Bernard of Clairvaux used similar language

---

[42] Bernard, *Sentences*, 3.61.

[43] *Ibid.*

[44] Hugh, *Didascalion*, 7.1 (PL 176:811-12).

[45] Maurer, *Medieval Philosophy*, p.72.

[46] This was one of the foundational verses for the Greeks' understanding of Trinitarian relationships.

[47] Robert Melun, *De Epistola ad Romanos*, 11.36 , Vol.2, p.148 (Italics in Martin edition).

[48] William, *Enigma*, 79, p.160 (p.100). David Bell writes that William saw the Holy Spirit as the *bonitas* of the Father and the Son that was 'transferred' to people in His economic role. D. Bell, *Image and Likeness*, p.211.

[49] *Ibid.*, 100, p.178 (p.116).

regarding the Holy Spirit's work in creation.⁵⁰

Richard of St. Victor used goodness in a different context in his *Benjamin Major*, writing about the effects of the Holy Spirit in the heart of the believer in terms of goodness. The Spirit is said to "inject the goodness of His heart into us through divine grace".⁵¹ This gives a person a love of goodness because of the work of the Holy Spirit who is called both goodness and sweetness in this passage. The importance for twelfth-century writers of tying together ideas on the immanent and economic states of the Holy Spirit is shown in these thoughts on the work of the Holy Spirit, which clearly reflect His identity as goodness in the immanent Trinity.

Conclusion

Twelfth-century writers were generally agreed on the application of the term goodness to the person of the Holy Spirit, despite the dispute that took place over Abelard's power, wisdom, goodness model. The opposition to this was based on the seeming exclusivity of the terms in Abelard's presentation and the lack of authoritative support given for the Spirit being named goodness. However, a more complete understanding of Abelard's use of these terms shows that he in no way intended to imply a lack of divinity in any of the persons, and the basis for the use of goodness in concepts such as love and unity led many writers from different backgrounds to teach that the Holy Spirit is the goodness of God.

The strength of the term goodness as an appropriate name for the Holy Spirit was shown in its use as a primary concept in the understanding of Abelard and Richard of St. Victor, as well as in the teaching that it received from various writers in connection with the procession of the Holy Spirit and the blasphemy against the Spirit. This analysis of its use across authors has also shown that goodness is a term that fits both the immanent and economic states of the Spirit, as most thought that deals with the Spirit as goodness covers both of these areas.

---

⁵⁰ Bernard surprisingly used the power, wisdom goodness formula in his *Sentences*. Abelard wrote of creation being 'fashioned' by the Holy Spirit as goodness; and also taught that the goodness of God ordered all things in comparing the Spirit to the World Soul. Bernard, *Sentences*, 3.61; Abelard, *Introductio*, 1.11, 17 (Vol. 3, p.324, 326).

⁵¹ Richard, *Benjamin Major*, 3.24 (PL 196:133-36).

CHAPTER 9

Will

The concept that the Holy Spirit is the will of God had surprisingly little analysis by the writers of the twelfth century, given its extensive use in the writings of Augustine. In Augustine's thought on the Trinity, and in the analogies that he created, will was an equivalent term with love in relevance to the third person, and the two terms were at times used interchangeably. However, whereas love was widely used as a primary understanding of the eternal person of the Holy Spirit, will was only incorporated by William of St. Thierry as a major part of his doctrine of the Spirit. Other writers did use will terminology, but this was generally done within the context of other thoughts on the person of the Spirit. There was teaching on the procession of the Holy Spirit as will, some linking of will to the blasphemy against the Holy Spirit and use of this idea in relation to the economy of the Spirit. However, this was not on the scale that might be expected given the writers' devotion to Augustine and the stress found on this concept in his work. For this reason alone, it is an interesting point of study in this book; but it is important also to analyse the use that was made of the Holy Spirit as will to provide a complete picture of twelfth-century thought on the third person of the Trinity.

Augustine

Augustine consistently held in his *De Trinitate* that there was one will in the godhead for all three persons, and yet that the Holy Spirit could also be conceived of as the will of the Father and the Son. Because, as with love, Augustine used the term will primarily in an analogical manner, it is unclear to what extent he would have understood the Spirit to be the will of God in relation to the world or, indeed, what role the Holy Spirit had as will in the immanent Trinity.[1] Certainly, Augustine's stress on the interrelationship of the three persons in all things would indicate his belief in a unity of will. It is disappointing therefore, given that Augustine makes a clear association of the will of God with the Holy Spirit from the analogies onwards, that there is no detailed teaching on the nature of God's will in the opening half of the *De*

---

[1] Augustine clearly states that the *operatio* of Father and Son is *inseparabilis*, but there is no connection made at this point to the Holy Spirit. Augustine, *De Trinitate*, 1.6, p.42 (pp.72-73). David Bell comments on this point that, in his opinion, Augustine does not link the memory, understanding, will triad too closely to the Trinitarian persons. Bell, *Image and Likeness*, p.45.

Trinitate that might clarify Augustine's thought.[2] The person of the Spirit is not described in terms of will in the first half which deals primarily with the Trinitarian persons, which to some extent clouds the meaning of the analogies.

In the second half of the *De Trinitate*, where Augustine seeks analogies for the Trinitarian persons he has previously outlined, will takes a major position alongside love as the third person representing the Holy Spirit. Gillian Evans notes that in book ten, Augustine begins to associate will with the Spirit,[3] although this is not yet part of the analogies. Yves Congar writes of eight triads found in the second part of the *De Trinitate* that reflect the Trinity, of which four have some concept of will as third in the analogy.[4] Three different Latin words for will are used: *voluntas*, *intentio* and *volitio*, and the four analogies all contain some variety for the first and second persons:

> *memoria, intelligentia, voluntas*; *res, visio, intentio*; *memoria, visio, volitio*; *memoria, scientia, voluntas*.[5]

This shows that, in his exploration of the godhead, will was an important term for Augustine in expressing the nature of the third person in relationship with the other two. This necessarily reflects back to his ideas on the procession of the Holy Spirit, as both will and love are divine characteristics that fit well into processional models for the third person. It is within the context of these analogies that Augustine makes some wider use of will terminology in discussing the Holy Spirit, linking this idea to other thoughts on the procession and nature of the third person.

One of the closest associations of terms in the *De Trinitate* is between will and love; indeed, at times, Augustine used the two terms interchangeably in his thoughts.[6] This is reflected in the fact that four of his triads used will, and four love, in describing the third person in the godhead. However, whereas love is a concept that is readily applicable to relations between divine persons, it is more difficult to grasp how will could fit into an intra-Trinitarian model. The close connection for Augustine between will and love provides some basis for understanding this element of the person of the Spirit, but Augustine also provides additional thought on how the Holy Spirit should be conceived of as will.

Edmund Hill shows in his edition of the *De Trinitate* how Augustine works with the will/love connection to elucidate the Holy Spirit in the Trinitarian

---

[2] In this lack of balance within the *De Trinitate*, Augustine's thought on love and will are the same.

[3] Evans, *Anselm and a New Generation*, 57.

[4] Congar, *I Believe in the Holy Spirit 3*, p.80. This section of Congar's work is taken from Cayre's *Bibliographie Augustiniennes* 16, p.587.

[5] Found respectively in Augustine's *De Trinitate* 10.11-12, 11.1-2, 11.3-5, 12.14-15; pp.330-32, 333-40, 340-45, 374-80 (pp.298-99, 304-07, 307-11, 334-37).

[6] One such occasion is at the end of book ten, when he inexplicably inserts love into a discussion that had revolved around the concept of will. *Ibid.*, 10.12, p.332 (p.299).

relations.[7] Hill notes that there is a potential problem with the mind, knowledge, will triad because, in the human mind, the will could be seen to maintain the word from the memory - indicating that the Holy Spirit would proceed before the Son. Augustine is shown to work with this analogy to show that the will results from the formation of the word as will is described as an act of love consequent upon an act of knowledge.

Another teaching that Augustine draws out from his analogies is that the Holy Spirit as will draws the Father and Son together. This is concluded from the analogies because the pictures of Father and Son indicate separate, although not mutually exclusive, positions relative to the object of their perception.[8] Augustine states that, as will, the Holy Spirit *conjungit utrumque*,[9] which illuminates the relational role of the Spirit in this capacity.

In writing of the Holy Spirit, therefore, Augustine gave almost equal weight to the concept of will as to that of love, although little was made of either term in his initial presentation of the divine persons. There was an even use of the two terms in the analogies that were taught. The remainder of this chapter will examine the extent to which twelfth-century writers appropriated this terminology in their writings on the Holy Spirit, and will then show how these authors used the idea of the Spirit as will in their broader thoughts about the identity of the Holy Spirit.

Use of Augustine's Thought on Will in the Twelfth Century

The weakness of Augustine's thought on the Holy Spirit as will is shown in the sparse use that was made even of the analogies that Augustine put forward on this issue. Many writers, including Anselm, Abelard and Richard of St. Victor, did not follow up Augustine's teaching, although both Abelard and Richard did write independently of the Spirit as the will of God in their work. As will now be shown, even those writers who did use Augustine's analogies which spoke of the third person as will either did not devote much space to these thoughts, or did not give them any foundational place in their understanding of the Holy Spirit.

Peter Lombard was the author who made the most direct use of Augustine's thought concerning the Holy Spirit as will in his theology. Lombard quotes Augustine on this point in *Distinctio* 3: "Therefore we principally discuss these three things, memory, intelligence and will".[10] In *Distinctio* 3, not only is this analogy from the mind given, but Lombard also notes that the terms *voluntas* and *dilectio* are often used interchangeably in Augustine's thought. Peter

---

[7] Hill introducing the second half of Augustine's, *The Trinity*, p.265.

[8] For example, *memoria* indicates memory of something, which is very different to *intelligentia*, or understanding of that same object. The two may be in harmony, but there is no necessity on the basis of these terms. It is only in the production of one *voluntas* from the two that they are joined.

[9] One example is the *memoria, visio, volitio* triad in book eleven. Augustine, *De Trinitate*, 11.3-5, pp.340-45 (pp.307-11).

[10] Lombard, *Sentences*, 1.3.2.2, p.72 (PL 192:531, 1.3.7).

Lombard thus shows a firm grasp of Augustine's teaching on this issue.

Given this, it is interesting that *Distinctio* 3 is not part of Lombard's definition of the person of the Holy Spirit, or the divine persons generally, but concerns how the creator is able to be perceived through creation. The fact that Peter Lombard includes Augustine's thought at this point, rather than in his more detailed examination of the Holy Spirit, shows the limitations that he perceived in Augustine's teaching. Will always remains tied into this analogical set-up in the *Sentences*, and is not transferred by Lombard to his discussion of either the immanent or economic states of the third person. It is also important to note that this section of *Distinctio* 3 is not intended to reflect the natures of the divine persons in relation to each other, but merely to support the fact that the three are all part of one God: "Haec ergo tria eo unum sunt, quo una vita, una mens, una essentia, et quidquid aliud ad seipsa singula dicuntur etiam simul, non pluraliter, sed singulariter dicuntur".[11] Lombard shows in the nature and position of his discussion of Augustine on this point the lack of depth that is present in Augustine's thought, despite its prominence in the *De Trinitate*.

Three writers extend Augustine's analogy into the economy of the Holy Spirit. Honorius Augustodunensis uses the memory, intelligence, will triad in describing the relationship of the three persons regarding their roles in creation. Immediately after stating that, "All things come from the Father, through the Son, in the Holy Spirit", Honorius goes on to write, "It is understood that the Father is memory, the Son intelligence and the Holy Spirit will" seemingly as a kind of explanation.[12] It is difficult to draw too many conclusions from the *First Book of Dialogue on the Whole Christian Faith* because the questions and answers are so brief.

Bernard of Clairvaux and William of St. Thierry use the memory, understanding, will triad identically in explaining the access to God and the experience of the believer in this. Both speak of the Christian "clinging" to God. The only difference is that Bernard writes of a person's action - "We cling to the Father through the power of memory; to the Son by reason or understanding; to the Holy Spirit through the will" - whereas William indicates the passivity of the believer as "the Father claims our memory, the Son our wisdom and the Holy Spirit our will".[13] Dechanet regards William's commentary on the *Song of Songs* as intending to show the image of God in this triad, yet this work seems to concentrate more on the Spirit as love.[14]

---

[11] Lombard, *Sentences*, 1.3.2.3, p.72 (PL 192:531, 1.3.7).

[12] Honorius Augustodunensis, *First Book of Dialogue on the Whole Christian Faith*, 2 (PL 172:1111).

[13] Bernard, *Sentences*, 3.5; William, *On the Nature and Dignity of Love* (tr. G. Webb and A. Walker). London: A.R. Mowbray, 1956), p.15.

[14] Dechanet, *William of St Thierry*, p.73. William does refer in the *Commentary on the Song of Songs* to the Holy Spirit as the 'substantial will of God', but this is an isolated reference, and is not part of an analogy. This concept will be studied in more detail later in this chapter.

Twelfth-Century Descriptions of the Holy Spirit as Will

There was thus little direct use of Augustine's thought on the Holy Spirit as will in the twelfth century, primarily because Augustine himself did not provide sufficient foundational teaching relating this idea to the immanent or economic person of the Spirit. However, several writers did use will as a term to refer to the third person based on their own broader understandings of His personhood, connected to related concepts, in order to clarify their broader picture of the Holy Spirit. The emphasis is thus on will not as an analogical term for the third person, but as a reasonable description of His immanent or economic person: that as a result of His procession from the Father and the Son, the Holy Spirit is the one will of the first two persons.

It should also be noted that writers in this period taught about the one will of the Trinity, without referring this to the Holy Spirit. Peter Lombard was one of these, identifying the will of God as "eternally part of the essence of God", and as such an unchangeable part of His character.[15] Richard of St. Victor also teaches the unity of the three persons in one will in book three of the *De Trinitate*. The context of this passage is the perfect love and community that exists between the three persons, which results for Richard in the existence of one will.[16] The author of the *Summa Sententiarum* uses Augustine's idea that whatever is in God is God, to discuss the will without reference to the Holy Spirit. He concludes from this that, "The will is not said to be God absolutely; but the will of God is God".[17] It is interesting that he then moves on to consider wisdom in the godhead in relation to the person of the Son despite not linking the will to the Holy Spirit.

Will and Love

Given the concentration that has been shown on the Holy Spirit as love in this period, and the fact that Augustine used will and love interchangeably in his writings, it is unsurprising that will is related most often to love. William of St. Thierry was one of the foremost thinkers on this approach, particularly in his *De Contemplando Deo*. Love and will are initially linked (along with unity) in the opening section on the person of the Holy Spirit.[18] Just before this, William defines a relationship between the two concepts, writing that "a well-ordered will wants to do nothing more than love".[19] This same idea is found in William's *On the Nature and Dignity of Love*, in which William describes the birth of love in the will.[20] David Bell notes William's interest in this area of teaching in his book, *The Image and Likeness*, showing the definition of love in the context of the will, and explaining this as the cooperation of will and grace

---

[15] Lombard, *Sentences*, 1.45.1, p.306 (PL 192:641, 1.45.1).

[16] Richard, *De Trinitate*, 3.12, pp.147-48 (PL 196:923).

[17] *Summa Sententiarum*, 1.11 (PL 176:59).

[18] William, *De Contemplando*, 11, p.98 (p.54).

[19] *Ibid.* 11, p.96 (p.54).

[20] William, *On the Nature*, p.15.

becoming love.²¹

Two other Cistercians make similar connections between will and love, although not to the same extent or depth as William of St. Thierry. Aelred identifies the will of God with the Holy Spirit as love in his *Mirror of Charity*, stating that the "will of God is itself his love, which is the Holy Spirit by whom charity is poured into our hearts".²² Bernard of Clairvaux likewise concentrates on this idea as it affects the work of the Holy Spirit. In *The Steps of Humility and Pride*, Bernard writes of the Holy Spirit as the will of God, uniting Himself with the human will in order to create charity.²³

Two other writers also connected will and love in their thoughts on the Holy Spirit. Hugh of St. Victor wrote in these terms regarding the nature of the Spirit in relation to the Father and the Son, that this love and will is the same in every view of it, and is one with these two persons.²⁴ Walter of Mortagne, who closely followed Augustine in his thought, wrote about the Holy Spirit as love and will in the context of one of Augustine's analogies: that of mind, self-knowledge and love. Walter focused on the inter-relatedness of these three terms, that it is not possible for any to exist without the other two, and concluded that love flows from the Father and Son, which love is also called their will.²⁵

Will and Goodness

Two writers, Richard of St. Victor and the author of the *Summa Sententiarum*, use will as part of their discussion of the power, wisdom, goodness triad, to clarify their understanding of the third person in this model. Another writer who makes a separate link between will and goodness is William of St. Thierry, who makes an obscure connection in his *Mirror of Faith* regarding the resurrection, which is said to be cause by the omnipotent, and willed by goodness.²⁶ As this comes in the context of teaching on the person of the Holy Spirit, it would seem that this second phrase refers to the Spirit. William also makes a brief reference to the two terms in his *Golden Epistle*, in reference to the person of the Holy Spirit.²⁷

Richard of St. Victor made the Spirit's identity as will a crucial part of his presentation of the trinity of power, wisdom and goodness. In showing the inter-relatedness of the three attributes in terms of procession, Richard states that it is possible to have both power and the wisdom that is born of it without

---

²¹ Bell, *Image and Likeness*, p.127. This idea is so fundamental that it is included in the section on William of St. Thierry in *An Introduction to the Medieval Mystics of Europe*, p.73.
²² Aelred of Rievaulx, *The Mirror of Charity* 2.18.53 (tr. E. Connor. Kalamazoo: Cistercian Publications, 1990).
²³ Bernard, *Opera*, Vol.3, p.32 (*Steps*, p.21).
²⁴ Hugh, *Didascalion*, 7.1 (PL 176:811-12).
²⁵ Walter of Mortagne, *De Trinitate*, 9 (PL 209:584-86).
²⁶ William, *Speculum*, 48, p.64 (p.55). This is strange terminology for William, reminiscent of the power, wisdom, goodness model that he had opposed in Abelard.
²⁷ William, *Golden Epistle*, 12.35.

having the proceeding goodness. He gives the devil as evidence of this opinion. The goodness that is then described as coming from power and wisdom is "good will, the will to do good".[28] The goodness is thus tied closely into wisdom, which creates the possibility to choose between good and bad. This discretion is required by the will for it to become goodness.

The other author who includes will as part of the power, wisdom, goodness formula is the author of the *Summa Sententiarum*. Having introduced this model, and made clear that the Holy Spirit should be considered to be the goodness of God, the author asks the question why there are not more than these three persons? The answer that is given is that everything is contained in these three: "to be able, to know and to will".[29] This will is then described as goodness, but it is interesting that the main verb chosen to represent this third person of the Trinity is will. Knoch includes this section as part of his analysis of Hugh of St. Victor's Trinitarian positions, and Hugh does include similar teaching in his meditation on the divine essence without using this direct language.[30]

Will and Unity

The final major term with which will was linked was that of unity, and this was only done to a large extent in the work of William of St. Thierry. William's emphasis on human experience of the divine through the uniting of the will with the Holy Spirit, Himself unity within the godhead, meant that these two concepts of the Spirit's identity were closely linked in William's thought. The desire to present a single, unchanging person of the Spirit in both immanent and economic states meant that William included will and unity together in some of his discussion of the third person in the godhead, although the greater application of these terms was naturally to the economic work of the Holy Spirit.

The foundational thought of the *De Contemplando Deo* concerning the Holy Spirit, that He is love, unity and will, has been noted already in this chapter in the section on "Will and Love".[31] The focus of this passage is on the uniting role of the Spirit, and it is interesting that will is one of the primary terms brought into this discussion. The uniting of Father and Son in the one will that is the Holy Spirit is also mentioned briefly in William's *Meditations*, in which he writes that there are not two or three wills in the godhead, but one, which is the Holy Spirit.[32]

The other relevant section of William's work is his study in the *Mirror of Faith* of the mutual recognition of Father and Son.[33] The focus of this is on the

---

[28] Richard, *De Trinitate*, 6.15, pp.247-48 (PL 196:979-80).

[29] *Summa Sententiarum*, 1.10 (PL 176:56-58).

[30] Knoch in "'*Deus unus est Trinus*'", p.211. Hugh, *Didascalion* 7.1 (PL 176:811-12).

[31] William, *De Contemplando*, 11, p.98 (p.54).

[32] William, *Meditativae*, 3.8, p,70 (p.105).

[33] This will be treated fully in the chapter on the Holy Spirit as unity.

Spirit as unity, but there is also significant teaching on Him as will, and this will being an integral part of the Spirit's identity. William wrote that the "recognition by which they recognise each other is nothing other than substance by which they are what they are".[34] This is connected to the Biblical idea that "no one knows the Father except the Son, and no one knows Son but Father and those he is revealed to (Matthew 11:27). William states that this is revealed through the Holy Spirit, who is the common knowing or common will of both Father and Son.[35] The inclusion of will terminology into this section on the mutual recognition of first and second persons is important because it shows the role of this aspect of the Spirit both in the relationship of Father and Son, and then in the communication of this relationship to the world.

Will and Blasphemy Against the Holy Spirit
As this book has examined the blasphemy against the Holy Spirit as being against His identity as love and goodness, it is right to note that one author used the idea that the Spirit is will in relation to this topic. The writer is Bernard of Clairvaux, and the passage occurs in his *Sentences*. This section begins by stating that the will of the Father and Son is understood to be the Holy Spirit. Bernard then goes on to describe and apply this concept: "The will is truly good, and one who is not a partner with it - that is, who is not of good will - sins against the Holy Spirit".[36]

There is in this some linking of will to goodness, but the emphasis is on the former. While the application being made by Bernard concerns the work of the Holy Spirit, it remains significant that this important Biblical teaching is connected to the idea that the Spirit is the will of the Father and Son.

Will and the Economic Role of the Holy Spirit
William of St. Thierry was the author who most used will terminology to describe the Holy Spirit and, given both this and the experiential links that William consistently sought between his understanding of the immanent and economic persons, it is unsurprising that the most significant writings concerning the role of the Holy Spirit as the will of God in creation were written by William. The main teachings on this point all come in the work, *The Mirror of Faith*, in which the Holy Spirit is described as the "substantial will" of the godhead in two separate sections.

The first of these deals with the creative work and revelation of the Holy Spirit. William begins by explaining that the will of God is not "divine", as a quality, but is itself God, the Holy Spirit, "who is the substantial will of God".[37] The Spirit is next described as the "will of God whereby God makes all that he wills: Everything that he willed he did", picking up on Psalm 135. The *Mirror*

---

[34] William, *Speculum*, 68, p.80 (p.75).

[35] *Ibid.*, 68, p.82 (p.76).

[36] Bernard, *Sentences*, 3.59.

[37] William, *Speculum*, 41, pp.58-59 (p.48).

then moves directly on from this to the revelation of the Spirit to people, stating that it is the same Holy Spirit who makes Himself known to those he lives in, the "very Will of God makes himself known to the person in whom it is accomplished".[38]

The second section concerns the activity of the Spirit as will in the life of the believer, who is made one spirit with the God to whom he is attracted by the Holy Spirit. This "process happens better when the Holy Spirit, who is the substantial will of the Father and Son, attaches the will of a person to Himself. In this case, the soul is transformed, not into the nature of divinity, but beyond human form. The recognition of God which is mutual to the Father and Son, is the very unity of both, which is the Holy Spirit".[39]

These two passages show the extension of the Spirit's immanent identity as the will of the Father and Son into His economic state. The Holy Spirit is shown to be active in fulfilling the will of the godhead in His creative work, and also in conforming the will of individuals to that of God in uniting their spirit with the relationship that exists in the Trinity.

Two other writers that include some teaching on the Spirit as will in the created world are William of Conches and Peter Abelard. Abelard deals with this in writing of the procession of the Holy Spirit from the Father and Son, and wrote that the Spirit makes and orders everything as the "good will of God" that comes from the Father and Son.[40] William of Conches includes the activity of the Holy Spirit as will as part of his use of the power, wisdom, will formula for the Trinity, stating that as will the Spirit shows the effects of God's power and wisdom.[41]

There is one additional point that needs to be included in this discussion, which is from Nico den Bok's analysis of Richard of St. Victor. Although Richard himself does not write of the Holy Spirit as the will of God, den Bok infers from Richard's writings that this may be understood. The closest Richard comes to the issue is in discussing the procession of the persons when presenting the power, wisdom, goodness model in book six. In this, goodness is described as "good will, the will to do good".[42] However, elsewhere in the *De Trinitate*, Richard affirms that there is one will in God.

Den Bok notes that there seems to be a problem of wills regarding the subject and object, which seems to differ depending on the person being referred to. He writes that the problem may be overcome if the Holy Spirit is seen as the one will of the Father and Son. The conclusion reached is that there is one thing willed, but three things willing.[43] It is interesting that this is put forward as a solution to the problem found in Richard's work when there is so

---

[38] William, *Speculum*, 41, pp.58-59 (p.48).

[39] *Ibid.*, 68, p.80 (p.75).

[40] Abelard, *Introductio*, 2.122-26 (Vol. 3, pp.468-71).

[41] William of Conches, *Philosophia Mundi*, 10 (PL 172:45).

[42] Richard, *De Trinitate*, 6.15, pp.247-48 (PL 196:979-80).

[43] Den Bok, *Communicating the Most High*, p.338.

little explicit teaching to back this up in the Victorine school. Given the use of the term will for the third person in Augustine's writing, it is possible that there was a deeper acceptance of this in twelfth-century thought beyond what was written. However, this would be surprising considering the wealth of writing on attributes appropriate for the Holy Spirit from every perspective that has been shown in this book.

Conclusion

The twelfth-century writers thus used will mostly to clarify their understanding of the Holy Spirit, rather than as a major part of His identity. Only William of St. Thierry seriously incorporated this element into his ideas on the immanent person of the Spirit. This seems to be remarkable given the importance that Augustine had given this term, yet it would seem that the temporary nature and need for an object prevented writers from transferring this term into their major pneumatological thoughts.[44] Another contributory factor in this may be the lack of depth in Augustine's own thought on this point, although there is little more on love, which would be used as the main word to describe the Spirit. This analysis is thus important for an overall understanding of the thoughts of twelfth-century writers, despite the fact that will was not a primary term used in connection with the Holy Spirit.

---

[44] Although, as will be seen later in this thesis, this does not seem to have hindered the use of gift terminology.

CHAPTER 10

Gift

The application of the word gift to the person of the Holy Spirit caused some of the greatest theoretical problems both for Augustine and for the twelfth-century writers because of the stress that it contains on the economy of the Spirit. These writers were seeking to present one person of the Spirit in both His immanent and economic states, but the idea that the Holy Spirit is a gift generally points towards His work in creation and in the lives of believers. And yet, Biblical teaching on the Spirit demands that gift be one of the terms used to describe the third person, as Dennis Ngien notes, "biblically, the word most commonly linked to the Spirit is 'gift'".[1] Therefore, it was important to these authors that they not only taught about the role of the Holy Spirit as a gift to the world, but that they also tied this into their understanding of His immanent personhood. Indeed, the focus of many writers seems to have been at least equally on this latter aspect. This chapter will again begin with a summary of Augustine's teaching to provide a context for the thoughts of twelfth-century writers. There will necessarily be an initial concentration in looking at the later writers on the economy of the Spirit because of the nature of gift terminology; but this will be undertaken with a view to clarifying the perception of the immanent Holy Spirit in this period.

Augustine

There is a basic dilemma raised by the term gift for any theologian seeking to present a uniform person of the Holy Spirit in His immanent and economic states. The fundamental problem is that a gift is given to someone or something, and yet in the Holy Spirit this would seem only to refer to His presence in the world. There is no indication in the Bible that the Father and Son either give or receive the Spirit in the immanent Trinity. It was thus important for Augustine to explain both the nature and the work of the Holy Spirit in some way that necessitated a link between His immanent identity in

---

[1] Ngien, *Apologetic for Filioque*, p.12. Ngien notes five passages of Scripture that refer to the Holy Spirit as gift: Acts 2.38, 8.20, 10.45, 11.17, Luke 11.13.

the Trinity and His economic role in creation.²

Burnaby addresses this problem at the beginning of his analysis of Augustine's use of the term gift. Having noted Scripture's limitations in the use of gift, Augustine's desire to understand the persons of the Trinity as internal relations in the godhead, and the question against the Spirit being an immanent gift,³ Burnaby states that, for Augustine, the "nature of God seems to require an external relation to the existence of the created world".⁴

In his presentation of the Holy Spirit in the first half of the *De Trinitate*, Augustine states that the best relational term that can be used to describe the Spirit in the Trinity is gift.⁵ He does this in the context of discussion of the Holy Spirit as the "inexpressible communion" of Father and Son, yet does not conclude from this that unity is the most helpful understanding of the third person. Instead, Augustine reasons from the Spirit's being as communion that the name Holy Spirit is applicable because it shows the commonality of being of Father and Son, as both of these persons are both Holy and Spirit. "Holy Spirit", therefore, while it reflects the identity of the third person, is not a relational name within the Trinity, as the Father is not father to the Holy Spirit nor the Son a son. It is in this context that Augustine states that gift is the best name. The extent to which Augustine holds this teaching is shown in book eight of the *De Trinitate*, by which stage he is able to refer to the third person only as gift, and not as Holy Spirit.⁶ Augustine also transfers the Holy Spirit's identity as unity and gift into His economic state:

> Through that which is common to the Father and the Son, they have willed that we should have communion with one another and with them, that we should be brought together into one through that one gift which is of them both the Holy Spirit, God and God's gift. By that gift are we reconciled to the divine and made to delight therein.⁷

It has been noted in the chapters above on love and will that the first half of the *De Trinitate* outlines and develops the Trinitarian persons, and it is interesting that Augustine only employs limited language of love at this stage, which would be the most used term to refer to the Holy Spirit in the twelfth

---

² Many writers have examined Augustine's use of gift terminology regarding the Holy Spirit. Some of the more helpful discussions are found in: J. Ratzinger, 'The Holy Spirit as Communio: Concerning the Relationship of Pneumatology and Spirituality in Augustine', *Communio* 25 (1998), pp.324-39; E. Teselle, 'Holy Spirit', in A. Fitzgerald, *Augustine Through the Ages: An Encyclopedia* (Grand Rapids: Eerdmans, 1999), pp.434-37; Clark, '*De Trinitate*', pp.91-102.

³ Because a gift implies not only a giver, but also a recipient.

⁴ Burnaby, *Amor Dei*, p.173.

⁵ Augustine, *De Trinitate*, 5.12, p.220 (pp.197-200).

⁶ "non enim Pater Trinitas, aut Filius Trinitas, aut Trinitas Donum". *Ibid.*, 8.Prologue, p.268 (p.241).

⁷ Burnaby, *Amor Dei*, p.177, quoting Augustine's Sermon 71.

Gift 153

century; instead it is as gift that the third person is primarily presented to the reader. It is also noteworthy that, when Augustine seeks to find analogies for the Trinity, he does not refer to the Spirit as gift, but as love or will.

When Augustine finally deals with the idea that the Holy Spirit is love in book fifteen of the *De Trinitate*, this is tied closely into the Spirit's identity as gift, involving God's love of people and their love of God.[8] Burnaby writes of Augustine's legacy in teaching that the Spirit is the self-giving love of Father and Son, but that Augustine did not make use of this idea to solve the problem of eternal giving.[9] Heron also notes that the Western church received the love/gift association with the Holy Spirit from Augustine, but again this applies to the common gift of the Spirit from Father and Son to the world, rather than a solution to the problem of the immanent state of the Spirit as gift.[10]

Augustine's answer to this problem of the temporary nature of the Spirit as gift comes in book five, and is briefly backed up in the later discussion in book fifteen. Augustine has stated that gift is the best relational term to describe the Holy Spirit, but later asks the question whether the Spirit was only a gift after He was given, which would indicate that the third person was not co-eternal with the Father and Son.[11] The response to this is that the Spirit proceeds eternally as that which is "giveable"; He is a gift eternally, and a donation after He has been given.[12] This concept is picked up again later in the *De Trinitate*, in relation to the gifts of the Spirit, which are all said to come from the same one gift, the Holy Spirit Himself. In this section, Augustine writes that the Spirit is God's gift in such a way that God the Holy Spirit also gives Himself.[13] This is unhelpfully not related to any concept of the immanent Spirit as gift.

Despite this lack of clarity at the end of Augustine's work, the overall use of gift terminology was intended to bring together the immanent and economic states of the Holy Spirit. Burnaby writes that the identification of the Holy Spirit as gift "involved the concentration of attention upon the Spirit as immanent".[14] The gift that is made is the Holy Spirit Himself, with no other content. Stanley Burgess notes the same stress in Augustine's thought, that the Holy Spirit is both God and the gift of God at the same time.[15] The unity in the person of the Spirit that Augustine seeks to present is perhaps best expressed by Ngien, who states that, for Augustine, there is a "congruence of the economic and immanent rendering of gift so that the Spirit may be called Gift (*donum*)

---

[8] Augustine, *De Trinitate*, 15.16-19, pp.500-14 (pp.418-26).

[9] Burnaby, *Amor Dei*, pp.173-74.

[10] Heron, *The Holy Spirit*, p.87.

[11] Augustine, *De Trinitate*, 5.15, p.224 (pp.199-200).

[12] Edmund Hill writes that the Spirit is considered to be a "the Gift, potentially, even before we are there to be given this divine Gift" (Hill, *The Mystery of the Trinity*, p.70).

[13] Augustine, *De Trinitate*, 15.19, pp.512-13 (p.424).

[14] Burnaby, *Amor Dei*, pp.175-76.

[15] S. Burgess, *The Spirit and the Church: Antiquity* (Peabody, Massachusetts: Hendrickson, 1984), p.181.

eternally prior to His being given (*donatum*) in history".[16]

Augustine had thus provided a great deal of groundwork concerning the concept that the Holy Spirit is gift for the twelfth-century writers. However, there was still a lack of clarity about the relationship between the economic role of the Spirit as the gift of God and His immanent state, which would be further explored by the later writers.

The Role of the Holy Spirit as Gift in the World

It is appropriate to begin the analysis of twelfth-century views on the Holy Spirit with a look at the economic role attributed to the Spirit both because this is the focus of the Biblical material from which the writers took their overall conception of this issue, and because this provides an important foundation for understanding the concept relating to the immanent person of the Spirit that would be drawn from these ideas. Unsurprisingly, there is some connection in this work of the Spirit to ideas that have already been studied, particularly love.

It would seem appropriate when discussing the experience of the Holy Spirit and His work in people's lives to begin with the Cistercians, and particularly William of St. Thierry, who were focused on this area in their presentations of the Holy Spirit. However, when it comes to gift terminology, William seems more interested in the immanent/economic issues concerning the Spirit's identity. There is some teaching by William and Bernard of Clairvaux on the work of the Holy Spirit as gift, mostly concentrating on the awakening of love in the heart of the believer. In *The Enigma of Faith*, William writes of the gifts of God that are given because the Spirit dwells in a person, being Himself the gift of God.[17] The gifts of the Spirit are said only to be profitable if there is love, and on this basis (and quoting Romans 5:5) William claims that "the Holy Spirit is not properly called gift unless it is because of love".[18] It is as the gift of God that the Spirit kindles love in the believer for both God and his neighbour. Bernard of Clairvaux writes of the Spirit as a gift giving love in *The Steps of Humility and Pride*, working with the passage in Romans 5 that speaks of the Holy Spirit pouring out His love into our hearts.[19] Stanley Burgess also notes Bernard's association of the kiss of God in the Song of Songs with the gift of the Holy Spirit.[20]

Both Bell and Gilson note that William of St. Thierry teaches about the Holy Spirit as a gift uniting the believer with God, although they disagree on the means by which this is achieved. Gilson writes that it is by the gift of the Holy Spirit that the believer participates in the divine life, and this is connected to the Spirit as a gift of love by which God loves himself in us.[21] This is backed up by

---

[16] Ngien, *Apologetic*, p.12.
[17] William, *Enigma*, 99, p.176 (pp.114-15).
[18] *Ibid.*, 99, p.176 (pp.114-15).
[19] Bernard, *Opera*, Vol.3, p.31 (*Steps*, p.20).
[20] Burgess, *The Holy Spirit*, p.57; Bernard, *Opera*, Vol.1, p.37 (*Song of Songs*, p.46).
[21] Gilson, *Mystical Theology*, p.95 n.121.

his examination of Bernard's treatment of the Spirit as gift, that the gift of charity was the same as the gift of the Holy Spirit for Bernard and the Cistercians.[22] Gilson states that it is as this gift that the Spirit plays the part of a bond of union between God and the spiritual life. Bell writes that people do not love by the Holy Spirit, but are made one with God in the Spirit.[23] The application of the role of the Spirit as gift is the same, however, in uniting the spirit with God.

Peter Lombard, despite the confusions that were noted in chapter six about his use of gift to describe the Holy Spirit, is the most thorough and helpful writer studied in this book concerning the economic role of the Spirit as gift. Lombard divides the mission of the Spirit as gift into two sections: the visible (*Distinctio* 16) and the invisible (*Distinctio* 17). The visible concerns the manifestations of the Spirit on occasions such as Pentecost, whilst the invisible is the work the Spirit undertakes in the heart of the believer. Lombard gives various elements of this invisible work throughout the *Sentences* such as taking care and holding, helping to remain in God, giving compassion, creating love and giving gifts.[24] Peter Lombard thus provides strong teaching on the work of the Spirit as gift in the world.

Two other writers have some significant teaching on this aspect of the Spirit. Peter Abelard uses the Holy Spirit's role as gift as support for his ideas on goodness, writing that it is as a gift that the Spirit dispenses grace and charity and is involved in the remission of sins;[25] and later in discussing the World Soul, Abelard teaches that the gift that is the Holy Spirit not only quickens life in the world, but also stimulates virtues in people's lives.[26] Richard of St. Victor restricts his teaching on the Spirit as gift to one section of book six of his *De Trinitate*, in which he says that the Holy Spirit is said to be the gift of God because He is the love of God.[27] This is disappointingly brief, especially considering the use of giving and receiving language that Richard employs to establish the differences and relationships between the divine persons.[28]

There is thus some analysis on the role of the Holy Spirit as gift, drawn from the Biblical witness, but only Peter Lombard uses the idea that the Spirit is gift to any great extent in his account of the work of the Spirit. This is surprising given the fact that, as will now be shown, there was a great deal of discussion in the twelfth century about how the Holy Spirit can be considered a gift before He was given, and how this then relates to His being given in time.

---

[22] *Ibid.*, p.23.

[23] Bell, *Image and Likeness*, pp.58-59.

[24] Lombard, *Sentences*, 1.3.1.7-9; 1.10.2.3; 1.14.2.5; 1.17.1.2; 1.18.1; pp. 70-71, 111-12, 129, 142, 152-53 (PL 192:530, 550, 557-58, 564, 569; 1.3.6; 1.10.5; 1.14.3-4; 1.17.2; 1.17.19).

[25] Abelard, *Introductio*, 1.64-68 (Vol. 3, pp.343-45).

[26] *Ibid.*, 1.20 (Vol. 3, p.327).

[27] Richard, *De Trinitate*, 6.14, pp.245-46 (PL 196:978).

[28] See above, Chapter 5.

The Holy Spirit as Gift in His Immanent State

There are several questions that are naturally raised when one considers the idea that the Holy Spirit might be called a gift before He was given to the world, which will now be discussed. The relationships that are said to exist between the Trinitarian persons do not seem to include the possibility that one of them is a gift, especially as the thought that one member of the godhead is a gift in relation to the other two would seem to deny equality of status of all three persons. Despite this, however, this discussion of the Holy Spirit as gift in His immanent state begins with those writers who did declare this basic position, and examines the manner in which they expressed this.

The Holy Spirit: Eternally a Gift

The fundamental importance for twelfth-century writers of presenting a united picture of the Trinity in their immanent and economic states meant that most writers included some teaching on the Spirit as immanent gift, even if this would later be clarified in their writings. As a result, much of what will now be presented was concluded from the thoughts outlined above on the work of the Holy Spirit as gift in the world. Peter Abelard, for instance, who has little to say on this issue, moves from writing on the identification of the Holy Spirit seen in the effects of his works back to Augustine's idea that the Spirit is a gift eternally, and is temporally given.[29]

It is appropriate to begin more lengthy study of this with William of St. Thierry, both because he is the author who most thoroughly matches his presentations of the immanent and economic persons of the Holy Spirit, and because he was most consistent in teaching that the Holy Spirit can be called gift in His immanent state without seeking qualifications on this point. Dechanet writes of this consistent application of the word gift to the Spirit in his study of William's mystical theology in the context of the inseparability of the divine persons by human terminology.[30] Given William's devotion to Augustine's thought, it is unsurprising that gift is a primary word used to describe the Spirit (being the best that Augustine could find); but it is more strange that William does not involve himself greatly in the other debates that will be discussed below in this chapter,[31] which also derive from Augustine's thought. Perhaps William's intention to present a clear picture of the person of the Spirit, in order that his readers could easily comprehend both this and the work of the Spirit in the life of the believer, led William to omit the more problematical elements of the term gift.

William's main writing that concerns this issue comes in the *Enigma of Faith*. The initial reference to the Spirit as gift merely states that He is the gift of God and of God's Son.[32] Later in the same work, William discusses the

---

[29] Abelard, *Summi Boni*, 3.4, pp.252-53.

[30] Dechanet, *William of St. Thierry*, p.84.

[31] Although William does include some minor teaching on these points, as will be seen.

[32] William, *Enigma*, 26, p.114 (p.55).

relative processions of Son and Spirit, and again uses the word gift to describe the Holy Spirit. Having stated that the Father is chiefly the principle of the Holy Spirit, though with the Son, William then writes that the "Holy Spirit is the gift of the God that gives", mainly again from the Father.[33] This primacy of the Father in the procession of the Spirit does not, however, imply any inequality, but instead leads to concord between the gift and givers. At this point, William leaves his discussion of the overall procession of the Spirit to deal with the economy of the persons, before returning later, albeit briefly, to the his former theme. Picking up on the idea of concord, William writes that the first two persons are united by the Holy Spirit, not that they exist "through participation or gift, but by the gift of themselves they maintain unity of the Spirit in the bond of peace".[34] William then returns again from this to the role of the Spirit as gift in creation. Through all this, it is clear that William is happy to transfer the name gift to the Spirit in His immanent state without seeking much clarification.

Peter Lombard was perhaps the most thorough writer on the Holy Spirit as gift, as was shown in the analysis of this in the chapter on his overall work on the Spirit. Within this complex, and at times confusing, presentation, Lombard states his belief that the Holy Spirit is a gift outside of time. This comes in his initial section on the procession of the Spirit: comparing this to the procession of the Son, Lombard states that the second person proceeds by birth, the third as a gift.[35] Whilst Lombard never seems to be satisfied with an easy answer on this issue, he twice returns to this basic point, in *Distinctio* 18 and *Distinctio* 26. The first of these is a debate on whether the Holy Spirit is a gift, or if He is given as a gift. Lombard twice writes that the Spirit is a gift outside of time, before He was given temporally.[36] The second *Distinctio* discusses why the Spirit is called *the* gift of God when there are many gifts of God described in the Bible. Lombard's answer is that the Holy Spirit is called the "eternal and immutable" gift of God, which distinguishes Him from the temporal gifts described as bestowed in creation.[37] At one level of Lombard's thought, then, is the idea that the Spirit can be called the gift of God in His immanent state, before He was given to the world. Peter Rosemann notes this in his study of Lombard's work, stating that Lombard reserved "gift" for the eternal person, and using "given" or "gifted" (*donum vel donatum*) for the temporal.[38]

The author of the *Summa Sententiarum* uses some language similar to Peter Lombard in writing of the procession of the Holy Spirit. Moving from the

---

[33] *Ibid.*, 77, pp.158-60 (p.99).

[34] William, *Enigma*, 98, p.176 (p.115). William is quoting here from Ephesians 4:3.

[35] Lombard, *Sentences*, 1.13.2, p.122 (PL 192:555, 1.13.2).

[36] *Ibid.*, 1.18.2.2-3, p.153 (PL 192:570, 1.18.2-3).

[37] *Ibid.*, 1.26.6.1, p.201 (PL 192:593-94, 1.26.6).

[38] Rosemann, *Peter Lombard*, p.85. It is surprising that Marcia Colish does not devote any major section to Lombard's analysis of gift terminology in her work, instead merely including a short section on the gifts given by the Holy Spirit. Colish, *Peter Lombard 2*, pp.507-10.

Spirit's role in sanctification back to the immanent person of the Spirit, the writer states that the Holy Spirit does not come without the Father and the Son, and is thus given and accepted outside of time.[39] This is then related to the procession, which is differentiated from that of the Son because the Holy Spirit is given, not born. The fact that this "being given" happens outside of time is reinforced by the author when he declares that the Holy Spirit is not created when He is given as a gift as the Spirit is able to be a gift before He is given.[40] This echoes some of Anselm of Canterbury's teaching regarding the procession of the Holy Spirit in his *De Processione*. In this passage, which focuses on the dual procession of the Spirit as gift, Anselm writes that being given or sent never happens to the Holy Spirit, as nothing previously non-existent in His person ever comes to be.[41] Anselm thus links the economic procession of the Holy Spirit into the immanent.

The idea that the Holy Spirit is always able to be given, included by Lombard, the author of the *Summa Sententiarum* and Anselm in their writings, is reminiscent of the solution that Augustine put forward, which was that the Spirit proceeded eternally as "giveable". It is surprising that these twelfth-century writers did not pick up on this language to answer some of the difficulties that are put forward by gift terminology. The only exception was William of St. Thierry, who quoted Augustine on this point in his *On the Errors of William of Conches* against the power, wisdom, will formula.[42]

Gift as a Relative Term for the Immanent Holy Spirit

We come now to the first of two issues that qualify the idea that the Holy Spirit is immanently the gift of God, and which affect the implications of this on the procession of the Spirit. This concerns the relational character of the term gift, and was most commented on by Peter Lombard, although William of St. Thierry and Richard of St. Victor also mentioned this point.

Lombard's first interaction with gift as a relative term comes in *Distinctio* 18, which is the main *Distinctio* dealing with the idea that the Holy Spirit is called a gift. In section nine, Lombard distinguishes between the immanent and economic processions of the Spirit by writing that He is eternally a gift, and temporally given as a gift.[43] This is clarified by the notion that the Holy Spirit is a gift in relation to the Father and Son (immanent) and is given as a gift in relation both to the giver and to those to whom the Spirit is given (economic). This is an interesting point in Lombard's overall presentation, as it affirms that he considers that the Spirit is able to be a gift without the necessity for any object.

Lombard returns to the same subject later in the *Sentences* when considering

---

[39] *Summa Sententiarum*, 1.6 (PL 176:50-52).

[40] *Summa Sententiarum*, 1.6 (PL 176:50-52).

[41] Anselm C, *De Processione*, 2, Vol.2, p.190 (p.404).

[42] William, *De Erroribus*, (PL 180:339).

[43] Lombard, *Sentences*, 1.18.4.1, p.157 (PL 192:572, 1.18.9).

the eternal procession of the Spirit. At this point, Lombard writes that we should not say that the Holy Spirit is the gift of the Father or the Spirit of the Father, because the relations between these persons work differently to those between the Father and the Son.[44] Instead, it is more correct to say that the Holy Spirit is the gift of the giver, and the Father the giver of the gift, which confirms to Lombard the usefulness of Augustine's designation of gift as the best relative term for the Spirit.

The relational importance of gift language is also found in Richard of St. Victor's conclusions about the person of the Holy Spirit drawn from his idea that the Spirit receives His entire personhood primarily from the Father, but also from the Son.[45] As such, the Spirit is purely gift, the Father purely giver, and the Son both giver and gift. This is Richard's basic position on the application of the term gift to the Spirit, from which he concludes his main teaching which concentrates on the economy of the Spirit as gift. William briefly mentions the Holy Spirit as gift in his relational teaching in the *Enigma of Faith*, showing that the Spirit is neither the Father or Son in teaching against Sabellianism.[46]

On Whether the Holy Spirit can be said to Give Himself

This second issue that concerns the Spirit's identity as gift relates His immanent person to the economic. The importance of presenting a unified picture of the Holy Spirit does mean that any indication that the Spirit is said to give Himself reflects on His eternal procession within the godhead. Anselm of Canterbury is quite clear on this point, stating that no person can proceed from himself, with the result that the Holy Spirit must proceed only from the Father and the Son.[47] However, as will now be shown, others were happy to make distinctions between the immanent and economic processions of the Spirit on this point.

Peter Lombard is clearest on this issue, addressing this issue directly in *Distinctio* 15 of the *Sentences*, and clarifying his thoughts in other sections. Lombard makes it quite clear in the main *Distinctio* that he believes that the Holy Spirit, in His temporal procession, is given by Himself. The basis of this is Lombard's upholding of Augustine's principle that the *operatio* of the Trinity

---

[44] *Ibid.*, 1.26.8, pp.202-03 (PL 192:594, 1.26.8).

[45] Richard's teaching on the immediate and mediate procession of the Holy Spirit, and the results of this for gift terminology, are found in *De Trinitate* 5.8,19, pp.203-05, 217 (PL 196:955, 962-63).

[46] William, *Enigma*, 64, p.152 (p.94).

[47] Anselm C, *De Processione*, 9, Vol.2, p.188 (p.402). This reasoning comes as part of Anselm's attempt to convince the Greeks of the dual procession of the Spirit, and it is thus unsurprising that Anselm rules out any possibility of a third method of procession. The reasoning leads onto Anselm's analogy of the waterfall, which would also not indicate that the Spirit proceeds from Himself.

regarding the world is indivisible.[48] Therefore, as the Holy Spirit is God, He must have been involved in giving Himself. This is confirmed by Lombard in a variety of ways. Firstly, from the teaching that the Holy Spirit breathes where He wills (*ubi vult spirat*), Lombard concludes that the Spirit gives Himself. Secondly, Lombard states that it is not possible for the Father and Son to be able to do something which the Holy Spirit cannot. Thirdly, it is stated that, as the Spirit sent the Son into the world, it should not be surprising that He also sent Himself.[49] At the beginning of the following *Distinctio*, Lombard makes clear that he does not believe that this teaching impacts the eternal procession of the Holy Spirit, which is from the Father and Son alone, "et non a seipso".[50] The later teaching on the immanent status of the Spirit as a gift confirms this. As was shown above, gift is later used as a relative term to the Father and Son, and not in relation to the Holy Spirit Himself.

The two Cistercian writers, William of St. Thierry and Bernard of Clairvaux, also made a similar distinction between the two identities of the Holy Spirit as gift. While both upheld the idea that the Holy Spirit was the gift of God before He was given, they also teach that the Holy Spirit was both giver and gift in His economic procession. William often uses the word gift to describe the person of the Holy Spirit, and teaches that this is a relational term (see above); and that the Spirit's identity as gift in relation to the other two members of the godhead does not imply any inequality in status.[51] Bernard makes the point that the Holy Spirit is both giver and gift in his letter to the brothers at Chartreuse, in relation to the *caritas* that God gives, which is the Holy Spirit. The Spirit is both this love of God and God Himself.[52] Both Bell and Davy draw out from William's writings the significant difference between the Spirit's dual identity as giver and gift. In God, Bell writes, the Holy Spirit is *unitas*, binding the godhead together, whereas in man He is *similitudo*, drawing people into the likeness of God.[53]

Given the determination that has been noted throughout this book by twelfth-century writers, and William of St. Thierry more than any, to teach the same identity of the Holy Spirit in His immanent and economic processions, it is surprising that these writers seem unconcerned by the extreme difference implied by the thought that the Holy Spirit gave Himself.

Conclusion: The Procession of the Holy Spirit as Gift

There are clearly complexities arising from the Biblical concept that the Holy Spirit is the gift of God that affect these writers' overall perception of the Spirit.

---

[48] Lombard, *Sentences*, 1.15.1.1-3, pp.130-31 (PL 192:559, 1.15.1) quoting from Augustine's *De Trinitate* 15.36, pp.512-13 (p.424).

[49] Lombard, *Sentences*, 1.15.1.4, pp.131-32 (PL 192:559, 1.15.2). This is backed up from Augustine's *De Trinitate* 6.6, pp.93-96 (pp.101-05).

[50] *Ibid.*, 1.16.1.1, p.138 (PL 192:562, 1.16.1).

[51] William, *Enigma*, 77, pp.158-59 (pp.98-99).

[52] Bernard, *Opera*, Vol.3, p.149 (*On Loving God*, p.127).

[53] Bell, *Image and Likeness*, pp.135-36.

Gift 161

This chapter will conclude by looking specifically at how writers described the procession of the Holy Spirit as gift, in order to shed what light there may be on this issue.

Anselm of Havelberg is one of the clearest writers on this in responding to Greek questions about the dual procession of the Holy Spirit. In writing of the manner of the Spirit's procession, Anselm states that it is not on account of His substance that the Spirit proceeds, because this is the same as the Father and the Son. Instead, the Holy Spirit is the gift from both given, and the love from both loving.[54] In response to this, the Greeks do not question the basic principle that Anselm is teaching, but ask whether the existence of two givers creates two gifts, and therefore two principles?[55] Anselm answers this question by showing the unsatisfactory nature of the Greek position on the Trinity in suggesting that only the Father gives the Holy Spirit. This, in Anselm's opinion, would create a middle position for the Son in the procession of the Spirit as neither giver nor gift, yet somehow involved in an undefined role. Whilst it is true that, debating as he was with the Greeks, Anselm had some concentration on the work of the Holy Spirit, the overall dialogue was intended to clarify the immanent procession of the Spirit, and it is clear that Anselm does not seek to separate this from the economic persons. In this context, the argument that he uses on the Spirit as gift is important because it shows that, in Anselm's mind, the dual procession of the Holy Spirit as the gift of Father and Son is a fundamental element of the personhood of the Spirit.[56]

Three other writers also teach that the procession of the Holy Spirit from the Father and the Son can be described in basic gift terminology, all of whom include this in sections whose context is the immanent person of the Spirit. Peter Lombard, as the foremost writer on the Holy Spirit as gift in this period, consistently refers to the procession of the third person in these terms, but nowhere more clearly than in *Distinctio* 13. In this passage, Lombard is comparing the processions of the second and third persons, and distinguishes them by the fact that the Son is born, whereas the Spirit is a gift.[57] The author of the *Summa Sententiarum* make the same distinction when dealing with the procession of the Holy Spirit, clarifying this by stating that the "Holy Spirit is not created when given as a gift, as a gift is able to be before it is given".[58] William of St. Thierry has one important comment that has not been developed so far in this book. In the initial comment on the Holy Spirit as gift in the *Enigma of Faith*, William is considering the extent to which it is possible to

---

[54] Anselm H, *Dialogi*, 2.10 (PL 188:1178-79).

[55] *Ibid.*, 2.11 (PL 188:1180).

[56] It is noticeable that when Anselm of Canterbury addresses the question of two Spirits as a result of dual procession in his *De Processione Spiritus Sancti*, he does not refer to gift terminology. This is consistent within the overall work, but highlights again the shortcomings of the *De Processione* because of Anselm's decision not to address the identity of the Holy Spirit as love, gift, will or any other attribute.

[57] Lombard, *Sentences*, 1.13.2, p.122 (PL 192:555, 1.13.2).

[58] *Summa Sententiarum*, 1.6 (PL 176:50-52).

delve into the mystery of the Trinity. It is in this context that William writes of the Spirit as the gift of God, and the gift of His Son, which is thus important processional teaching on the Holy Spirit, in addition to the earlier references to the Spirit as love and unity.[59]

One other writer whose views on this issue need mentioning is Anselm of Canterbury. In writing about the dual procession of the Holy Spirit in the *De Processione Spiritus Sancti*, Anselm outlines two options for the Spirit's procession: either consisting of His being from the Father; or as being sent or given by the Father.[60] If the latter is a procession of the Spirit, Anselm concludes that the Spirit also proceeds from the Son, since the Son sends and gives the Holy Spirit. However, Anselm states that the Spirit is only given or sent to creatures, and must therefore proceed in both ways: "I do not think that we can deny this if we understand each procession in its own signification".[61] Anselm is unwilling to restrict his understanding of the Spirit's procession to gift terminology because of the need for an object: "if the Holy Spirit's procession in only his being sent or given, he is distinct from the Father and proceeds from the Father only when he is given or sent, something that no one to my knowledge understands".[62] Anselm later returns to the idea that the Spirit proceeds from God as regards His being without mentioning gift terminology, but still upholding dual procession.

The significance of this is that Anselm of Canterbury clearly distinguishes between the procession of the Holy Spirit as a gift and His immanent procession. No other writer so clearly divides the person of the Spirit in His two states. It is interesting, given the importance of Anselm on the rise of scholasticism in twelfth-century Europe, that no writer following him upheld his teaching on this issue. The judgement of his successors seems to be that the Holy Spirit proceeds as a gift as an integral part of his personhood.

---

[59] William, *Enigma*, 23. p.114 (p.55).
[60] Anselm C, *De Processione*, 2, Vol.2, p.188 (p.402).
[61] *Ibid.*
[62] *Ibid.*, 2, Vol.2, p.188 (p.402).

CHAPTER 11

Union

This was the most difficult chapter in the book to name because the twelfth-century writers used so many words to express the concept that the Holy Spirit joins the Father and Son (and sometimes the Holy Spirit Himself) together as one God in three persons. In this role, the Spirit is variously described as union, unity, fellowship, communion, concord, commonness and harmony. The idea is well-expressed by Joseph Ratzinger in his article on Augustine and communio:

> The particularity of the Holy Spirit is evidently that he is what the Father and Son have in common. His particularity is being unity ... Spirit is the unity which God gives himself. In this unity, he himself gives himself. In this unity, the Father and the Son give themselves back to one another. The Spirit's paradoxical and unique property is being *communio*, having his highest selfness precisely in being fully the movement of *communio*.[1]

One of the principle reasons for this line of thought is based on the name Holy Spirit, signifying two attributes that are common to the Father and Son. As such, the name does not seem to imply a relationship in the same manner that Father and Son do, but an identity and position within the Trinitarian relationships that results from the identity of the first two persons.

It is this concept that is at the root of twelfth-century writers' thoughts concerning the person of the Holy Spirit, and which is expressed in the various ways and terms that have been analysed in this book. Whether these men were describing the Holy Spirit as love, goodness, will or gift, it seems that the basis for these images is the understanding that the primary place, role or identity of the Spirit is as the uniting bond within the Trinity. This was the case even in the writings of individuals that do not place great emphasis on developing this role because it is so fundamental to each of the other concepts that are described as pertaining to the Holy Spirit.

This chapter will again begin with an assessment of Augustine's contribution, before moving on to an analysis of the various ways in which this concept was described by the writers of the twelfth century. There will be a section on the relation of unity to love because, of the other terms used, this was the most common link that was made, and also because love (rather than unity) may be seen from the frequency of references as the central concept in describing the person of the Holy Spirit. Finally, the application that was made

---

[1] Ratzinger, 'The Holy Spirit as Communio', p.327.

of this idea to the economy of the Spirit will be discussed as this affected the overall presentations of the Spirit's person.

Augustine

Augustine wrote of the unifying identity of the Holy Spirit in the Trinity in both his *De Trinitate* and *De Doctrina Christiana*. However, the modest teachings (relative to other topics) that are found in these works is over-emphasised in secondary scholarship that draws out Augustine's belief that the Spirit is unity within the Trinity. This supports the thrust of this book, that the volume of writing on this issue in the twelfth century is not necessarily indicative of the underlying importance of this concept in understanding the person of the Holy Spirit. For Augustine, as for the later writers, the identity of the Holy Spirit as the communing bond of Father and Son is crucial for the application of terms such as love and will, which draw out this central role or identity of the Spirit.

Augustine does not use the language of attributes to describe the person of the Holy Spirit very often in the *De Doctrina Christiana*, but he does write about the connection of the three persons in his presentation of the Trinity. The triad that is included here is that of unity (Father), equality (Son) and harmony (Holy Spirit).[2] It is important to note that the application of the term "unity" here to the Father does not imply that the first person is the uniting bond, but that, as the source of the other two persons, the Father is the root of the Trinity and as such is the cause of the "oneness" of God; it is the harmony, which is the Holy Spirit within the Trinitarian relations, that brings the three persons together. O'Donovan writes on this:

> The unity of the Father and the Son, of course, is a unity of being and as such has its source not in the third but in the first Person of the Trinity, who is the "fount of deity". But at the level of relational subsistence in the Godhead its unity is its love, the Holy Spirit who binds the Father and the Son in one.[3]

Augustine writes about the Holy Spirit as the unity of God in chapters five and six of the *De Trinitate*. In this work, he initially makes it clear that the three persons are united on account of their substance: "The Father, Son and Holy Spirit present divine unity in inseparable equality of one substance".[4] In book five, dealing with the person of the Holy Spirit, Augustine describes the role he perceives the Spirit playing in this unity. Dealing with the dual procession of the Holy Spirit as the Spirit of the Father and the Son, Augustine draws on the idea that the Holy Spirit is the gift of God, and concludes that the Spirit is a

---

[2] Augustine, *De Doctrina*, 1.5 (pp.16-17). It is noticeable that even when dealing with the concept of love, so important in the *De Trinitate*, Augustine does not relate his thoughts to the person of the Holy Spirit in the *De Doctrina*.

[3] O. O'Donovan, *The Problem of Self-Love in St. Augustine* (New Haven: Yale University Press, 1980), pp.130-31.

[4] Augustine, *De Trinitate*, 1.4, pp.34-36 (p.69).

kind of inexpressible communion or fellowship of the Father and Son.[5] Canning writes of this passage that the "Holy Spirit is coeternally and consubstantially equal to the Father and the Son ... whose own gift of unity the Spirit is".[6] This relational position of the Holy Spirit is drawn by Augustine not only from the gift language, where Father and Son are united in the giving of one gift, but also from the name Holy Spirit, as noted in the introduction to this chapter.[7] Augustine writes that, as the Father and Son are both holy and spirit in themselves, the name Holy Spirit becomes a relational guideline in showing His role as the communion of the first two persons. Augustine does not apply this thought too deeply to the experience of the believer, although Joseph Ratzinger writes of the implication that "becoming a Christian means becoming *Communio* and thereby entering into the mode of being of the Holy Spirit".[8]

Augustine further develops these thoughts in the next chapter, linking in the idea that the Holy Spirit is the love of the Father and Son for each other, and also their mutual holiness.[9] These attributes are seen as being results of the fundamental identity of the Spirit as that which is common to Father and Son, their "very commonness or communion".[10] Although Augustine himself concludes from this that *caritas* is one of the best words to describe the Holy Spirit, it seems clear that this is a result of the Spirit's identity, rather than the prime existence of the Holy Spirit in His immanent state.

David Coffey raises methodological objections to Augustine's argument in this link between ontological communion and love.[11] While Coffey supports Augustine's thought that "the Holy Spirit proceeds as a hypostasis from the Father and the Son, it is ... as He is a hypostasis that He is the communion between them", Coffey sees no necessity for this to lead to the conclusion that the mutual love is one of the properties of the Holy Spirit.[12] However, Coffey does not argue with the basic identity of the Spirit in Augustine's work as whatever is common to Father and Son; indeed, he supports Augustine in concluding this identity from the idea of dual procession from Father and Son.

John Burnaby provides a good summary of Augustine's outline of the Holy Spirit in the *De Trinitate* in his book, *Amor Dei*. In this, Burnaby shows the

---

[5] Augustine, *De Trinitate*, 5.11, pp.218-20 (p.197).

[6] Canning, *The Unity of Love*, p.304.

[7] Marc Ouellet notes how Augustine used the Spirit's name to imply *communio* in his 'The Spirit in the Life', p.202.

[8] Ratzinger, 'The Holy Spirit as *Communio*', p.324. David Bell supports this idea, stating that the "Holy Spirit is the communion of man with God and the communion and unity of the Trinity in itself" (Bell, *Image and Likeness*, p.61).

[9] Augustine, *De Trinitate*, 6.5, pp.235-36 (p.209).

[10] *Ibid.*

[11] Although he does note that Augustine was writing in a different academic climate to that of today.

[12] Coffey, 'Holy Spirit as mutual love', p.200. Coffey goes on in the same article to argue from a Biblical basis that the Holy Spirit is mutual love, thus supporting Augustine's theory without necessarily giving full backing to his methodology.

close links that Augustine makes between the concepts of gift, communion and love.[13] Burnaby also develops this thought through Augustine's other works to show how his identity of the Holy Spirit as union in God affected the economy of the Spirit in the lives of people: "Through that which is common to the Father and the Son, They have willed that we should have communion with one another and with Them, that we should be brought together into one through That one Gift which is of Them Both – the Holy Spirit, God and God's Gift".[14]

Two other writers who draw out Augustine's thought on the Spirit as union are Stanley Burgess and Alistair Heron, both again in connection to the concept of love. Heron agrees with David Coffey's analysis of Augustine, that communion is a valid, logical result of the idea of dual procession. In particular, he picks out Augustine's phraseology of the Holy Spirit as the *vinculum caritatis* as a good means of asserting that the Spirit proceeds from Father and Son.[15] Burgess, looking at the impact of Augustine on the history of pneumatology, writes about the "communion of divine mutual love" that is found in the *De Trinitate*.[16] He shows in this that Augustine's use of love to refer to the Holy Spirit was based on the Spirit's identity as that which joined Father and Son as one.

Augustine's thought on the Holy Spirit and his application of terms such as love, gift and will, were thus founded on his initial presentation of the Spirit as one who proceeds from Father and Son, and who is thus whatever is common to both, and their communion and fellowship. Whilst this aspect of Augustine's teaching does not always receive due consideration, it is fundamental to understanding the identity of the Holy Spirit in his work. It was also vital in the writings of the twelfth century, as authors sought to engage with, and expand upon, Augustine's ideas.

The Holy Spirit as Union in Twelfth-Century Thought

In Augustine's thought, as well as in commentary on Augustine, the idea of union was closely linked to that of love. This was also true in the twelfth century, as will shortly be shown, but there was also a great deal of writing focusing on the immanent person of the Holy Spirit simply as the commonness of Father and Son, and their communion. This will be examined first, followed by a consideration of the association of this concept with thoughts on love.

William of St. Thierry was the clearest writer in his teaching on the Holy Spirit as union in the immanent Trinity. This was undoubtedly helped by the fact that communion was central to his ideas on the work of the Spirit. However, this economic aspect did not dominate William's thought, but was used as an application of the Holy Spirit's immanent identity. William was also able to extend this concept in his portrayal of Trinitarian relationships, without

---

[13] Burnaby, *Amor Dei*, pp. 173-76.
[14] Augustine, *Sermon* 71.18 quoted in *Ibid.*, p.177.
[15] Heron, "'Who proceedeth from the Father and the Son'", pp.149-66.
[16] Burgess, *The Spirit and the Church: Antiquity*, p.181.

needing to add in other significant attributes, in order to clarify his thought on the position and role of the Holy Spirit in the Trinity.

The foundational significance of the Spirit being unity for William is most clear in his meditative writings, although it permeates every aspect of his thought, as Odo Brooke recognised. Brooke commented on the idea that the Holy Spirit is the mutual union of Father and Son that this is a "Trinitarian theme of great importance in William's theology".[17] This is the basis for William's person of the Spirit in *The Enigma of Faith*, in which the Holy Spirit is introduced as the "unity of Father and Son"; it is from this that William constructs his whole understanding of the immanent third person, and people's experience of the Holy Spirit.[18] David Bell notes that the work of the Spirit for William is rooted in the fact that He "is the communion and unity of the Trinity within itself".[19] One of the clearest passages that William writes on this comes in his *Meditations*, in which he writes that, "the Father is in the Son and the Son in the Father: the bond that unites is the Holy Spirit, who comes not as it were from somewhere else to be the link between you, but who exists as such by the virtue of his unity of being with you both".[20]

William does not only use this basis in order to develop the person of the Holy Spirit with ideas of love, will or gift. On two occasions, he expands this concept to build up a more complete picture of the Spirit in the Trinity. The first of these comes in William's commentary on the letter to the Romans, in which he writes that the Holy Spirit is the "divinity" of the Father and the Son because of His existence as their commonality.[21] The context is Romans 1:20, in which Paul is writing of the divine nature of God that is visible in creation. William states that this is not only seen in the Holy Spirit, but that this is a result of the Spirit's being that which unites the Father and the Son. Even given the context, this remains a strange teaching, but it again shows the importance for William of the identity of the Spirit as union in the godhead.

The second development of this concept is found in the *Mirror of Faith*. Here, William writes about the Holy Spirit as the mutual recognition or likeness of Father and Son, that the "recognition of God which is mutual to the Father and Son, is the very unity of both, which is the Holy Spirit".[22] One of the sources of this idea for William is the teaching of Jesus that no one knows the Father except the Son, and no one knows the Son except the Father and those to whom He is revealed (Matthew 11:27). William goes on to write that this mutual recognition and knowledge is based on their common substance, which commonality is that Holy Spirit. This again shows the strength for William of

---

[17] Brooke, 'The Trinitarian Aspect', p.117. The importance of the concept for William is shown in the brief article on William's thought by Stiegman in *The Medieval Theologians*, pp.140-42.

[18] William, *Enigma*, 6, p.96 (p.39).

[19] Bell, *Image and Likeness*, p.62.

[20] William, *Meditativae*, 6.11-12, p.114 (p.128).

[21] William, *Expositio*, p.22 (p.38).

[22] William, *Speculum*, 68, p.80 (p.75).

this aspect of the Spirit in the intra-Trinitarian relationships, and its foundational importance for his overall pneumatology.

Bernard of Clairvaux is less dependent on this idea in his presentation of the person of the Holy Spirit. Whilst he does use this thought occasionally, as in sermon twenty on the *Song of Songs*, there is much less indication of it as a basis for Bernard. In sermon twenty, Bernard writes that, "the Son lives and reigns with the Father in the unity of the Holy Spirit".[23] The overt weakness of this concept in Bernard's work is shown in sermon seventy-one, in which Bernard writes about unity in God, and the unity of Father and Son, without referring to the Holy Spirit.[24] It is interesting given the paucity of references that Etienne Gilson includes the concept in his *Mystical Theology of St. Bernard*, writings of the Holy Spirit as the "bond of union" in the Trinity as a result of His dual procession.[25] There is an indication in this that Gilson thought that this idea did influence Bernard's ideas, despite the fact that it was not directly used very much in his work.

The latent strength of this concept in the writings of the Cistercians is also shown in McDonnell's book, *The Other Hand of God*. This work deals only with early debates in Christian history regarding the immanent procession of the Holy Spirit, but its focus is very much on the mission of the Spirit; and yet the conclusion includes an attempt to construct an overall theology of the Spirit, of both His immanent and economic persons. McDonnell writes as part of this that, "the Holy Spirit is communion (koinonia), sharing, participation, fellowship in Trinitarian life".[26] Even this inference, which is drawn from ideas relating to the immanent procession, is directed at the mission of the Holy Spirit. However, despite the questionable methodology behind this statement, the impact which the concept of unity has on the reader throughout the works of both William and Bernard is revealed by this assertion.

The clearest teaching on this point in the writings of Richard of St. Victor is found in his letter to Bernard about the properties of the divine persons. The first part of this letter seems to address a query from Bernard about Augustine's Trinity of unity, equality and concord that has been examined already in this chapter. Richard is concise in his reply: the Father is unity because the other two subsist from Him, and He is thus the principle of the godhead; the Son is equality as the image of the Father;[27] in the Holy Spirit is then found the completion of the Trinity, on which basis He can be said to be the concord of the Trinity.[28] Richard then clarifies the person of the Holy Spirit by writing that all connection in the Trinity is attributed to the Holy Spirit alone because only

---

[23] Bernard, *Opera*, Vol.1, p.121. Other references to this concept are linked to thoughts on love, and will be dealt with below.

[24] *Ibid.*, Vol.2, pp.214-24 (pp.47-61).

[25] Gilson, *Mystical Theology*, p.94.

[26] McDonnell, *Other Hand*, p.228.

[27] The Holy Spirit cannot be said to be equality because there is no origin of a divine person in Himself, according to Richard.

[28] Richard, *De Tribus* (PL 196:991-94).

He has the same relation to both other members.[29] This is a useful passage for examining the position of the Holy Spirit as unity because there is no attempt to apply these characteristics to the economy of the persons – Richard is simply dealing with the immanent persons in their relationships.[30]

Peter Lombard writes about the Holy Spirit as union at different points, and in various ways, in his *Sentences*. The first major section, in *Distinctio* 10, follows Augustine's thought on the name of the third person: "That the Holy Spirit, as he is the communion of the Father and the Son, so also it is right for Him to have the name of that communion".[31] Lombard concludes that the Holy Spirit is so-called because both words pertain to both Father and Son. This line of thought is not really extended much beyond that found in Augustine. There is a second section of the *Sentences* dealing solely with this aspect of the Holy Spirit, which is part of a passage about the nature of the Spirit. Lombard notes that the third person is referred to in Scripture both as the Spirit of God and the Spirit of Christ, and raises the question from this whether the Holy Spirit is both God and of God? The answer that he gives is: "that the Holy Spirit is a thing of the same nature as the Father and the Son, and is also that nature".[32] This passage focuses on Biblical teachings about the work of the Holy Spirit, but Lombard's solution to the problems raised is important for understanding his views on the immanent person of the Spirit.

Peter Abelard has less significant teaching on this particular point, although he does include in both the *Introductio ad theologiam* and the *Theologia Christiana* the idea from Augustine that the name Holy Spirit implies that the third person is the commonness of the first two in His procession.[33] Anselm does not pick up on the idea that the Holy Spirit is unity in any direct teaching, although its influence can be seen in parts of the *Monologion* and *Proslogion*. The only major teaching on this subject in Anselm's works is found in the *Proslogion*, in which he states that "each part of the Trinity is none other than supremely simple unity and supremely unitary simplicity".[34] Gillian Evans notes in her work on Anselm's images of the Trinity that Thierry of Chartres picks up on Augustine's teaching of unity, equality and harmony in the *De Doctrina Christiana*. Based on this work, Thierry writes of the role of the Holy Spirit binding all things together in the Trinity.[35]

It is important to note these passages in which the authors deal purely with the idea that the Holy Spirit is union in the Trinity both because a grasp of their thought at this level informs our understanding of their application of this

---

[29] Richard, *De Tribus* (PL 196:991-94).

[30] The teaching in the *De Trinitate* on this issue is consistently linked into concepts of love, and will thus be examined below.

[31] Lombard, *Sentences*, 1.10.2.5, p.113 (PL 192:551, 1.10.7).

[32] *Ibid.*, 1.34.1.4, pp.247-48 (PL 192:614, 1.34.2).

[33] Abelard, *Introductio*, 1.12 (Vol. 3, p.324); *Theologia Christiana*, 1.5 (Vol. 2, p.73).

[34] Anselm, *Proslogion*, 23, Vol. 1, p.117 (p.100).

[35] Evans, 'St. Anselm's Images', pp.46-57.

directly to other attributes of the person and work of the Spirit, and also because this is influential in their overall conception of the Holy Spirit, even where there is no explicit link made to His identity as union in the Trinity.

Association of Unity with Love in the Person of the Holy Spirit

Although there was a lot of discussion of the Spirit purely as union in the twelfth century, secondary scholarship seems to have focused more on the connection between union and love, in particular, than on the main concept alone. It is possible that this is due to the concentration that writers had on the idea that the Holy Spirit is love without explicitly drawing this back to His more foundational identity as the communion of Father and Son. O'Donovan, writing about Augustine, shows how the love that is seen to be the Holy Spirit is based on His role as unity: "All love originates in the immanent love of the Godhead, which is at once a mutual relation between subject and object (the first and second Persons), the expression of the unity between them (which has its ground in the identity of being), and at the same time an independent subsistent (a third Person) alongside them".[36]

Peter Lombard wrote on many occasions in his *Sentences* about the Holy Spirit being that which was common to the Father and the Son, and thus being the connection between them. He also wrote a substantial amount on the Spirit's identity as love (as was shown in the chapter on that theme above). However, there was little direct interaction between these two concepts. *Distinctio* 32 is one section that does directly link them, discussing whether the Father and Son love through the Holy Spirit, if love is part of what God is. Lombard states in response to this that the "Holy Spirit is the communion of Father and Son by which they love each other".[37] Schupp, writing on the person of the Holy Spirit found in the *Sentences*, unites the two concepts as the primary identity of the Spirit.[38] In supporting this, Schupp quotes all the words and phrases connected to unity or love used by Lombard throughout the *Sentences*. The indication is that the love that is the Holy Spirit is a product of His more fundamental identity as communion, which is shown in the quote from Lombard given above.

Bernard of Clairvaux was one writer who wrote about unity more in connection with love, although there was little explicit teaching about the Spirit as union in Bernard's work as a whole. Sermon eight of Bernard's series on the Song of Songs, in which Bernard wrote more clearly about the attributes of the Holy Spirit than at any other time, linked unity and love together; and Bernard also mentioned the two ideas in the letter to Chartreuse, writing that it was charity (the Holy Spirit) that maintained unity in the Trinity.[39] Etienne Gilson uses the latter passage in his study of Bernard's mystical theology, and writes

---

[36] O'Donovan, *The Problem of Self-Love*, p.128.
[37] Lombard, *Sentences*, 1.32.1.1, pp.232-33 (PL 192:607, 1.32.1).
[38] Schupp, *Gnadenlehre*, p.216.
[39] Bernard, *Opera*, Vol. 3, p.149 (*On Loving God*, p.127).

that Bernard saw charity as the root of the Holy Spirit's identity as unity.[40] This is not particularly clear in Bernard's work, nor does Gilson convince in arguing this. Immediately before writing this passage, Gilson states that the Holy Spirit is the bond of union because of His procession from the Father and the Son.

Gilson goes on to contrast Bernard's position with that of William of St. Thierry. This is much more easy to understand, both in the corpus of William's works, and in Gilson's analysis. Union is the core of William's whole spirituality; and love, both within God and in the relationship between God and people, is a result of this union. Tomasic shows this basic position of William in his writing in his chapter on 'Neoplatonism and the Mysticism of William of St. Thierry'.[41]

The strength of William's teaching on the Holy Spirit as unity, discussed above in the previous section of this chapter, was consistently used to support ideas on the concept of love. In his commentaries both on Romans and on the Song of Songs, William is quick to include both concepts together, in order to draw out the message that he is seeking to teach from the relevant passages. In the latter commentary, William writes that the Holy Spirit is "nothing else than the unity of the Father and the Son of God, their Kiss, their Embrace, their Love, their Goodness, and whatever in that supremely simple Unity is common to both".[42] The concept of embrace, which joins the two ideas together, is also used in the commentary on Romans.[43] William takes a similar approach in his *On Contemplating God*, weaving together unity and love in the person of the Holy Spirit as preparation for a meditation on these themes in the experience that people have of the Spirit.[44]

In other works, such as the *Enigma of Faith*, William begins with a more thorough grounding in his basic perception of the Holy Spirit as union in the godhead before he moves on to other applications. The *Enigma* in particular has a great deal of discussion of the Trinitarian persons themselves and their relationships, in which the Holy Spirit is primarily described as unity; and only then does William introduce the concept of love as one result of this identity of the Spirit.[45]

In the writings of both Richard of St. Victor and Peter Abelard, it appears that love is the dominating attribute. However, even here, it is the unity that the Holy Spirit provides that remains at the root of His personhood. Richard's idea of *condilectio*, of the Holy Spirit not only joining Father and Son in love but of loving Himself as part of this relationship, is one that seems to place the stress on love, but when considered reveals the importance of communion in the Spirit's identity. Bligh shows this in referring to Richard teaching that the

---

[40] Gilson, *Mystical Theology*, pp.94-95.
[41] Tomasic, 'Neoplatonism and the Mysticism', p.73.
[42] William, *Song of Songs*, 8.95, pp.202-04 (p.78).
[43] William, *Expositio*, p.162, (p.224).
[44] William, *De Contemplando*, 11, pp.94-100 (pp.54-56).
[45] William, *Enigma*, 6, p.96 (p.39); 98, p.176 (p.115).

perfection of love is when two wills are united in the love of a third.[46] Nico den Bok follows the same line in his study of Richard, and traces this idea of divine plenitude back to Abelard, who in turn drew on Gregory the Great's thought that there cannot be love without at least two persons.[47] Mary Melone states that *condilectio* refers more to "communication" than "fusion" between the first two persons.[48]

The progression of thought from the Spirit purely as union to a connection between this and love is part of a journey for these writers towards the experience of the Holy Spirit in their spirituality. As will shortly be shown, William remains at the forefront of this thought, but all of those studied thus far conceived of the Spirit primarily as drawing the Trinity together as one, resulting from His procession from both Father and Son. Whilst love was the prime name they gave to the resulting relationship between the Trinitarian persons, union remained the fundamental identity of the Holy Spirit.

The Holy Spirit as Union in His Economic State

Just as union is the root concept for the various terms attributed to the immanent Holy Spirit, it is also a foundational thought from which the experience of the Spirit in the life of the believer can be better understood. This will be fully drawn out in the concluding chapter below, which will seek to tie together the various ideas that have been discussed in this book. In this present section, the writings that deal specifically with this point will be studied to show the strength of this thought in its basic form. The concept is found to some extent in Lombard's *Sentences*, but only William of St. Thierry meditated on this specific theme at any length, his reflections showing both the outworking of the Spirit's immanent identity as unity and being a guide for understanding the overall conception of the person of the Holy Spirit in the twelfth century.

The recurring image throughout William's spirituality is of the believer being drawn into communion with the godhead by the person who is Himself communion.[49] This is not only used in reference to ecstatic experiences of God, but is also seen as being the hidden reality of the Christian life. The result of this union is the transformation of the person, either in the gradual change of the will into line with that of God, or in the sudden experience of the intimate presence of the Trinity in the life of the believer.

This idea is found throughout the corpus of William's works, in his

---

[46] Bligh, 'Richard of St. Victor's *De Trinitate*', pp.118-39.

[47] Den Bok, *Communicating the Most High*, p.287; Abelard, *Introductio*, 2.123 (Vol. 3, p.469).

[48] "La *condilectio* esprime un'idea particolare de comunione intradivine: nello Spirito la comunione del Padre e del Figlio si realizza non come fusione, ma come *comunicazione*, nella reciprocità della loro apertura verso la terza persona". Melone, 'Lo Spirito Santo', p.60 (Melone's italics).

[49] Thomas sees this as the overall focus of William's spirituality. R. Thomas, 'William of St. Thierry: Our Life in the Trinity', *Monastic Studies* 3 (1965), pp.139-165.

meditations and commentaries as well as his more theological treatises. The *De Contemplando Deo* has a lot of material on the Spirit as unity both relating to human experience and identity: "We become one in God through God's unity in us";[50] and this idea is followed up in his *Meditations*.[51] The commentary on the Song of Songs is rightly more poetical in its description of the experience of the Holy Spirit: "This embrace extends to man, but it surpasses man. For this embrace is the Holy Spirit. He is the Communion, the charity, the Friendship, the Embrace of the Father and of the Son of God; and he himself is all these things in the love of Bridegroom and Bride".[52] In the *Mirror of Faith*, William takes a more philosophical line, working with the idea outlined above that as the communion of Father and Son, the Holy Spirit is their mutual recognition and knowing. William goes on from this to argue that people know the Father and Son because of their mutual knowing, the Holy Spirit; and that unity is accomplished in the hearts of people because of the likeness of God that is integrated through the grace that the Spirit imparts.[53]

This element of William's teaching has received a lot of comment from writers examining his spirituality. One aspect of this that many stress is the participation that people are able to have in the Trinity because of the work and person of the Holy Spirit. McDonnell is one writer who picks up on this, stating that the human experience of God is a result of the union that is accomplished through the Holy Spirit.[54] David Bell writes of this that "man participates in the Holy Spirit, who is the substantial unity of the Father and Son".[55] Renna summarises William's thought thus: "as the Holy Spirit unites Father and Son, the Holy Spirit unites the holy soul with the other two persons of the Trinity."[56] Gilson also picks up on this idea from William and from Bernard, writing that for both these men, the "Holy Spirit therefore plays the part of the bond by which the soul is united to God and the spirit participates in the divine";[57] or again, "The Father and the Son are one by the Holy Spirit. It is therefore by the Holy Spirit that we are enabled to enter into union with God ... in receiving the Holy Spirit under the form of a gift, namely the gift of grace, we thereby participate in the Divine Life".[58]

Other writers draw out the difference that is found in William's thought between the union that the Holy Spirit is in the Trinity and that which He effects in the hearts of men. Verdeyen, for example, notes that "dans la Trinité, le Saint-Esprit *est* la charité et l'unité mutuelle des Personnes; en nous, il *fait* ou

---

[50] William, *De Contemplando*, 11, p.104 (p.57).
[51] William, *Meditativae*, 6.11-12, p.114 (p.128), 6.11-12, p.114 (p.128).
[52] William, *Song of Songs*, 11.132, pp.282-84 (p.106).
[53] William, *Speculum*, 68-70, pp.80-82 (pp.74-78).
[54] McDonnell, *Other Hand*, p.177.
[55] Bell, *Image and Likeness*, p.176.
[56] Renna, 'Augustine and the Early Cistercians', pp.388-89.
[57] Gilson, *Mystical Theology*, p.23.
[58] *Ibid.*, p.94.

il *réalise* la même charité et unité d'Esprit".[59] Both Bell and Brooke teach on the same lines, that the union effected in people is more a resemblance than true unity. Brooke states that the Holy Spirit restores our resemblance to God, which process is due to participation in the life of the Holy Spirit by sharing in the mutual union of Father and Son.[60] David Bell also sees a similar difference, writing that the Holy Spirit is *unitas* in God, whereas He is *similitudo* in man.[61] Whilst these are vaild observations that the Holy Spirit is not identical as union in His immanent and economic identities, the concept that He draws people into fellowship with the Father and Son because He is that fellowship in the Trinity does illuminate this important, basic view of the person of the Holy Spirit.

It is unfortunate that more writers do not focus on applying this attribute of the Spirit to His economic mission. Peter Lombard does give indications in two minor parts of the *Sentences*, both of which concentrate on the immanent identity of the Holy Spirit as that which unites Father and Son, but do so in the context of the economy of the Spirit.[62] The first of these sections is part of a discussion of the language used in the Bible regarding the Spirit being both "of God" and "of Christ". In between these references to the Spirit's work and passages from Paul about the mission of the Holy Spirit, Lombard stresses the unifying role of the Spirit in the immanent Trinity, thus implying a similar role in His economic state without explaining what this entails. The second *Distinctio* looks at the Spirit's union of the immanent godhead with Christ when He lived on earth, something that was achieved by the "grace of union".[63] The fact that this bond was achieved on the basis of the Spirit's immanent identity indicates an extension of His work as union with regards to believers.

Conclusion

It is important that this treatment of the Holy Spirit as communion or fellowship in the Trinity comes at the end of the thematic section because each of the preceding chapters feeds into this root thought for the writers of the twelfth century. All of the attributes that were ascribed to the Holy Spirit were based on two ideas: that He proceeded from both the Father and the Son; and that He was that which somehow joined the first two persons together.[64]

This belief about the person of the Holy Spirit was the key not only to basic pneumatological understandings, but also to the interrelationships of the Trinitarian persons, and to writers' mystical thought concerning the godhead, the interaction of the divine with the created order, and people's experience of God. The Cistercians (and particularly William of St. Thierry) devoted more

---

[59] Verdeyen, *Le Théologie Mystique*, p.93 (his italics).
[60] Brooke, 'The Trinitarian Aspect', p.107.
[61] Bell, *Image and Likeness*, p.134.
[62] The relevant sections are 1.34 and 1.37 (PL 192:613-17, 620-26).
[63] Lombard, *Sentences*, 1.37.1 (PL 192:620).
[64] These ideas will be discussed at length in the concluding chapter on the procession of the Holy Spirit.

attention to this specific idea because of their focus on mysticism and the experience of the Spirit. Other writers showed the importance of this aspect in their fewer explicit teachings, which indicated its foundational significance for their overall understanding of the persons of the Holy Spirit.

The various terms that are included in this chapter were not prominent in the writings of Augustine (although the basic idea is included in both the *De Trinitate* and the *De Doctrina Christiana*), and it seems that theological thought gathered together the various terms that Augustine did use under this one principle in the twelfth century.

CHAPTER 12

The Procession of the Holy Spirit

It should be clear by this stage that the major writers studied in this book from Anselm of Canterbury to Peter Lombard provided significant ideas on the immanent procession of the Holy Spirit. This chapter will seek to summarise their contribution in two ways: the first of these will examine basic processional issues, looking at dual procession, primacy in procession, equality in procession and divine interrelationships; and the second will deal with the mode of procession of the Holy Spirit, as commonness, mutual love and other terms that were applied to the third person of the Trinity.[1] The concentration throughout this last chapter will be exclusively on the immanent procession of the Spirit, which has been the major concentration of the whole book.

Basic Processional Issues

It is important to begin this conclusion by drawing out fundamental thoughts on the procession of the Holy Spirit that were discussed in the studies of individual writers in the first half of this book, but which were not analysed in the second, thematic section. The various topics analysed here are significant for understanding the nature of the procession from Father and Son, and particularly so as regards the controversy with the Greeks; and are the foundation from which the personhood of the Spirit is explored regarding the mode of His procession.

The Dual Procession of the Holy Spirit

It is right to start, albeit briefly, with the simple affirmation that the Holy Spirit proceeded from both the Father and the Son, in light of the debate that was taking place with the Orthodox church over the *filioque* clause. This needs little depth of analysis at this stage because the following parts of the "basic processional issues" section deal with issues resulting from this first belief. Anselm of Canterbury and Anselm of Havelberg both, of course, had dual procession at the centre of their respective presentations of the Latin position in debate with the Greek church.

It is noticeable that the two other writers who wrote "systematic" studies of Christian thought, Peter Abelard and Peter Lombard, both felt that they needed

---

[1] This chapter is largely a summary of the second, thematic part of this thesis, and so there will be fewer references to secondary material because these have been included in the relevant previous chapters.

to present direct answers to the Greek position. Lombard includes this at the beginning of his teaching on the immanent procession of the Holy Spirit, in *Distinctio* 11 of the *Sentences*. Having reasoned from Biblical evidence for dual procession, he shows his awareness of this issue by entitling one part of this *Distinctio*: "This shows from the Greek authorities that the Holy Spirit also proceeds from the Son".[2] He concludes his evidence from four earlier writers by stating: "See that we have clear testimony from the Greek doctors, which shows that the Holy Spirit proceeds from the Father and the Son".[3] Peter Abelard uses the same method to support dual procession in the face of Greek opposition, although he leaves this section until much later in his *Introductio*. It does not appear until late in book two, but Abelard does have a greater thoroughness in his evidence against the Greeks from both Biblical and Patristic material.[4]

The fact that both Abelard and Lombard included these direct passages supporting the Latin position shows that this issue was of significance throughout the period covered by this book. The remainder of this first section of the chapter will examine ways in which dual procession was used to support the position of the Holy Spirit and the relationships within the Trinity.

Primacy in Procession

There are two elements in the issue of primacy in procession, which concerns whether the Holy Spirit proceeded more from one of the first two persons than the other. The first is a question surrounding appropriation of Augustine's teaching that the Holy Spirit, whilst He proceeded from both Father and Son, proceeded primarily from the Father. The second is a solution to this dilemma which states that the Holy Spirit proceeded from the "unity of the divine nature".

Augustine wrote in book fifteen of the *De Trinitate* that the Holy Spirit proceeded primarily from the Father because the Son received the capability to have a person proceeding from Him as a result of His generation.[5] There is a simple logic to this line of thinking: if the Father had not begotten the Son, then there would be no Son from whom the Holy Spirit could proceed. The watercourse analogy supports this idea: the water rises in the spring (Father), and then flows down the river (Son) to collect in the pool (Holy Spirit). The water does get to the pool from the river, but only because the spring has created the river.

When this concept was discussed by twelfth-century writers, they generally agreed with Augustine. Mews notes that Peter Abelard writes that the Holy Spirit proceeds principally from the Father in his *Theologia Christiana*,[6] which is the same idea that William of St. Thierry teaches in his *Enigma of Faith* and

---

[2] Lombard, *Sentences*, 1.11.2-5, pp.116-17 (PL 192:552-53, 1.11.5).
[3] *Ibid*.
[4] Abelard, *Introductio*, 2.157-60 (Vol. 3, p.483-85).
[5] Augustine, *De Trinitate*, 15.17, pp.503-04 (p.419).
[6] Mews, *Development of the Theologia*, p.130.

Anselm of Havelberg used in discussion with Nechites.[7] Only Peter Lombard writes that neither of the first two persons has primacy in the procession of the Holy Spirit.[8] Even this statement is qualified in an analysis by Peter of Augustine's views, in which Lombard allows that Augustine was correct in what he had written.

The problem that is raised by the above discussion is that it does seem to indicate levels in the godhead regarding the procession of the Spirit that might lead readers to hold that the Father is greater than the Son, and both greater than the Holy Spirit. In order to avoid this implication, some writers focused on the unity of the first two persons as being the source of the procession of the third. Anselm of Canterbury is very clear on this point in his *De Processione*, using the idea to underpin much of his argument. The most helpful part of this is his analysis of the Nicene Creed's statement that the Holy Spirit proceeds from the Father.[9] Anselm shows that this cannot mean procession from the Father *in that He is* Father, as this would make the Spirit a son. Instead, the meaning must be from the Father *as He is God*, which indicates to Anselm procession from the Son (who is also God) as well. This idea answers a major Greek objection to dual procession, which is that this might imply the existence of two spirits. The focus on the unity of Father and Son in producing the procession of the Holy Spirit clarifies the western position on this point.[10]

Two other writers take up a similar position to Anselm of Canterbury. Anselm of Havelberg provides Nechites with a more simple version early in his debate, based on John 10:30, which teaches that the Son and the Father are one. In light of this, Anselm challenges Nechites to explain how the Spirit can proceed from only one of these divine persons?[11] Peter Lombard also writes that the Father and Son are one principle of the Holy Spirit because the Spirit proceeds or is given in the same way by both.[12]

This solution to the quandary concerning primacy in procession is useful because it focuses solely on the Holy Spirit, and how He proceeds. In addition, there is already an indication in this basic teaching of the extension that would be made about the Spirit's identity as that which joins together the first two persons.

Unique Relationships Within the Trinity

Two writers in this period taught regarding the uniqueness of the three persons as a result of their respective processions. In this, the procession of the Holy Spirit from Father and Son was an important factor in the models that were

---

[7] William, *Enigma*, 77, pp.158-59 (pp.98-99); Anselm H, *Dialogi*, 2.25 (PL 188:1205).
[8] Lombard, *Sentences*, 1.12.1.1-3, p.118 (PL 192:553, 1.12.1-2).
[9] Anselm C, *De Processione*, 2, Vol.2, p.190 (p.404).
[10] Gillian Evans notes the strength of this in Anselm's *De Processione* in her book *Anselm and a New Generation* (pp.54-55).
[11] Anselm H, *Dialogi*, 2.3 (PL 188:1170).
[12] Lombard, *Sentences*, 1.29.4.1, pp.219 (PL 192:602, 1.29.4).

created. Anselm of Canterbury used this method as part of his arguments in the *De Processione* against the Greeks, while Richard of St. Victor sought to explain why the godhead exists in its Trinitarian form using a similar technique.

Anselm introduced his set of associations late in the *De Processione*, seeking to show how the western position provided complementary yet unique relationships which maintained the unity of the three persons in one godhead.[13] The basis for his approach was that each person had two characteristics in common with the other persons, and one that distinguishes them: the Holy Spirit, for instance, was the only person not to have a person proceeding from Himself, but shared with another person not having the Father as Father, and not having the Son as Son.[14] The whole model is slightly tautological, but does present a neatness concerning divine relations that cannot be created from the Greek position. The most important feature is the distinctiveness of the Son and Holy Spirit, which the Monarchical approach does not allow for in the same way.

Richard gives his model in book five of the *De Trinitate* as he works logically from the standpoint of no knowledge towards the Trinity. He begins his ideas by stating that there are two possibilities for procession: immediate and mediate. Having declared that there must be one person who must exist from Himself, his next step is to write that one person must proceed immediately from the first. He then argues (in a style that brings to mind the "unity of divine nature") that the third person must proceed from the perfection of the first two.[15] Richard tests his model further, enquiring why a fourth person does not proceed from the third, and responds that there are no further unique processions that exist (*ex nihilo*, immediate or mediate) and that there must therefore be one divine person from whom no other proceeds.[16] As part of this discussion, Richard writes that the persons are defined by their origin, and if two persons had the same origin there would be no method of definition. This strikes at the Greek position on the procession of the Son and Holy Spirit, but Richard gives no indication that he had this in mind.

The two models created by Anselm and Richard provide further evidence of the strength of the Western position on the respective processions of Son and Spirit. They show that the *filioque* theory creates clarity not only in differentiating between the two processions, but also in understanding the interrelationships of the divine persons.

The Equality of the Holy Spirit in His Procession

One more brief point that should be made about the basic procession of the

---

[13] Anselm C, *De Processione*, 16, Vol.2, pp.216-17 (p.431).

[14] Hopkins writes of the effectiveness of this model in showing that the different properties of the persons prevent them from being seen to be identical. Hopkins, *Companion to the Study of Anselm*, pp.96-97.

[15] Richard, *De Trinitate*, 5.8, pp.203-05.

[16] He also notes that, if this were not the case, then there would be an infinite number of divine persons.

Holy Spirit concerns the equality of the three persons that was seen to be reinforced by the concept of dual procession. This was implied in Augustine's teaching, first on the inseparableness of the three persons, and then in the procession of the Spirit from the one substance of Father and Son. Two authors, Anselm of Canterbury and Peter Lombard, devoted sections of their work to state this idea directly.

Anselm of Canterbury's focus in part four of the *De Processione* actually centres on the equality of the Son in the dual procession of the Spirit, with implications arising from this regarding the status of the Spirit Himself.[17] Anselm is considering in what way the Bible talks of the Son sending the Holy Spirit, and argues that this must be done in the same way as He is sent by the Father. The reasoning behind this is that, if the Spirit proceeds from the Father alone, then the Father has something which the Son does not after the generation of the second person. This would imply inequality in the status of the first two persons. The Greek position, which places the Son in the middle position in the sending of the Spirit, does not solve the problem for Anselm, but enhances the lack of equality between the persons.[18] In asserting the identical status of Father and Son in this way, Anselm supports the view that the person proceeding from these two must also be equal in every way.

Peter Lombard stresses the equality of the Holy Spirit with the Father and Son in His procession fairly late in his ideas on the Spirit in the *Sentences*. It might be expected that this would result from teaching about primacy in procession (*Distinctio* 12), but it is not until *Distinctio* 20 that Lombard deals with the status of the Spirit, in the context of teaching on the equality and indifference of all three persons.[19] The generation of the persons is said not to show priority in any way, but merely origin. The attributes of the godhead are transferred to Son and Spirit as a result of their respective processions.

There was thus clear teaching in the writings of twelfth-century authors concerning the basic procession of the Holy Spirit from Father and Son. The next stage in this chapter is to analyse how the different writers developed the mode in which the Spirit proceeded, extending from these foundational thoughts.

The Mode of Procession of the Holy Spirit

This second part of the chapter will examine the various attributes that were studied in the second half of the book to show how writers used the terms to describe the mode of the Spirit's procession. The emphasis here will thus be on how each idea expressed not the identity of the Holy Spirit, but the way in which the Spirit proceeded from the Father and Son. This will begin by looking at the concept of communion, which is central to understanding twelfth-century thought on both the identity and procession of the Holy Spirit.

---

[17] Anselm C, *De Processione* 4, Vol. 2, pp.191-94 (pp.405-08).
[18] Anselm of Havelberg argued with Nechites about this 'media relatione' position of the Son in the Greek understanding of the Spirit's procession.
[19] Lombard, *Sentences*, 1.20, pp.172-74 (PL 192:579-80, 1.20).

The Holy Spirit Proceeding as the Unity of Father and Son

The best description of this foundational thought about the procession of the Holy Spirit is by Joseph Ratzinger, which was quoted at length in the introduction to the previous chapter: "The Spirit's paradoxical and unique property is being *communio*, having his highest selfness precisely in being fully the movement of *communio*".[20] The Holy Spirit proceeded as that which drew the first two persons together in communion with each other. The writers of the twelfth century held strongly to this view, and expressed it in a variety of forms. They took this on from Augustine, who had taught on these lines in his exploration of the person of the Spirit in His procession in book five of the *De Trinitate*;[21] and whose unity, equality, harmony triad, found in the *De Doctrina Christiana*, implied a similar mode of procession.[22] One element from Augustine that found repeated favour was his work with the name Holy Spirit, signifying that which the Trinitarian persons held in common.

William of St. Thierry was the most consistent writer in his portrayal of the Holy Spirit as the communion of Father and Son. Indeed, the first section of this chapter shows that William did not greatly involve himself in discussions of more basic processional issues. Throughout the corpus of William's work, the emphasis is on the role of the Spirit as He proceeds in the Trinity, "existing as unity" and creating concord between the first two persons.[23] It is this that forms the basis of all that William writes about the identity and work of the Holy Spirit.

Richard of St. Victor does not have clear teaching on this element of the Spirit's procession in the *De Trinitate*, although as will be shortly be shown, it is implied in the terminology that he does use. His most direct writing on this point comes in his letter of explanation to Bernard of Clairvaux about the use of Augustine's unity, equality, harmony to describe the three persons of the Trinity. Richard states that, as the Holy Spirit is the completion of the Trinity, all connection in the Trinity is attributed to Him.[24] This point is backed up by the fact that only the Holy Spirit has the same relationship with the other two members of the godhead.

It is interesting that Peter Lombard begins his processional teaching on the Holy Spirit with love and unity before progressing to the more basic issues discussed above. Whilst it is true that love is the first term ascribed to the Spirit, Lombard shows later in the same *Distinctio* that this is based on His procession as the communion of Father and Son. He explains this both from his teaching

---

[20] Ratzinger, 'The Holy Spirit as Communio', p.327.
[21] Augustine, *De Trinitate*, 5.12, pp.218-20 (p.197).
[22] Augustine, *De Doctrina*, 1.5, pp.16-17.
[23] He writes in the meditations that unity in the Trinity is "effected" by the Holy Spirit. William, *Meditations*, 8.5.
[24] Richard, *De Tribus* (PL 196:991-93).

on love, and from Augustine's use of the name "Holy Spirit".[25] Anselm of Havelberg is one other writer who uses this concept centrally in his thinking when discussing the procession of the Holy Spirit with Nechites.[26] This is the idea to which Anselm repeatedly returns when questioned about different aspects of the Spirit's procession, and never appears to be denied by his opponent.

The mode of procession of the Holy Spirit is thus seen as that which joins the Trinity together. He exists by virtue of the need for unity and completeness in the godhead, and this is reinforced by other terms that expand upon this theme.

The Holy Spirit's Procession as Mutual Love

The importance of Augustine in the association of love with the person of the Holy Spirit cannot be overemphasised. In the *De Trinitate*, this idea, regarding procession, comes in book six, following the teaching that has just been examined on communion. Augustine wrote that love was one of the best terms to describe the mutual interaction of Father and Son that resulted in the procession of the Holy Spirit.

This line of thought was taken, and expanded upon, by authors in the twelfth century. All of the writers studied in this book used love as one of the processional models for the Holy Spirit as it had been suggested by Augustine. However, some went beyond this in their thoughts, detailing further how the Holy Spirit proceeded within the divine essence as love. Peter Lombard sought to show in his initial presentation of the procession of the Spirit how love was able both to exist in the first two persons, and yet be the mode by which the third person proceeded.[27]

Two other authors, Anselm of Canterbury and Hugh of St. Victor, transformed one of Augustine's analogies of the Trinity (mind, knowledge, love) into their main processional teaching about the persons. Anselm of Canterbury took this approach in his *Monologion*, writing that self-love is consequent upon self-consciousness and self-knowledge.[28] Anselm strengthens his argument by showing from his model the interrelationships and equality of the three persons, as well as supporting the concept of dual procession. Hugh of St. Victor takes the same approach in his meditation on the divine essence.[29]

Both of the Victorine writers, Hugh and Richard, brought additional teaching about the procession of the Spirit as love with their respective ideas about *complaceo* and *condilectio*. These terms, which seek to understand more deeply the relative positions of Father and Son towards the Holy Spirit, also bring the third person into the love relations on account of this mode of His

---

[25] Lombard, *Sentences*, 1.10.2.5, p.113 (PL 192:558, 1.10.7).

[26] Anselm H, *Dialogi*, 2.10 (PL 188:1178-79).

[27] Lombard, *Sentences*, 1.10.1.4-2.1, p.111 (PL 192:550, 1.10.3-4).

[28] Anselm C, *Monologion*, 49-54, Vol.1, pp.64-66 (pp.60-62).

[29] Hugh, *Didascalion* 7.21 (PL 176:831).

procession. The community of Trinitarian persons that is created as a result in turn strengthens the overall concept of the identities and work of the members of the godhead.

The ideas on mutual love in the twelfth century must be recognised as part of the wider processional teaching on the Holy Spirit as that which draws the Father and Son together. This is a particularly significant aspect because of the Biblical teaching about the nature of God as love, and because it is a powerful characteristic showing the bonds between the persons of the Trinity.

Other Processional Terms Regarding the Holy Spirit

In order to conclude correctly, it is important to note briefly the processional importance of other terms that have been looked at in the main body of this book. Of these attributes, will was not used by twelfth-century writers as a major concept for the procession of the Holy Spirit; and gift, despite the best attempts of authors to achieve a united picture of the immanent and economic states of the Spirit, and the use of "giveable" to solve this dilemma, remained tied to the overall picture of the Holy Spirit rather than His immanent procession. There was some support from gift terminology for dual procession, but again this relied on the language of "sending" thus linking to the economic state.

However, it is important to state the processional teaching that Peter Abelard and Richard of St. Victor both gave regarding goodness, both in the context of a power, wisdom, goodness trinity. Marcia Colish stated in her book on Peter Lombard that the power, wisdom, goodness model "does not solve processional issues".[30] However, both Peter and Richard use this idea precisely as the basis for understanding the procession of the Holy Spirit. For Abelard, the strength of this idea is in the completeness that these three terms give to the overall godhead: nothing is lacking where there is power, wisdom and goodness, and together they create perfection.[31]

Richard of St. Victor begins the *De Trinitate* with power, wisdom, goodness as a processional proof for the Trinity. Book six, however, contains his more solid teaching on the processional significance of this model, supporting the idea of the dual procession of the Holy Spirit because of the impossibility for goodness to exist without true power and true wisdom.[32] These terms are thus used to support the identity, equality and nature of the procession of the Spirit from the Father and the Son.

A Twelfth-Century Perspective of the Procession of the Holy Spirit

This chapter has sought to put together and summarise the thoughts of the writers studied in this book concerning the procession of the Holy Spirit. The importance of the propriety of dual procession was stressed throughout the

---

[30] Colish, *Peter Lombard 1*, p.249.

[31] Abelard, *Summi Boni*, 1.2, p.6.

[32] Richard, *De Trinitate*, 6.15, pp.247-48 (PL 196:980).

period, and this was not simply in opposition to the Greek position, but a result of the character and relationships of the Spirit as He proceeded from the Father and the Son. The procession and the identity of the Holy Spirit were thus one and the same in the minds of these authors, and were that He was that which joined together the first two persons as a uniting bond, symbolised by the attributes of love (primarily), goodness, will and gift.

It must be noted that this position is arrived at as a result of the synthesis of the various writings studied. However, while few writers' pneumatology was clearly expressed in these terms, this definition helps to understand the thought of each of the individuals included in this study.

Anselm of Havelberg was perhaps the closest in his presentation to the conclusions of this book, helped by his interaction with Greek opposition, and by the concentration on the person of the Spirit. Peter Lombard's *Sentences* contained all the major ideas that have been looked at, but they were less connected due to the wide scope of his work. William of St. Thierry's work best represents the focus on the Holy Spirit as that which unites the Father and Son, and is the most consistent over an extremely wide range of styles. If there is a weakness in William's work, it is the lack of sustained theological reflection due to his desire to engage himself and his readers with an experience of the Spirit. Richard was the most innovative writer, and the most significant in many areas (such as love). His "systematic" work, along with the more devotional material, does almost leave out some of the areas studied, such as will and gift, but the overall tenor of his writings are certainly in line with the thrust of this book.

Anselm of Canterbury's position at the beginning of scholasticism shows in comparison with these other authors, as there is less depth in his work on the identity of the Holy Spirit. His metaphysical appropriation of Augustine's analogies was valuable as a root from which later writers studied the person of the Spirit, but Anselm himself seems less convinced by the use of attributes to describe the Holy Spirit, as was shown in the *De Processione*. Peter Abelard's logical strength, and the depth of his wide theology, mean that the person of the Holy Spirit does not figure as greatly in his work as in that of other writers (except in contentious passages such as that on the World Soul). However, when the Spirit is referred to, Abelard supports all of the terms and ideas that have been looked at through this book. Hugh of St. Victor had similar weaknesses, as regards this study, to Peter Abelard. Bernard of Clairvaux's concentration on the economy of the Holy Spirit meant that he left little systematic teaching on the immanent procession, but what he did write supported his friend, William of St. Thierry.

The writers studied in this book thus shared a common perception of the Holy Spirit, both in His procession and His identity, as the unifying bond between Father and Son. Whilst the basic terminology was inherited from Augustine, these authors used Biblical, Patristic and rational means to explore further the person of the Holy Spirit. Despite their varying backgrounds and approaches, the common view of the Spirit was expressed through systematic, meditative and experiential writings. This study has shown how other concepts were tied into the root idea to deepen the understanding of the nature and mode of the immanent procession of the Holy Spirit.

CHAPTER 13

Conclusion

This book has sought to fill an important gap in the history of pneumatology. The different backgrounds, interests and approaches of the writers studied created a breadth and depth of writing on the Holy Spirit in this period, which was helped by the close proximity in which they lived and worked.[1] In order to study twelfth-century thought on the immanent Holy Spirit, it has been important both to look at individual perspectives within the diverse positions, and to analyse the collective contribution of all the authors to the various aspects of the Spirit that have been highlighted.

The analysis has shown that there was agreement between the writers about the nature of the immanent Holy Spirit and the mode of His procession. This accord existed despite the public disputes over terminology, and the different foci of individual authors. All believed that the Holy Spirit is the communion of Father and Son, drawing the first two persons together in one love, one goodness, one will. This is the basis for His economic procession to creation as the gift of the Trinity, in order that He might show God's goodness and draw people into the unity of the godhead by imparting love and communicating the will of God.

The discovery and existence of this consensus is important for many areas of historical theology, and this conclusion will discuss three major contributions that this study can make. The most immediate subjects that are affected are twelfth-century theology and spirituality. The pneumatology that has been expressed through the preceeding chapters has been generally overlooked in works on the period, excepting studies of the writings of William of St. Thierry. Instead, the focus has either been on Gilbert of Poitiers's refusal to attribute specific characteristics to immanent divine persons, or on the debates over Peter Abelard and William of Conches' thoughts on Plato's World Soul.

However, this book has shown that there was a strong, positive train of thought on the Holy Spirit in the twelfth century, continuing the work begun by Anselm of Canterbury in his appropriation of Augustine's descriptions of the Spirit. In their teaching, the authors clearly emphasised a correct presentation of the Holy Spirit in both His immanent and economic states, even when an individual was not seeking to write 'spiritual' work (Peter Abelard and Peter

---

[1] The Cistercians may not have lived in Paris, but it is clear from their involvement with Abelard, and from their writings, that they were in contact with the schools there.

Lombard are the best examples of this). The concentration of this work on the ideas about the immanent person is important for two reasons: firstly, it reflects the importance of this aspect for the twelfth-century writers (which is often not shown in works on this period); and secondly, the discussions that took place about the various aspects of the Spirit's personhood illuminate the work ascribed to the Holy Spirit in creation, and in relationship with people. The conclusions reached here should, therefore, impact future study of the spirituality of each of the writers included in the book.

One significant effect should be a recognition of a basic unity in the perception of the different authors about the identity of the Holy Spirit. The debates about attributes and personhood in the Trinity between the Cistercians and Peter Abelard have received so much comment that secondary scholarship seems to teach that there was no major consensus between the writers studied in this book. However, this analysis, particularly that of William and Bernard's use of goodness and will, shows that there was a fundamental agreement about the nature of the immanent third person.

There are wider implications here beyond the pneumatology of these writers. Three sets of relations in particular need reviewing. The first of these is the impact of Anselm of Canterbury on the generations following him. The 'father of scholasticism' opened the way for more reason-based enquiry into theology and the Trinity, but it is clear from this research that his initial work on Augustine's thoughts about the Holy Spirit was quickly extended by the more definite application of attributes to the person of the Spirit. William's use of the communion concept, Richard's work on the Spirit as love and Peter Lombard's discussion of gift terminology all move these ideas far beyond those expressed by Augustine and Anselm. As a result, it is unclear to what extent these writers viewed Anselm as a forerunner of their work, if at all.

The second set of relations that requires comment is between Peter Abelard on the one hand, and William of St. Thierry and Bernard of Clairvaux on the other. There has been a lot of analysis on the disputes and the trials of Abelard, but this book indicates that there remained fundamental agreement on significant areas under dispute. This seems to have been the case even with those accusations that involve the Holy Spirit, but whether this is mirrored in the other charges remains to be seen.

The final, fascinating relationship that has been ignored by secondary writers is that between Bernard of Clairvaux and Richard of St. Victor. The letter from the latter to the former, included in Migne's collection of Richard's works, has not received major comment from any writer on the period. Given the significance of this document, particularly for the power, wisdom, goodness debate, this is surprising. The influence of the school of St. Victor in this and other discussions may prove important, especially as the letter would seem to indicate that Bernard sought Richard's advice on the appropriateness of these three designations. The fact that Hugh also taught a version of the power, wisdom, goodness model, yet was not involved on either side in the accusations against Peter Abelard, is another interesting component of the relationship of the Victorine school to the surrounding academic world.

This book thus provides both a contribution and a challenge to study of the twelfth century. Besides the main goal, to examine the immanent person of the Holy Spirit in this period, this work also gives a greater context for work on the spirituality of individual writers. In addition to the pneumatological impact, the consensus of views found in the different individuals and groups studied shows that we must be aware of the influence of many different 'schools' in studying any author in the twelfth century.

The second issue in historical theology that has been addressed is the addition of *filioque* to the Nicene Creed that led to the split between the Eastern and Western churches. This was not simply the case because of renewed contact at the end of the eleventh century, leading to discussions for both Anselm of Canterbury and Anselm of Havelberg with Greek opponents on this subject. The application of their pneumatology to the Greek position by later writers such as Peter Abelard and Peter Lombard was partly due to the historical climate, but was also a result of the identity of the Spirit that they were teaching, which challenged the Monarchical model taught by the Orthodox church.

The discussion of Anselm of Havelberg with Nechites is particularly instructive in this matter. The main question put to Anselm was whether dual procession implied the existence of two Spirits, one from the Father and the other from the Son. Anselm's response concentrated on the unity of the first two persons in the procession of the third. In arguing his case, Anselm spoke of the Holy Spirit as the communion of Father and Son, and their mutual love. Throughout the debate, Nechites does not deny this identity of the Spirit, and because of this suggests at the end a common council to affirm the *filioque*.

The writers studied above teach much that strengthens Anselm's case. The idea that the Holy Spirit should be seen in some way to be that which draws the Father and Son together was expanded on in a variety of helpful ways by different writers in the twelfth century, including more work on the concept of mutual love, and other terms that are used to describe the Spirit. Much of this speculation surrounded the immanent third person, and attempted to explore how the Biblical witness implied the nature of the procession of the Holy Spirit. The immanent identity of the Spirit was crucial for Western thinkers for their belief in the inclusion of *filioque* in the creedal clause. This is shown in the relational models put forward by Anselm of Canterbury and Richard of St. Victor that distinguish the immanent persons on the basis of exclusive relations which demand the dual procession of the third person of the Trinity.

The book therefore provides another basis for discussion between East and West on this vital issue. Given the response of Nechites at the end of his discussion with Anselm of Havelberg, the Eastern Church is challenged to state a position on the immanent person of the Holy Spirit that would reject the inclusion of the *filioque*. This has added importance given the witnesses cited from the Greek position by writers such as Anselm of Havelberg, Peter Abelard and Peter Lombard that support the idea of dual procession. The concept that the Holy Spirit proceeds from the Father through the Son does seem to have validity in the economy of the Spirit. However, if this is transferred to the

Conclusion

immanent procession, then questions must be raised about the equality and relationships of the three persons in light of the 'middle position' given to the Son. This model is also unsatisfactory because the Greeks hold that the Spirit proceeds from the Father alone, but in a different way than the Son. This makes the nature of the two processions difficult to distinguish, and further complicates the idea that the third person proceeds 'through' the second.

The solution that it is impossible to know in what way the second and third persons proceed in their immanent states may seem the most helpful, and yet this would seem to validate modalist teaching that there is only one person in God who 'appears' in different forms at different times in creation, which Scripture does not seem to allow. These twelfth-century writers thus pose a challenge and possible solution to the continuing debate which needs to be addressed.

The third main contribution is to the overall history of pneumatology, and particularly the continuation and development of Augustinian spirituality. The twelfth century was an important time in the history of ideas, which has been recognised by the application of the term 'renaissance' to this period. The development from schools to universities, accompanied by a more reasoned approach to theological study, created good conditions for a fresh impetus to the study of the Bible and the Church Fathers, and the writings of this time would form the basis of later scholastic thought. However, the importance of this time in the area of pneumatology has not been widely recognised.

The second half of the book showed how the writers in the twelfth century took Augustine's teaching that related attributes to the person of the Holy Spirit and developed this thought in many ways. Taken together, these authors present a strong case for belief in the Spirit as the harmony of Father and Son, drawing the first two persons together as their love, goodness, will and gift. Much of the focus from Augustine in secondary material has been on the concept of mutual love, with some discussion also of communion. However, the thematic studies showed that Augustine's ideas on these topics was limited, and this is emphasised by the collected thoughts presented from the twelfth century.

This research contributes to three separate parts of the history of pneumatology. The first of these is the writing of Augustine. For the most part, the writers of the twelfth century supported the teaching of Augustine on the Holy Spirit, particularly his ideas on communion and mutual love. Studies of these areas of Augustinian spirituality can gain from the greater depth and clarity offered by the later thinkers. However, two parts of Augustine's work on the Holy Spirit are challenged by this analysis of twelfth-century thought, if not directly by the writers of the period. The first of these is Augustine's use of will to describe the Holy Spirit. Whilst this fits well into analogical models of the Trinity, the authors studied here reserve their application of this attribute almost completely to the economic person of the Spirit. The second questionable term used by Augustine is gift (although, as has been noted above, this is also a common Biblical word used to describe the Holy Spirit). The problems associated with the need for an object found little more resolution in the twelfth century than they did in Augustine's own writing. However, the analyses that were carried out in the later period do provide a greater framework for future discussion of the applicability of 'gift' to the third person of the Trinity.

The second period of studies that should gain from this study is the medieval, scholastic age that began in the twelfth century. Too often, studies of the history of thought on the Holy Spirit have leapt from Augustine to Aquinas without assessing the background for the latter's work. Given the prominence of Lombard's *Sentences* for later study, and the impact on these books by the other writers studied in this book, it is surprising that more has not been done to examine the wealth of material that was written in the time from Anselm of Canterbury to Peter Lombard. It is hoped that there will be a study undertaken at some point that will assess the influence of these authors on Aquinas and later scholastic theologians.

The final stage in the history of pneumatology that may gain from this work is the present. Given the work of David Coffey and others on Augustine's mutual love theory, and the challenges that have been made to these concepts, this book provides a new perspective from the history of ideas to add to the ongoing discussion. The writers who are studied here were in a privileged position, being part of the first major group of thinkers in the West interacting with one another since the time of the Church Fathers. As a result, they were working with established material without the influence of predecessors' paradigms, and were free to explore their Biblical and Patristic inheritance. It is time that the work done in the twelfth century receives due consideration in current study on the Holy Spirit.

Given the wealth of writing on the Holy Spirit in the twelfth century, this study has much to offer on the individual authors, the period as a whole, and the history of pneumatology. The greater context given to each individual writer studied here gives greater clarity to the spirituality of each, and illuminates the mutual interaction and dependence in their theological explorations. The renewed discussions with the Eastern Church over *filioque* added an impetus to work on the Holy Spirit, and made this time important in the overall history of debate on the nature and procession of the third person of the Trinity. It now remains to see how far-reaching the effects of writers from Anselm of Canterbury to Peter Lombard can be on thought about the immanent and economic Holy Spirit.

Bibliography

Primary Sources

In J.P. Migne's Patrologia Latina

Abelardian School, *Epitome theologiae Christianae* in PL 178.
Aelred of Riveaulx, *Speculum charitatis* in PL 195.
Anon, *Summa sententiarum* in PL 176.
Anselm of Havelberg, *Dialogi* in PL 185.
Augustine, *De Doctrina Christiana* in PL 34.
- *De Trinitate* in PL 42.

Bernard of Clairvaux, *Apologia ad Guillelmum* in PL 182.
- *De gradibus humilitatis et superbiae* in PL 182.
- *De diligendo Deo* in PL 182.
- *De gratia et libero arbitrio* in PL 182.
- *Capitula haeresum Petri Abaelardi* in PL 182.
- *Sententiae* in PL 183.
- *Sermones in Cantica canticorum* in PL 183.

Honorius Augustodunensis, *Elucidarium* in PL 172.
Hugh of Saint Victor, *De laude charitatis* in PL 176.
- *De sacramentis* in PL 176.
- *De potestate et voluntate Dei* in PL 176.
- *De Tribus Diebus* in PL 176.

Peter Abelard, *Introductio ad theologiam* in PL 178.
- *Theologica Christiana* in PL 178.
- *Sic et Non* in PL 178.
- *Responsio* in PL 180.

Peter Lombard, *Sententiae in IV Libris Distinctae* in PL 192.
Richard of Saint Victor, *De Trinitate* in PL 196.
- *De tribus appropriatis personis in Trinitate* in PL 196.
- *Quomodo Spiritus Sanctus est amor Patris et Filii* in PL 196.
- *Sermo de missione Spiritus Sancti* in PL 196.
- *De spiritu blasphemiae* in PL 196.
- *De gradibus charitatis* in PL 196.
- *De quatuor gradibus violentae charitatis* in PL 196.

Robert Pullen, *Sententiae* in PL 186.
Rupert of Deutz, *De Trinitate et operibus ejus* in PL 167.
- *De Voluntate Dei* in PL 170.
- *De Omnipotentia Dei* in PL 170.

Walter of Mortagne, *Liber de Trinitate* in PL 209.
William of Conches, *De philosophia mundi* in PL 172.
William of St. Thierry, *Epistola ad fratres de Monte Dei* in PL 180.
- *Disputatio adversus Abaelardum* in PL 180.
- *De contemplando Deo* in PL 180.

- *De natura et dignitate divini amoris* in PL180.
- *Disputatio altera adversus Abaelardum* in PL 180.
- *De erroribus Guillelmi de Conchis* in PL 180.
- *Commentarius in Cantica canticorum* in PL 180.
- *Expositio in Epistolam ad Romanos* in PL 180.
- *Orationes meditativae* in PL 180.
- *De natura et dignitate amoris* in PL 184.

Other Primary Sources

Aelred of Rievaulx, *The Mirror of Charity*, (tr. E. Connor). Kalamazoo: Cistercian Publications, 1990.

Anselm of Canterbury, *Opera Omnia* Vols.1-6, (ed. F.S. Schmitt). Edinburgh: Thomas Nelson, 1946-9.
- *Anselm of Canterbury: The Major Works*, (tr. B. Davies and G.R. Evans). Oxford: OUP, 1998.

Augustine, *De Trinitate* in *Corpus Christianorum Series Latina* 16, (ed. W. Mountain). Turnholt: Brepols, 1968.
- *The Trinity*, (ed. J. Rotelle, tr. E. Hill). Brooklyn: New City Press, 1991.
- *De Doctrina Christiana*, (ed. R. Green). Oxford: OUP, 1995.

Bernard of Clairvaux, *Opera* Vols.1-8, (ed. J. Leclerq). Rome: Editions Cistercienses, 1957-77.
- *On Loving God*, (tr. R. Walton). Washington, D.C.: Cistercian Publications, 1974.
- *Sermons on the Song of Songs*, (tr. S. Eales). London: Elliot Stock, 1895.
- *Parables and Sentences*, (tr. M. Casey). Kalamazoo: Cistercian Publications, 1989.
- *The Steps of Humility and Pride; On Loving God*, (tr. M. Ambrose Conway, R. Walton). Kalamazoo: Cistercian Publications, 1973.

Dutton, P. (ed), *The* Glosae Super Platonem *of Bernard of Chartres*. Toronto: Pontifical Institute of Medieval Studies, 1991.

Eadmer, *The Life of St. Anselm, Archbishop of Canterbury*, (ed., tr. R.W. Southern). Oxford: OUP, 1962.

Häring, N., *Commentaries on Boethius by Thierry of Chartres and his School*. Toronto: Pontifical Institute of Medieval Studies, 1971.
- *Life and Works of Clarembald of Arras: A Twelfth-Century Master of the School of Chartres*. Toronto: Pontifical Institute of Medieval Studies, 1965.

Hugh of St. Victor, *The Divine Love*, (tr. A Religious of C.S.M.V.). London, A.R. Mowbray, 1956.
- *De Tribus Diebus* in CCCM 177, (ed. D. Poirel). Turnhout: Brepols, 2002.

Martin, R.M. (ed), *Oeuvres de Robert de Melun Tomes 1-4*. Louvain: Spicilegium Sacrum Lovaniense, 1932, 38, 47

Kirchberger, C., *Richard of Saint-Victor: Selected Writings on Contemplation*. London: Faber and Faber, 1957.

McCallum, J., *Abelard's Christian Theology*. Merrick, New York: Richwood, 1976.

Peter Abelard, *Dialectica*, (ed. L.M. De Rijk). Assen: Van Gorcum, 1956.
- *Historia Calamitatum*, (ed. J. Monfrin). Paris, J. Vrin, 1967.
- *Apologia Contra Bernardum*, (ed. E.M. Buytaert). Turnholt: Brepols, 1969.
- *Theologia Summi Boni*, (ed. U. Niggli). Hamburg: Felix Meiner, 1997.
- *Theologia Christiana* in CCCM 12, (ed. E.M. Buytaert). Turnholt: Brepols, 1969.
- *Theologia Scholarium* in CCCM 13, (ed. E.M. Buytaert). Turnholt: Brepols, 1987.

Peter Lombard, *Sententiae in IV Libris Distinctae Vols. 1-2*, (3rd Edition). Grottaferrata:

Collegii S. Bonaventurae ad Claras Aquas, 1971, 1981.
Richard of Saint Victor, *De Trinitate*, (ed. J. Ribaillier). Paris: J. Vrin, 1958.
William of Conches, *Glosae Super Platonem*, (ed. E. Jeauneau). Paris: J. Vrin, 1965.
William of St. Thierry, *Expositio Super Epistolam ad Romanos* in CCCM 86, (ed. P. Verdeyen). Turnholt: Brepols, 1989.
- *Exposition on the Epistle to the Romans*, (ed. J.H. Anderson). Kalamazoo: Cistercian Publications, 1980.
- *On the Nature and Dignity of Love*, (tr. G. Webb and A. Walker). London: A.R. Mowbray, 1956.
- *Deux Traités sur la Foi: Le Miroir de la Foi, L'Énigme de la Foi*, (ed. M.-M. Davy). Paris: J. Vrin, 1959.
- *The Mirror of Faith*, (tr. T. Davis). Kalamazoo: Cistercian Publications, 1979.
- *The Enigma of Faith*, (tr. J.D. Anderson). Kalamazoo: Cistercian Publications, 1974.
- *Exposé sur le Cantique des Cantiques*, (ed. J.-M. Déchanet). Paris: Les Éditions du Cerf, 1998.
- *Exposition on the Song of Songs*, (tr. C. Hart). Shannon: Irish University Press, 1970.
- *La Contemplation de Dieu*, (ed. J. Hourlier). Paris: Les Éditions du Cerf, 1999
- *The Works of William of St. Thierry Volume 1: On Contemplating God; Prayer; Meditations*, (tr. Sister Penelope). Kalamazoo: Cistercian Publications: 1977.
Zinn, G.A., *Richard of St. Victor: The Twelve Patriarchs, The Mystical Ark, Book Three of the Trinity*. London: SPCK, 1979.

Secondary Sources

Arendt, H., *Love and Saint Augustine*. Chicago: University of Chicago Press, 1996.
Aubé, P., *Saint Bernard de Clairvaux*. Fayard, 2003.
Ayres, L., 'Augustine on God as Love and Love as God', *Pro Ecclesia* 5 (1966), pp.470-487.
Backus, I. (ed.), *The Reception of the Church Fathers in the West Volume I: From the Carolingians to the Maurists*. Leiden: E.J. Brill, 1997.
Badcock, G., *Light of Truth and Fire of Love: A Theology of the Holy Spirit*. Grand Rapids: Eerdmans, 1997.
Bainvel, J., 'Sainte Anselme', in A. Vacant, E. Mangenot, É. Amann, *Dictionnaire de Théologie Catholique*. Paris: Letouzet et Ané, 1930-1950, 1(1):36-55.
Baltzer, O., *Die Sentenzen des Petrus Lombardus: Ihre Quellen und ihre dogmengeschichtliche Bedeutung*. Leipzig: Dieterich'sche Verlags-Buchhandlung, 1902.
Barmann, L., 'Reform Ideology in the "Dialogi" of Anselm of Havelberg', *Church History* 30 (1961), pp.379-395.
Baron, R., *Études sur Hughes de Saint-Victor*. Angers: Desclée de Brouwer, 1963.
Bell, D.N., *The Image and Likeness: The Augustinian Spirituality of William of St. Thierry*. Kalamazoo: Cistercian Publications, 1984.
- 'Greek, Plotinus, and the Education of William of St. Thierry', *Cîteaux Commentarii Cistercienses* XXX (1979), pp.221-248.
Berlière, V., 'Anselme de Havelberg', in A. Vacant, E. Mangenot, É. Amann, *Dictionnaire de Théologie Catholique*. Paris: Letouzet et Ané, 1930-1950, 1(2):1327-1360.
Berschin, W., 'From the Middle of the Eleventh Century to the Latin Conquest of

Constantinople 5: The Metropolis Constantinople', in J. Frakes, *Greek Letters and the Latin Middle Ages: From Jerome to Nicholas of Cusa.* The Catholic University of America Press, 1988. The Myriobiblos online website (July 2005, http://www.myriobiblos.gr/texts/english/Walter_Berschin_35.html).

Bertold, G.C., 'Saint Anselm and the *Filioque*', in G.C. Bertold, *Faith Seeking Understanding: Learning and the Catholic Tradition.* Manchester, New Hampshire: Saint Anselm Press, 1991, pp.227-234.

Blastic, M., *Condilectio: Personal Mysticism and Speculative Theology in Works of Richard of Saint Victor.* Michigan: UMI, 1991.

Bligh, J., 'Richard of St. Victor's *De Trinitate*: Augustinian or Abelardian?', *Heythrop Journal 1* (1960), pp.118-139.

Boh, I, 'Divine Omnipotence in the Early *Sentences*', in T. Rudavsky, *Divine Omniscience and Omnipotence in Medieval Philosophy: Islamic, Jewish and Christian Perspectives.* Dordrecht: D. Reidel, 1984, pp.185-212.

Böhnke, M. & Heinz, H. (eds.), *Im Gespräch mit dem Dreieinigen Gott: Elemente Einer Trinitärischen Theologie.* Düsseldorf: Patmos Verlag, 1985.

Boss, G., 'Le combat d'Abélard', *Cahiers de Civilisation Médiévale* 32:1 (1988), pp.17-28.

Bougerol, J-G., 'The Church Fathers and the *Sentences* of Peter Lombard', in I. Backus, *The Reception of the Church Fathers in the West Volume 1.* Leiden: E.J. Brill, 1997, pp.113-164.

Bourassa, F., '"Dans la communion de l'Esprit Saint"': étude théologique', *Science et Esprit* (1982), pp.31-56, 135-149, 239-268.

Brague, R. (ed.), *Saint Bernard et la Philosophie.* Paris: Presses Universitaires de France, 1993.

Bray, G., 'The Filioque Clause in History and Theology', *Tyndale Bulletin* 34 (1983), pp.91-144.

Bredero, A.H., *Bernard of Clairvaux: Between Cult and History.* Grand Rapids: Eerdmans, 1996.

- 'The early Cistercians and the old monasticism', in D. Loades, *The End of Strife: Papers Selected from the Proceedings of the Colloquium of the Commission Internationale d'Histoire Ecclésiastique Comparée.* Edinburgh: T & T Clark, 1984, pp.180-199.

Broderon, A.H., *Christendom and Christianity in the Middle Ages.* Grand Rapids: Eerdmans, 1993.

Bromily, G., *Historical Theology: An Introduction.* Edinburgh: T & T Clark, 1978.

Brooke, C., *The Twelfth-Century Renaissance.* London: Thames and Hudson, 1969.

Brooke, O., 'The Trinitarian Aspect of the Ascent of the Soul to God in the Theology of William of St. Theirry', *Récherches de Théologie ancienne et médiévale* 26 (1959), pp.85-127.

- 'The Speculative Development of the Trinitarian Theology of William of St. Thierry in the *Aenigma fidei*', *Récherches de Théologie ancienne et médiévale* 27 (1960), pp.193-211 and 28 (1961) pp.26-58.

- 'Towards a theology of connatural knowledge', *Citeaux Commentarii Cistercienses* 18 (1967), pp.275-290.

- *Studies in Monastic Theology.* Kalamazoo, Cistercian Publications, 1980.

Brooks, P. (ed), *Christian Spirituality: Essays in Honour of Gordon Rupp.* London: SCM, 1975.

Brower, J.E., 'Trinity', in J.E. Brower and K. Guilfoy, *The Cambridge Companion to Abelard.* Cambridge, CUP, 2004, pp.223-257.

Burgess, Stanley M., *The Holy Spirit: Medieval Roman Catholic and Reformation*

Traditions. Peabody, Massachusetts: Hendrickson, 1997.
- *The Spirit and the Church: Antiquity*. Peabody, Massachusetts: Hendrickson, 1984.
Burleigh, J.H.S., 'The Doctrine of the Holy Spirit in the Latin Fathers', *Scottish Journal of Theology* 7 (1954), pp.113-132.
Burnaby, J., *Amor Dei: A Study of the Religion of St. Augustine*. London: Hodder and Stoughton, 1938.
Butler, C., *Western Mysticism: The teaching of SS. Augustine, Gregory and Bernard on Contemplation and the Contemplative Life*. London, New York: Keegan Paul International, 2000.
Buytaert, E.M. (ed), *Peter Abelard: Proceedings of the International Conference Louvain May 10-12, 1971*. Leuven: Leuven University Press, 1974.
Campbell, R., 'Anselm's Theological Method', *Scottish Journal of Theology* 32:6 (1979), pp.541-562.
Canning, R., *The Unity of Love for God and Neighbor in St. Augustine*. Louvain: Augustinian Historical Institute, 1993.
Carfanton, J. (tr.), *William, Abbot of St. Thierry: A Colloquium at the Abbey of St. Thierry*. Kalamazoo: Cistercian Publications, 1987.
Casey, M., *Athirst for God: Spiritual Desire in Bernard of Clairvaux's Sermons on the Song of Songs*. Kalamazoo: Cistercian Publications, 1988.
Cavallera, F., 'La doctrine de Saint Augustine sur l'Esprit-Saint à propos du *De Trinitate*', *Récherches de Théologie ancienne et mediévale* 2 (1930), pp.365-387.
Chenu, M.-D., *La Théologie au Douzieme Siècle (Études de Philosophie Médiévale XLV)*. Paris: J. Vrin, 1957.
- 'Un essai de Méthode théologique au XIIe siècle', *Revue des Sciences Philosophiques et Théologiques* 24:2 (1935), pp.258-267.
Clanchy, M.T., 'Abelard's Mockery of St. Anselm', *The Journal of Ecclesiastical History* 41 (1990), pp.1-23.
- *Abelard: A Medieval Life*. Oxford: Blackwells, 1999.
Clark, Mary T., 'The Trinity in Latin Christianity', in B. McGinn and J. Meyendorff, *Christian Spirituality: Origins to the Twelfth Century*. New York: Crossroad, 1987, pp.276-290.
- '*De Trinitate*', in E. Stump and N. Kretzmann, *The Cambridge Companion to Augustine*. Cambridge: CUP, 2001), pp.91-102.
- *Augustine*. London: Continuum, 1994.
Coffey, D., 'The Holy Spirit as the Mutual Love of the Father and the Son', *Theological Studies* 51.2 (1990), pp.193-229.
- *Grace: The Gift of the Holy Spirit*. Sydney: Catholic Institute of Sydney, 1979.
- *Deus Trinitas: The Doctrine of the Triune God*. New York, Oxford: OUP, 1999.
- 'The Roman "Clarification" of the Doctrine of the Filioque', *International Journal of Systematic Theology* 5:1 (2003), pp.3-21.
- 'Spirit Christology and the Trinity', in B.E. Hinze and D.L. Davney, *Advents of the Spirit: An Introduction to the Current Study of Pneumatology*. Milwaukee: Marquette University Press, 2001, pp.315-338.
- 'A Proper Mission of the Holy Spirit', in *Theological Studies* 47.2 (1986), pp.227-250.
- The "Incarnation" of the Holy Spirit in Christ', in *Theological Studies* 45.3 (1984), pp.466-480.
Colish, M, 'St. Anselm's Philosophy of Language Reconsidered', in *Anselm Studies I*. Milwood, New York: Kraus, 1983, pp.113-124.

- *Peter Lombard: Volumes 1 & 2.* Leiden: E.J. Brill, 1994.
- '"... *Quae hodie locum non habent*": Scholastic Theologians Reflect on Their Authorities' in *Proceedings of the PMR Conference Volume 15.* Villanova: Augustinian Historical Institute, 1990, pp.1-18.
- '*Psalterium Scholasticorum*: Peter Lombard and the Emergence of Scholastic Psalms Exegesis', *Speculum* 67.3 (1992), pp.531-548.
- 'Systematic theology and theological renewal in the twelfth century', *The Journal of Medieval and Renaissance Studies* 18:2 (1988), pp.135-156.
- 'Peter Lombard', in G.R. Evans, *The Medieval Theologians: An Introduction to Theology in the Medieval Period.* Oxford: Blackwells, 2001, pp.168-186.

Colle, R. Del, *Christ and the Spirit: Spirit-Christology in Trinitarian Perspective.* Oxford: OUP, 1994.

Congar, Y.M.J., *I Believe in the Holy Spirit* (tr. D. Smith). New York: Seabury Press, 1983.

Copleston, F.C., *Medieval Philosophy.* London: Methuen, 1952.

Coulton, G.G., *Studies in Medieval Thought.* London: Thomas Nelson, 1940.

Courtney, F., *Cardinal Robert Pullen: An English Theologian of the Twelfth Century (Analecta Gregoriana LXIV).* Rome: Apud Aedes Universitatis Gregorianae, 1954.

Cowburn, J., *Love and the Person: A philosophical theory and a theological essay.* London: Geoffrey Chapman, 1967.

Crouse, R., 'What is Augustinian in Twelfth-Century Mysticism?', in F. Van Fleteren, J. Schnaubelt and J. Reino, *Augustine: mystic and mystagogue.* New York: Peter Lang, 1994, pp.401-414.
- 'Honorius Augustodunensis: Disciple of Anselm?', *Analecta Anselmiana* 4:2. Frankfurt: Minerva, 1975, pp.131-140.

Davy, M.-M., *Théologie et Mystique de Guillaume de Saint-Thierry.* Paris: J. Vrin, 1954.

Dawe, D.G., 'The Divinity of the Holy Spirit', *Interpretation* 28.1 (1979), pp.19-31.

Dawson, C., *Religion and the Rise of Western Culture.* New York: Doubleday, 1991.

Deanesly, M. *History of the Medieval Church 590-1500.* London: Methuen, 1965.

Dechanet, J.-M., *William of St Thierry: The Man and his Work.* Spencer, Massachusetts: Cistercian Publications, 1972.
- '*Amor ipse intellectus est.* La doctrine de l'amour-intellection chez Guillaume de Saint-Thierry', *Revue de Moyen Age Latin* 1 (1945), pp.349-375.
- 'L'amitié d'Abélard et de Guillaume de Saint-Thierry', *Revue d'Histoire Ecclésiastique* 35 (1939), pp.761-773.

De Ghellinck, S., *Le Mouvement Théologique De XIIe Siècle.* Bruges: Éditions "De Tempel", 1948.
- 'Pierre Lombard', in A. Vacant, E. Mangenot, É. Amann, *Dictionnaire de Théologie Catholique.* Paris: Letouzet et Ané, 1930-1950, 12(2):1941-2019.

Del Colle, R., 'A Response to Jurgen Moltmann and David Coffey', in B.E. Hinze and D.L. Dabney, *Advents of the Spirit: An Introduction to the Current Study of Pneumatology.* Milwaukee, Wisconsin: Marquette University Press, 2001, pp.339-346.
- *Christ and the Spirit. Spirit-Christology in Trinitarian Perspective.* Oxford: OUP, 1994.

Delhaye, P., *Pierre Lombard: Sa Vie, Ses Oeuvres, Sa Morale.* Montreal: Institute d'Études Médiévales, 1961.

Deme, D, *The Christology of Anselm of Canterbury.* Aldershot: Ashgate, 2003.

Den Bok, N., *Communicating the Most High: A Systematic Study of Person and Trinity*

in the *Theology of Richard of St. Victor.* Paris: Brepols, 1996.
De Wulf, M., *History of Medieval Philosophy Volume One: From the Beginnings to the End of the Twelfth Century.* London: Thomas Nelson, 1952.
Dreyer, E.A., 'An Advent of the Spirit: Medieval Mystics and Saints', in B.E. Hinze and D.L. Dabney, *Advents of the Spirit: An Introduction to the Current Study of Pneumatology.* Milwaukee, Wisconsin: Marquette University Press, 2001, pp.123-162.
Dronke, P., *A History of Twelfth-Century Western Philosophy.* Cambridge: CUP, 1988.
Fabula: Explorations into the Uses of Myth in Medieval Platonism. Leiden: E.J. Brill, 1974.
- 'Thierry of Chartres', in P. Dronke, *A History of Twelfth-Century Western Philosophy.* Cambridge: CUP, 1988, pp.358-385.
Elder, E., 'William of Saint Thierry: rational and affective spirituality' in J. Leclercq, F. Vandenbroucke and L. Bouyer, *Spirituality of Western Christendom.* Kalamazoo: Cistercian Publications, 1976, pp.85-105.
Elford, D., 'William of Conches', in P. Dronke, *A History of Twelfth-Century Western Philosophy.* Cambridge: CUP, 1988, pp.308-327.
English, E.D. (ed), *Reading and Wisdom: The De Doctrina Christiana of Augustine in the Middle Ages.* Notre Dame: University of Notre Dame Press, 1995.
Evans, G.R. (ed), *The Medieval Theologians: An Introduction to Theology in the Medieval Period.* Oxford: Blackwells, 2001.
- 'Anselm of Canterbury', in G.R. Evans, *The Medieval Theologians: An Introduction to Theology in the Medieval Period.* Oxford: Blackwells, 2001, pp.94-101.
- *Anselm.* London: Geoffrey Chapman, 1987.
- *Old Arts and New Theology: The Beginnings of Theology as an Academic Discipline.* Oxford: OUP, 1980.
- *The Mind of Bernard of Clairvaux.* Oxford: OUP, 1983.
- *Anselm and Talking About God.* Oxford: OUP, 1979.
- *Anselm and a New Generation.* Oxford: OUP, 1980.
- 'St. Anselm's Analogies', *Vivarium* 14 (1976), pp.81-93.
- 'The Cur Deus Homo: The Nature of St. Anselm's Appeal to Reason', *Studia Theologica* 31 (1977), pp.33-50.
- 'Past, Present and Future in the Theology of the Late Eleventh and Early Twelfth Century', *Studia Theologica* 32 (1978), pp.133-149.
- 'St. Anselm's Images of the Trinity', *Journal of Theological Studies* 27 (1976), pp.46-57.
- 'Unity and diversity: Anselm of Havelberg as ecumenist', *Analecta Praemonstratensia* 67 (1991), pp.42-52.
- 'Anselm of Canterbury and Anselm of Havelberg: the controversy with the Greeks', *Analecta Praemonstratensia* 53 (1977), pp.158-175.
- 'Putting Theory in Practice: Anselm and the Augustinian Model', in F. Van Fleteren, J. Schnaubelt and J. Reino, *Augustine: mystic and mystagogue.* New York: Peter Lang, 1994, pp.367-378.
Every, G., 'Peter Lombard and II Lyons', *Eastern Churches Review* 9 (1977), pp.85-90.
Farkasfalvy, D., 'Bernard the theologian: Forty years of research', in *Communio* 17 (1990), pp.580-594.
Fatula, M., 'A Problematic Western Formula', *One in Christ* 17 (1981), pp.324-334.
Fitzgerald, A. (ed.), *Augustine Through the Ages: An Encyclopedia.* Grand Rapids: Eerdmans, 1999.

Flasch, K. (ed), *Parusia: Studien zu Philosophie Platons und zur Problemgeschichte des Platonismus: Festgabe für Johannes Hirschberger*. Frankfurt: Minerva, 1965.

Flint, V., 'The Place and Purpose of the Works of Honorius Augustodunensis', *Revue Bénédictine* 87 (1977), pp.97-127.

Fortin, J. (ed.), *Saint Anselm - His Origins and Influence*. Lewiston: Edwin Mellen, 2001.

Fortman, E.J., *The Triune God: A Historical Study of the Trinity*. London: Hutchinson, 1972.

Fritz, G., 'Richard de Saint-Victor', in A. Vacant, E. Mangenot, É. Amann, *Dictionnaire de Théologie Catholique*. Paris: Letouzet et Ané, 1930-1950, 13(2):2676-2695.

Gandillac, M. de, 'Sur quelques interprétations récentes d'Abélard', *Cahiers de Civilisation Médiévale* 4 (1961), pp.293-302.

Gasper, G., *Anselm of Canterbury and his Theological Inheritance*. Aldershot: Ashgate, 2004.

Gemeinhardt, P., *Die Filioque-Kontroverse zwischen Ost- und Westkirche im Frühmittelalter*. Berlin: Walter de Gruyter, 2002.

Gersh, S., 'Anselm of Canterbury', in P. Dronke, *A History of Twelfth-Century Western Philosophy*. Cambridge: CUP, 1988, pp.255-278.

Gilbert, P, 'La confession de foi dans le *De Processione Spiritus sancti* de Saint Anselme', M. Hoegen, *L'Attualità Filosofica di Anselmo D'Aosta*. Rome: Ateneo S. Anselmo, 1990, pp.229-262.

Gilson, E., *A History of Christian Philosophy in the Middle Ages*. London: Sheed and Ward, 1955.

- *The Mystical Theology of St. Bernard* (tr. A.C. Downes). Kalamazoo: Cistercian Publications, 1990.
- 'Abélard et Platon', in E.M. Buytaert, *Peter Abelard: Proceedings of the International Conference Louvain May 10-12, 1971*. Leuven: Leuven University Press, 1974, pp.38-64.

Giusberti, F., *Materials for a Study on Twelfth-Century Scholasticism*. Bibliopolis, 1982.

Godet, P., 'Guillaume de Saint-Thierry', in A. Vacant, E. Mangenot, É. Amann, *Dictionnaire de Théologie Catholique*. Paris: Letouzet et Ané, 1930-1950), 6(2):1981-2.

Gollnick, J.T., 'The Monastic-Devotional Context of Anselm of Canterbury's Theology', *Monastic Studies* 12 (1976), pp.239-248.

Grane, L., *Peter Abelard: Philosophy and Christianity in the Middle Ages*. London: George Allen and Unwin, 1970.

Gregory, T., *Anima Mundi: La Filosofia di Guglielmo di Conches e la Scuola di Chartres*. Firenze: G.C. Sansoni, 1956.

- 'The Platonic Inheritance', in P. Dronke, *A History of Twelfth-Century Western Philosophy*. Cambridge: CUP, 1988, pp.54-80.
- 'Le platonisme du XIIe siècle', *Revue des Sciences Philosophiques et Théologiques* 71:2 (1987), pp.243-259.

Guimet, F., '*Caritas ordinata et amor discretus* dans la théologie trinitaire de Richard de Saint-Victor', *Revue de Moyen Age Latin* 4 (1948), pp.225-236.

Gunton, C., *The Promise of Trinitarian Theology*. Edinburgh: T & T Clark, 1991.

Haskins, C.H., *The Renaissance of the Twelfth Century*. Cambridge, Massachusetts: Harvard University Press, 1927.

Haven, M., *Medieval Thought: The Western Intellectual Tradition from Antiquity to the Thirteenth Century*. London: Macmillan, 1992.

Hendry, G.S., *The Holy Spirit in Christian Theology*. London: SCM Press, 1965.
Heron, A., *The Holy Spirit: The Holy Spirit in the Bible in the History of Christian Thought and in Recent Theology*. Philadelphia: Westminster, 1983.
- 'Anselm and the *Filioque*: A Responsio pro Graecis', *Anselm Studies* I. Milwood, New York: Kraus International, 1983, pp.259-264.
- '"Who proceedeth from the Father and the Son"; the problem of the Filioque', *Scottish Journal of Theology* 24.2 (1971), pp.149-166.
Hill, E., *The Mystery of the Trinity*. London: Geoffrey Chapman, 1985.
Hinze, B.E and Dabney, D.L. (eds), *Advents of the Spirit: An Introduction to the Current Study of Pneumatology*. Milwaukee, Wisconsin: Marquette University Press, 2001.
Hofmann, P., 'Die Triniätslehre als tragende Struktur der Fundamentaltheologie: Das Beispiel Richards von St.-Victor', *Zeitschrift Für Katholische Theologie* 123 (2001), pp.211-236.
Hofmeier, J., *Die Trinitätslehre des Hugo von St. Viktor*. München: Max Hueber, 1963.
Hopkins, J., *A Companion to the Study of Anselm*. Minneapolis, Minnesota: University of Minnesota Press, 1972.
Horst, U., *Die Trinitäts- und Gotteslehre des Robert von Melun*. Mainz: Matthias-Grünewald-Verlag, 1964.
Javelet, R., *Image et Ressemblance au Douzième Siècle: De Saint Anselme a Alain de Lille* Vols 1-2. Paris: Letouzey & Ané, 1967.
Johnson, O.A., 'God and St. Anselm', *Journal of Religion* 45 (1965), pp.326-334.
Jolivet, J., *Arts du Langage et Théologie Chez Abélard*. Paris: J. Vrin, 1969.
Jordan, M.D. and Emery Jr., K., *Ad Litteram: Authoritative Texts and Their Medieval Readers*. Notre Dame: University of Notre Dame Press, 1992.
Kantorowicz, E., 'Plato in the Middle Ages', *The Philosophical Review* 51 (1942), pp.312-323.
Kaufman, P., '*Caritas non est nisi a Spiritu Sancto*. Augustine and Peter Lombard on Grace and Personal Righteousness', *Augustiniana* 30 (1980), pp.209-220.
Klibansky, R., *The Continuity of the Platonic Tradition During the Middle Ages*. London: Warburg Institute, 1939.
Klimartin, E., 'The Active Role of Christ and the Holy Spirit in the Sanctification of the Eucharistic Elements', *Theological Studies* 45.2 (1984), pp.225-253.
Knoch, W., '"*Deus unus est Trinus*": Beobachtungen zur frühscholastischen Gotteslehre', in M. Böhnke and H. Heinz, *Im Gespräch mit dem Dreieinigen Gott: Elemente Einer Trinitärischen Theologie*. Düsseldorf: Patmos Verlag, 1985, pp.209-230.
Kohlenberger, H., 'Konsequenzen und inkonsequenzen der Trinitätslehre in Anselms Monologion', *Analecta Anselmiana* 5. Frankfurt: Minerva, 1976, pp.149-178.
Kohlenberger, H. (ed.), *Sola Ratione: Anselm-Studien für F.S. Schmitt*. Stuttgart: Friedrich Frommann Verlag, 1970.
Kretzmann, N., Kenny, A., Pinborg, J. (eds.), *The Cambridge History of Later Medieval Philosophy: From the Rediscovery of Aristotle to the Disintegration of Scholasticism 1100-1600*. Cambridge: CUP, 1982.
Lancel, S., *St. Augustine*. London: SCM, 1999.
Landgraf, A., *Dogmengeschichte der Frühscholastik*. Regensburg: Friedrich Pustet, 1953-6.
Lawrence, C.H., *Medieval Monasticism: Forms of Religious Life in Western Europe in the Middle Ages*. London: Longman, 1987.
Lardreau, G., 'Amour Philosophique et amour spirituel', in R. Brague, *Saint Bernard et la Philosophie*. Paris: Presses Universitaires de France, 1993, pp.27-48.

Latourette, K.S., *The Thousand Years of Uncertainty: 500 A.D. – 1500 A.D.* Grand Rapids: Zondervan, 1980.
- *A History of Christianity.* London: Eyre and Spottiswoode.

Leclercq, J. (ed.), *The Influence of Saint Bernard.* Oxford: SLG Press, 1976.
- *Monks and Love in Twelfth-Century France: Psycho-Historical Essays.* Oxford: OUP, 1979.
- *Bernard of Clairvaux and the Cistercian Spirit.* Kalamazoo: Cistercian Publications, 1976.
- 'Études récentes sur Guillaume de Saint-Thierry', *Bulletin de Philosophie Médiévale* 19 (1977), pp.49-54.
- 'Les lettres de Guillaume de Saint-Thierry à saint Bernard', *Revue Bénédictine* LXXIX:4 (1969), pp.375-391.

Leclercq, J, Vandenbroucke, F., Bouyer, L., *The Spirituality of the Middle Ages.* London: Burns and Oates, 1968.

Leff, G., *Medieval Thought: Augustine to Ockham.* Harmondsworth, Middlesex: Penguin, 1965.

Lemoine, F. and Kleinhenz, C. (ed.), *Saint Augustine the Bishop: A Book of Essays.* New York: Garland, 1994.

Lewicki, J., 'Saint Anselme et les doctrines des Cisterciens du XIIe Siècle', *Analecta Anselmiana* 2. Frankfurt: Minerva, 1970, pp.209-216.

Loades, D. (ed.), *The End of Strife: Papers Selected from the Proceedings of the Colloquium of the Commission Internationale d'Histoire Écclesiastique Comparée.* Edinburgh: T & T Clark, 1984.

Lortz, J., *Bernard von Clairvaux: Mönch und Mystiker: International Bernhardkongress.* Wiesbaden: Franz Steiner, 1955.

Lottin, O., 'Questions inédites de Hugues de Saint-Victor', *Récherches de Théologie ancienne et médiévale* 26 (1959), pp.177-263.
- *Psychologie et Morale aus XIIe et XIIIe Siècle I: Problèmes de Psychologie.* Louvain: Abbaye du Mont César, 1942.

Louis, R. *Pierre Abélard, Pierre Le Vénérable: Les Courants Philosophiques, Littéraires et Artistiques en occident au Milieu Du XIIe Siècle.* Paris: Centre National de la Recherche Scientifique, 1975.

Luscombe, D.E., *The School of Peter Abelard: The Influence of Abelard's Thought in the Early Scholastic Period.* Cambridge: CUP, 1969.
- 'Peter Abelard', in P. Dronke, *A History of Twelfth-Century Western Philosophy.* Cambridge: CUP, 1988, pp.279-307.
- 'Peter Abelard: Some Recent Interpretations', *The Journal of Religious History* 7 (1972), p.69-75.
- 'St. Anselm and Abelard', *Anselm Studies* I. Milwood, New York: Kraus International, 1983, p.207-230.

Luscombe, D.E. & Evans, G.R. (eds), *Anselm: Aosta, Bec and Canterbury: Papers in Commemoration of the Nine-Hundredth Anniversary of Anselm's Enthronment as Archbishop, 25 September 1093.* Sheffield: Sheffield Academic Press, 1996.

Lynch, J.H., *The Medieval Church: A Brief History.* London: Longman, 1992.

Marenbon, J. (ed), *Medieval Philosophy.* London: Routledge, 1998.
- *The Philosophy of Peter Abelard.* Cambridge: CUP, 1999.
- 'Gilbert of Poitiers', in P. Dronke, *A History of Twelfth-Century Western Philosophy.* Cambridge: CUP, 1988, pp.328-352.

Marsh, T., *The Triune God. A Biblical, Historical and Theological Study.* Connecticut: Twenty-Third Publications, 1994.

Martinich, A.P., 'Identity and Trinity', *Journal of Religion* 58 (1978), pp.169-181.

Maurer, A.A., *Medieval Philosophy*. Toronto: Pontifical Institute of Medieval Studies, 1982.

McCabe, J., *Peter Abelard*. London: Duckworth and Co., 1901.

McDonald, S., 'The Divine Nature', in E. Stump and N. Kretzmann, *The Cambridge Companion to Augustine*. Cambridge: CUP, 2001, pp.71-90.

McDonnell, K., *The Other Hand of God: The Holy Spirit as the Universal Touch and Goal*. Collegeville, Minnesota: Liturgical Press, 2003.

McGinn, B., 'The Role of the Anima Mundi as Mediator between the Divine and Created Realms in the Twelfth Century', in J.J. Collins and M. Fishbane, *Death, Ecstasy, and Other Worldly Journeys*. New York: State of New York Press, 1995, pp.285-316.

- *The Growth of Mysticism. Gregory the Great through the 12th Century*. New York: Crossroad, 1994.

- 'Love, Knowledge and Mystical Union in Western Christianity: Twelfth to Sixteenth Centuries', *Church History* 56 (1987), pp.7-24.

- 'Christ as Saviour in the West', in B. McGinn and J. Meyendorff, *Christian Spirituality: Origins to the Twelfth Century*. London: Routledge and Kegan Paul, 1986, pp.253-259.

McGinn, B. and Meyendorff, J. (eds), *Christian Spirituality: Origins to the Twelfth Century*. London: Routledge and Kegan Paul, 1986.

McGrath, A., *Historical Theology: An Introduction to the History of Christian Thought*. Oxford: Blackwell, 1994.

McFarlane, G., *Why Do You Believe What You Believe About the Holy Spirit?* Carlisle: Paternoster, 1998.

McIntyre, J., *St. Anselm and his Critics: A Re-Interpretation of the Cur Deus Homo*. Edinburgh: Oliver and Boyd: 1954.

McLaughlin, M., 'Abelard as Autobiographer: The Motives and Meaning of his "Story of Calamities"', *Speculum* 42 (1967), pp.463-488.

Melone, M., 'Lo Spirito Santo nel *De Trinitate* di Riccardo di San Vittore: L'originalità di una proposta', *Antonianum* 71:1 (2002), pp.33-67.

Mews, C.J., *The Development of the Theologia of Peter Abelard*. Oxford: DPhil Thesis, 1980.

- 'The List of Heresies Imputed to Peter Abelard', *Revue Bénédictine* 95 (1985), pp.73-110.

- 'On Dating the Works of Peter Abelard', *Archives d'Histoire Doctrinale et Littéraire du Moyen Age* 52 (1985), pp.73-134.

- 'In Search of a Name and Its Significance: A Twelfth-Century Anecdote about Thierry and Peter Abaelard', *Traditio* XLIV (1988), pp.171-200.

- 'Peter Abelard's (*Theologia Christiana*) and (*Theologia 'Scholarium'*) re-examined', *Récherches de Théologie ancienne et médiévale* 52 (1985), pp.109-158.

- 'The *Sententiae* of Peter Abelard', *Récherches de Théologie ancienne et médiévale* 53 (1986), pp.130-184.

- 'A neglected gloss on the *Isagogue* by Peter Abelard', *Freiburger Zeitschrift Für Philosophie und Theologie* 31 (1984), pp.35-55.

Michel, B., 'La consideration et l'unitas spiritus', in R. Brague, *Saint Bernard et la Philosophie*. Paris: Presses Universitaires de France, 1993, pp.109-128.

Moltmann, J., 'The Trinitarian Personhood of the Holy Spirit', in B.E. Hinze and D.L. Dabney, *Advents of the Spirit: An Introduction to the Current Study of Pneumatology*. Milwaukee, Wisconsin: Marquette University Press, 2001, pp.302-314.

- *History and the Triune God: Contributions to Trinitarian Theology* (tr. J. Bowden). London: SCM Press, 1991.
Moonan, L., 'Abelard's Use of the *Timaeus*', *Archives d'Histoire Doctrinale et Littéraire du Moyen Age* 56 (1986), pp.7-90.
Mühlen, H., *Der Heilige Geist Als Person: Beitrag zur Frage nach der dem Heiligen Geiste Eigentümlichen Funktion in der Trinität, bei der Inkarnation und im Gnadenbund.* Munster: Aschendorffsche Verlagsbuchhandlung, 1963.
Nef, F., '"Caritas dat caritatem". La Métaphysique de la charité dans les sermons sur le Cantique de cantiques et l'ontologie de la contemplation', in R. Brague, *Saint Bernard et la Philosophie*. Paris: Presses Universitaires de France, 1993, pp.87-108.
Ngien, D., *Apologetic for Filioque in Medieval Theology*. Bletchley: Paternoster, 2005.
- 'Richard of St. Victor's Condilectus: The Spirit as Co-beloved', *European Journal of Theology* 12 (2003), pp.77-92.
- 'The *Filioque* Clause in the Teaching of Anselm of Canterbury', *Churchman* 118 (2004), pp.105-122, 219-234.
Nielson, L.A., *Theology and Philosophy in the Twelfth Century: A Study of Gilbert Porreta's Thinking and the Theological Expositions of the Doctrine of the Incarnation During the Period 1130-1180*. Leiden: E.J. Brill, 1982.
- 'Peter Abelard and Gilbert of Poitiers', in G.R. Evans, *The Medieval Theologians: An Introduction to Theology in the Medieval Period*. Oxford: Blackwells, 2001, pp.102-128.
O'Donovan, O., *The Problem of Self-Love in St. Augustine*. New Haven, Yale University Press, 1980.
Opsahl, P.D. (ed.), *The Holy Spirit in the Life of the Church: From Biblical Times to the Present*. Minneapolis: Augsburg, 1978.
Osborne, C., 'The nexus amoris in Augustine's Trinity', *Studia Patristica* (1989), pp.309-314.
Ott, L., 'Die platonische Weltseele in der Theologie der Frühscholastik', in K. Flasch, *Parusia: Studien zur Philosophie Platons und zur Problemgeschichte des Platonismus*. Frankfurt am Main: Minerva, 1965, pp.307-331.
Ouellet, M., 'The Spirit in the Life of the Trinity', *Communio* 25 (1998), pp.199-213.
Penido, M., 'Gloses sur la procession d'amour dans la Trinité', *Ephemerides Theologicae Lovanienses* 14.1 (1937), pp.33-68.
- 'A propos de la procession d'amour en Dieu', *Ephemerides Theologicae Lovanienses* 15.2 (1938), pp.338-344.
Perino, R., *La dottrina trinitaria di S. Anselmo: nel quadro del suo metodo teologica e del suo concetto di Dio*. Roma: Herder, 1952.
Pennington, B., 'The Cistercians', in B. McGinn and J. Meyendorff, *Christian Spirituality: Origins to the Twelfth Century*. London: Routledge and Kegan Paul, 1986, pp.196-204.
Poirel, D., 'Love of God, Human Love: Hugh of St. Victor and the Sacrament of Marriage', *Communio* 24 (1997), pp.99-109.
- *Livre de la nature et débat trinitaire au xii siècle: le tribus diebus de Hughes de Saint-Victor*. Turnhout: Brepols, 2002.
Portalié, E., 'Pierre Abélard', in A. Vacant, E. Mangenot, É. Amann, *Dictionnaire de Théologie Catholique*. Paris: Letouzet et Ané, 1930-1950, 1(1):36-55.
Pranger, B, 'Sic et non: Patristic Authority between Refusal and Acceptance: Anselm of Canterbury, Peter Abelard and Bernard of Clairvaux', in I. Backus, *The Reception of the Church Fathers in the West: Volume 1* (ed I. Backus). Leiden: E.J. Brill, 1997, pp.165-193.
Rahner, K., *The Trinity* (tr. J. Donceel). Tunbridge Wells, Kent: Burns and Oates, 1986.

Raitt, J., 'Deus caritas est', in F. Lemoine and C. Kleinhenz, *Saint Augustine the bishop*. New York: Garland, 1994, pp.197-199.

Ratzinger, J., 'The Holy Spirit as Communio: Concerning the Relationship of Pneumatology and Spirituality in Augustine', *Communio* 25 (1998), pp.324-339.

Reid, D., *Energies of the Spirit: Trinitarian Models in Eastern Orthodox and Western Theology*. Atlanta, Georgia: Scholars Press, 1997.

Renna, T., 'Augustine and the Early Cistercians', in F. Van Fleteren, J. Schnaubelt and J. Reino, *Augustine: mystic and mystagogue*. New York: Peter Lang, 1994, pp.379-400.

- 'Bernard versus Abelard: An Ecclesiological Conflict', in J.R. Sommerfeldt, *Simplicity and Ordinariness: Studies in Medieval Cistercian History* IV. Kalamazoo: Cistercian Publications, 1980) pp.94-138.

Ristschl, D., 'The History of the Filioque Controversy', in H. Kung and J. Moltmann, *Conflicts About the Holy Spirit*. New York: Seabury Press, 1979, pp.3-14.

Rosemann, Philipp W., *Peter Lombard*. Oxford: OUP, 2004.

Ruh, K. 'Die Augen der Liebe bei Wilhelm von St. Thierry', *Theologische Zeitschrift* 45:2-3 (1989), pp.103-114.

Rusch, W.G., 'The Doctrine of the Holy Spirit in the Patristic and Medieval Church', in P.D. Opsahl, *The Holy Spirit in the Life of the Church: From Biblical Times to the Present*. Minneapolis: Augsburg, 1978, pp.66-98.

Saarinen, R., 'Ipsa Dilectio Deus Est: Zur Wirkungsgeschichte von 1. Sent. dist. 17 des Petrus Lombardus bei Martin Luther', in T. Mannermaa, A. Ghiselli and S. Peura, *Thesaurus Lutheri: Auf der Suche nach neuen Paradigmen de Luther-Forschung*. Helsinki: Vammalan Kirjapaino Oy, 1987, pp.185-204.

Schaff, P., *History of the Christian Church Volume V: The Middle Ages*. Grand Rapids: Eerdmans, 1907.

Schmaus, M., 'Die metaphysisch-psychologische Lehre über den Heiligen Geist im *Monologion* Anselms von Canterbury', in H. Kohlenberger, *Sola Ratione: Anselm-Studien für F.S. Schmitt*. Stuttgart: Friedrich Frommann Verlag, 1970, pp.189-220.

- 'Die theologiegeschichtliche Tragweite der Trinitätslehre des Anselm von Canterbury', *Analecta Anselmiana* 4:1. Frankfurt: Minerva, 1975.

Schmidt, M.A., *Gottheit und Trinität nach dem Kommentar des Gilbert Porreta zu Boethius, De Trinitate*. Basel: Verlag fur Recht und Gesellschaft, 1956.

- 'Zur Trinitätslehre der Frühscholastik', *Theologische Zeitschrift* 40:2 (1984), pp.181-192.

Schupp, J., *Die Gnadenlehre des Petrus Lombardus*. Freiburg im Breslau: Herder, 1932.

Sikes, J., *Peter Abailard*. Cambridge: CUP, 1932.

Simonis, W., *Trinität und Vernuft: Untersuchungen zur Möglichkeit einer rationalen Trinitätslehre bei Anselm, Abaelard, den Viktorinern, A. Günther und J. Frohschammer*. Frankfurt: J. Knecht, 1972.

Smalley, B., *Studies in Medieval Thought and Learning: From Abelard to Wyclif*. London: The Hambledon Press, 1981.

Sommerfeldt, J.R., *The Spiritual Teachings of Bernard of Clairvaux: An Intellectual History of the Early Cistercian Order*. Kalamazoo: Cistercian Publications, 1991.

- 'Bernard of Clairvaux and Scholasticism', *Papers of the Michigan Academy of Sciences, Arts and Letters* 48 (1963), pp.265-278.

Sommerfeldt, J.R. (ed.), *Bernardus Magister: Papers Presented at the Nonacentenary Celebration of the Birth of Saint Bernard of Clairvaux*. Kalamazoo Cistercian Publications, 1992.

- *Simplicity and Ordinariness: Studies in Medieval Cistercian History* IV.

Kalamazoo: Cistercian Publications, 1980.
Sontag, F., 'Anselm and the Concept of God', *Scottish Journal of Theology* 35:3 (1982), pp.213-218.
Southern, R.W., *The Making of the Middle Ages*. London: Pimlico, 1993.
- *Western Society and the Church in the Middle Ages*. Harmondsworth, Middlesex: Penguin, 1970.
- *St. Anselm and his Biographer*. Cambridge: CUP, 1966.
- *Saint Anselm: A Portrait in a Landscape*. Cambridge: CUP, 1990.
Southern, R.W. (ed.), *Essays in Medieval History*. London: MacMillan, 1968.
Spijker, I.V., 'Exegesis and Emotions: Richard of St. Victor's *De Quatuor Gradibus Violentae Caritatis*', *Sacris Erudiri* 36 (1996), pp.147-160.
Stiegman, E., 'Bernard of Clairvaux, William of St. Thierry, the Victorines', in G.R. Evans, *The Medieval Theologians: An Introduction to Theology in the Medieval Period*. Oxford: Blackwells, 2001, pp.129-155.
Studer, B., 'Zur Pneumatologie des Augustinus von Hippo (*De Trinitate* 15, 16, 17-27, 50)', Augustinianum 35:2 (1995), pp.567-586.
Stump, E. (ed.), *Reasoned Faith: Essays in Philosophical Theology in Honor of Norman Kretzmann*. Ithaca, London: Cornell University Press, 1993.
Swete, S., *On the History of the Doctrine of the Procession of the Holy Spirit: From the Apostolic Age to the Death of Charlemagne*. Cambridge: Deighton, Bell, 1876.
Szermach, P. (ed.), *An Introduction to the Medieval Mystics of Europe*. Albany: State University of New York Press, 1984.
TeSelle, E., *Augustine the Theologian*. London: Burns and Oates, 1970.
- 'Holy Spirit', in A. Fitzgerald, *Augustine Through the Ages: An Encyclopedia*. Grand Rapids: Eerdmans, 1999, pp.434-437.
Thomas, R., 'William of St. Thierry: Our Life in the Trinity', *Monastic Studies* 3 (1965), pp.139-165.
Thomas, R. (ed.), *Petrus Abelardus: Person, Werk und Wirkung*. Trier: Paulinus-Verlag, 1980.
Tomasic, T., 'Neoplatonism and the Mysticism of William of St. Thierry', in P. Szermach, *An Introduction to the Medieval Mystics of Europe*. Albany: State University of New York Press, 1984, pp.53-76.
Toon, P, Spiceland, J.D., *One God in Trinity*. London: Samuel Bagster, 1980.
Treadgold, W. (ed.), *Renaissances Before the Renaissance: Cultural Revivals of Late Antiquity and the Middle Ages*. Stanford, California: Stanford University Press, 1984.
Vacandard, E., 'Sainte Bernard', in A. Vacant, E. Mangenot, É. Amann, *Dictionnaire de Théologie Catholique*. Paris: Letouzet et Ané, 1930-1950) 2(1):746-785.
Van Engen, J.H., *Rupert of Deutz*. Berkeley: University of California Press, 1983.
Van Fleteren, F., Schnaubelt, J., Reino, J. (eds.), *Augustine: mystic and mystagogue*. New York: Peter Lang, 1994.
Verdeyen, P., *La Théologie Mystique de Guillaume de Saint-Thierry*. Paris: FAC-editions, 1990.
- 'Un Théologien de L'Expérience', in *Bernard de Clairvaux: Histoire, Mentalité, Spiritualité*. Paris: Les éditions du Cerf, 1992, pp.557-578.
Verger, J. and Jolivet, J., *Bernard-Abélard ou Le Cloître et L'école*. Paris: Fayard-Mame, 1982.
Vernett, F., 'Hughes de Saint-Victor', in A. Vacant, E. Mangenot, É. Amann, *Dictionnaire de Théologie Catholique*. Paris: Letouzet et Ané, 1930-1950, 7(1):240-308.
Vischer, L., *Spirit of God, Spirit of Christ: Ecumenical Reflections on the* Filioque

Controversy. London: SPCK, 1981.
Von Balthasar, H.U., *Homo Creatus Est.* Einsiedeln: Johannes Verlag, 1986.
- *Spiritus Creator.* Einsiedeln: Johannes Verlag, 1967.
- 'Retrieving the Tradition: The Council of the Holy Spirit', *Communio* 17 (1990), pp.595-612.
Van den Eynde, D., 'La *Theologia Scholarium* de Pierre Abelard', *Récherches de Théologie ancienne et médiévale* 28 (1961), pp.225-241.
- 'William of St. Thierry and the Author of the *Summa Sententiarum*', *Franciscan Studies* 10 (1950), pp.241-256.
Verhees, J., 'Heiliger Geist und Inkarnation in der Theologie des Augustinus von Hippo: Unlöslicher Zusammenhang zwischen Theo-logie und Ökonomie', *Revue des Études Augustiniennes* 22 (1976), pp.234-53.
- 'Heiliger Geist und Gemeinschaft bei Augustinus von Hippo', *Revue des Études Augustiniennes* 23 (1977), pp.245-64.
Von den Steinen, W., *Vom Heiligen Geist des Mittelalters: Anselm von Canterbury, Bernhard von Clairvaux.* Darmstadt: Wissenschaftliche Buchgesellschaft, 1968.
Ward, B., 'Anselm of Canterbury and His Influence', in B. McGinn and J. Meyendorff, *Christian Spirituality: Origins to the Twelfth Century.* London: Routledge and Kegan Paul, 1986, pp.196-204.
Watkin-Jones, H., *The Holy Spirit in the Medieval Church: A Study of Christian Teaching Concerning the Holy Spirit and His Place in the Trinity from the Post-Patristic Age to the Counter-Reformation.* London: Epworth Press, 1922.
Weinandy, T., *The Father's Spirit of Sonship: Reconceiving the Trinity.* Edinburgh: T & T Clark, 1995.
Weingart, R., *The Logic of Divine Love: A Critical Analysis of the Soteriology of Peter Abailard.* Oxford: OUP, 1970.
Weisweiler, S., 'La "Summa Sententiarum" source de Pierre Lombard', *Récherches de Théologie ancienne et médiévale* 6 (1934), pp.143-183.
Welker, M., *God the Spirit.* Minnepolis, Minnesota: Fortress Press, 1994.
Westra, H.J. (ed.), *From Athens to Chartres: Neoplatonism and Medieval Thought.* Leiden: E.J. Brill, 1992.
Wielcockx, R., 'La Sentence *De Caritate* et la Discussion Scolastique sur L'amour', *Ephemerides Theologicae Lovanienses* 58-59 (1982-3), pp.50-86.
Williams, C., *The Descent of the Dove: A Short History of the Holy Spirit in the Church.* London: Faber and Faber, 1939.
Williams, W., *Saint Bernard of Clairvaux.* Manchester: Manchester University Press, 1913.
Wimsatt, J., 'St. Bernard, the Canticle of Canticles, and Mystical Poetry', in P. Szermach, *An Introduction to the Medieval Mystics of Europe.* Albany: State University of New York Press, 1984, pp.77-95.
Wipfler, H., *Die Trinitätsspekulation des Petrus von Poitiers und Die Trinitätsspekulation des Richard von St. Viktor (Beiträge Zur Geschichte der Philosophie und Theologie des Mittelalters* XLI).1. Münster: Aschendorffsche, 1965.
Zakara, Y. (ed.), *Aspects de la Pensée Médiévale dans la philosophie politique moderne.* Paris: Presses Universitaires de France, 1999.
Zemler-Cizewski, W., 'The Holy Spirit in Medieval Thought: Some Examples in the Individual, Ecclesial and Scholarly Areas', in B.E. Hinze and D.L. Dabney, *Advents of the Spirit: An Introduction to the Current Study of Pneumatology.* Milwaukee, Wisconsin: Marquette University Press, 2001, pp.163-172.
- '"The Lord, the Giver of Life:" A Reflection on the Theology of the Holy Spirit in

the Twelfth Century', *Anglican Theological Review* 83:3 (2001), pp.547-556.

Zerbi, P., 'William of St. Thierry and His Dispute with Peter Abelard', in J. Carfanton, *William, Abbot of St. Thierry: A Colloquium at the Abbey of St. Thierry*. Kalamazoo: Cistercian Publications, 1987, pp.181-203.

Zigon, F., 'Der Begriff der Caritas beim Lombarden und der hl. Thomas', *Divus Thomas* 4 (1926), p.404-424.

Zinn, G.A., 'The Influence of Augustine's *De Doctrina Christiana* upon the Writings of Hugh of St. Victor', in E.D. English, *Reading and Wisdom: The* De Doctrina Christiana *of Augustine in the Middle Ages*. Notre Dame: University of Notre Dame Press, 1995, pp.48-60.

- 'The Regular Canons', in B. McGinn and J. Meyendorff, *Christian Spirituality: Origins to the Twelfth Century*. London: Routledge and Kegan Paul, 1986, pp.196-204.

Index

Aelred of Rievault, 146
Ambrose, 40
Anselm of Canterbury, 2, 4, 5, 8, 9, 10, 11, 13, 61, 79, 85, 97, 101, 119, 120, 124, 158, 159, 162, 169, 176, 178, 179, 180, 182, 184, 186, 188
   Ontological Argument, 5, 25
Anselm of Havelberg, 5, 13, 26, 35, 36, 116, 120, 121, 161, 176, 178, 182, 184, 188
Archbishop Nechites, 24, 26, 36, 38, 121, 178, 188
Archbishop Nicetas, 5
Arendt, H., 20
Athanasian Creed, 48
Athanasius, 58, 97
Augustine, 1, 3, 4, 6, 7, 9, 19, 27, 40, 46, 57, 58, 65, 66, 73, 85, 87, 95, 98, 99, 101, 103, 105, 110, 113, 117, 122, 124, 126, 129, 141, 151, 164, 177, 181, 182, 186, 189
Badcock, G., 11, 81, 87
Bell, D., 15, 16, 68, 70, 126, 145, 154, 160, 167, 173, 174
Bernard of Clairvaux, 2, 6, 9, 14, 18, 44, 52, 59, 61, 79, 84, 93, 110, 117, 126, 131, 134, 139, 144, 146, 148, 154, 160, 168, 170, 181, 184, 187
Bertold, G., 12
Blasphemy against the Holy Spirit, 39, 88, 125, 135, 148
Bligh, J., 19
Boethius, 3, 9
Bredero, A., 18
Brooke, O., 17, 167, 174
Brower, J., 14

Burgess, S., 8, 153, 154, 166
Burnaby, J., 113, 114, 152, 165
Butler, C., 18, 79
Buytaert, E., 15
Canning, R., 20, 126, 165
Chartrains, 2, 14, 49, 139
Chrysostom, 40, 58, 97, 116
Church Fathers, 4
Cistercians, 2, 6, 15, 18, 62, 79, 187
Clanchy, M., 13
Clarembald of Arras, 116, 130
Clark, M., 20, 90, 94, 113
Coffey, D., 10, 113, 165, 190
Colish, M., 15, 21, 63, 96, 101, 102, 106, 110, 129, 135, 183
Condilectio, 182
Congar, Y., 10, 28, 142
Council of Bari, 3, 5, 25
Cyril, 40, 58, 97
Davy, M.-M., 17, 160
Dechanet, J.-M., 17, 144
Deme, D., 12, 28
Den Bok, N., 19, 80, 149, 172
Didymus, 40, 58, 97
Dreyer, E., 18
Dronke, P., 21
Evans, G., 9, 11, 35, 142, 169
Filioque, 3, 8, 12, 24, 26, 31, 40, 176, 188
Fortman, E., 11
Gemeinhardt, P., 12
Gilbert of Poitiers, 4, 11, 67, 186
Gilson, E., 9, 18, 69, 154, 168, 170, 173
Grane, L., 13
Gregory the Great, 58, 59, 89
Gregory, T., 51
Heloise, 44

Heron, A., 11, 12, 22, 153, 166
Hilary, 40
Hildegard of Bingen, 4, 8
Hill, E., 142
Hofmeier, J., 86
Holy Spirit
  Communion, 1, 3, 6, 20, 37, 55, 57, 126, 152, 186
  Condilectio, 90, 118
  Gift, 1, 3, 6, 55, 57, 72, 77, 80, 108, 120, 151, 166, 183
  Goodness, 1, 3, 6, 19, 30, 43, 47, 64, 74, 90, 129, 138, 186
  Love, 3, 6, 16, 18, 19, 27, 30, 37, 47, 55, 70, 80, 85, 102, 113, 130, 136, 142, 145, 153, 154, 165, 170, 186
  Mutual Love, 1, 10, 20, 28, 36, 71, 87, 115, 182
  Ontological Argument, 30
  Power, 3
  Power, Wisdom, Goodness, 13, 21, 45, 46, 65, 80, 81, 110, 125, 129, 146, 183
  Procession, 32, 36, 39, 58, 76, 91, 97, 119, 133, 156, 176
  Sweetness, 71, 117
  Union, 17, 22
  Unity, 18, 29, 30, 37, 66, 93, 107, 147, 163, 181, 184
  Will, 1, 3, 6, 47, 54, 56, 64, 65, 73, 125, 137, 141, 183, 186
  Wisdom, 3, 29
  World Soul, 13, 21, 43, 45, 49, 62, 138, 184
Honorius Augustodunensis, 144
Horst, U., 21
Hugh of St. Victor, 6, 22, 48, 79, 118, 124, 125, 131, 146, 182
Hypostasis, 4
Isidore, 40
Jerome, 40, 55, 116
Kant, I., 12
Kaufman, P., 107

Knoch, W., 22
Luscombe, D., 9, 13, 21
Mühlen, H., 11
Marenbon, J., 13, 49
McDonnell, K., 11, 168, 173
McGinn, B., 1, 21, 22, 51
Melone, M., 115, 172
Mews, C., 14, 44, 177
Moltmann, J., 10
Moonan, L., 21, 51
Ngien, D., 8, 12, 151, 153
Nicene Creed, 3, 4, 24, 40, 188
Nielson, L., 47
O'Donovan, O., 164, 170
Origen, 66
Orthodox Church, 3, 4, 5, 24, 31, 36, 58, 83, 92, 97, 120, 161, 176, 188
Ott, L., 21, 63
Peter Abelard, 2, 5, 6, 9, 11, 13, 16, 21, 35, 43, 61, 73, 74, 77, 80, 98, 110, 116, 122, 124, 127, 132, 136, 138, 149, 155, 156, 169, 171, 176, 183, 184, 186, 188
Peter Lombard, 1, 2, 4, 5, 15, 80, 96, 118, 119, 120, 123, 124, 125, 126, 129, 131, 135, 138, 143, 145, 155, 157, 158, 159, 161, 169, 170, 174, 176, 178, 180, 181, 182, 184, 187, 188
Peter the Venerable, 45
Pinnock, C., 80
Plato, 49, 62, 138, 186
Pranger, B., 9
Primacy in procession, 39
Ratzinger, J., 20, 163, 181
Reason, 2, 22, 24, 62, 79
Renna, T., 68, 173
Richard of St. Victor, 6, 8, 11, 15, 18, 79, 97, 110, 115, 118, 119, 121, 123, 125, 127, 133, 135, 136, 140, 145, 146, 149, 155, 159, 168, 171, 179, 181, 183,

Index

184, 187
Robert Melun, 5, 22, 134, 135, 139
Robert Pullen, 5
Roscelin of Compiegne, 44
Rosemann, P., 16, 96, 157
Rupert of Deutz, 4, 8
Rusch, W., 8
Saarinen, R., 16
Sabellianism, 159
Scholasticism, 22, 24, 61, 84, 184, 187
Schupp, J., 16, 104, 105, 107, 170
Sens, 44
Sentences, 1, 5, 15, 96, 169
Sikes, J., 21
Soissons, 14, 44, 130
Sommerfeldt, J., 18
Studer, B., 114
Summa Sententiarum, 122, 124, 137, 146, 147, 157, 161
Thierry of Chartres, 6, 21, 52, 116, 169
Thomas Aquinas, 9, 15

Tomasic, T., 22, 171
Trinity, 3, 4, 9, 13, 27, 80, 139
Verdeyen, P., 17, 173
Victorines, 2, 6, 18, 121, 182
Virgil, 52
von den Steinen, W., 8
Walter of Mortagne, 5, 130, 146
Watkin-Jones, H., 8, 28
Weingart, R., 14
William of Champeaux, 44
William of Conches, 2, 5, 6, 9, 16, 21, 52, 61, 62, 73, 74, 77, 131, 149, 186
William of St. Thierry, 2, 6, 14, 16, 21, 22, 44, 47, 49, 50, 61, 80, 110, 116, 117, 122, 124, 126, 131, 137, 139, 144, 145, 146, 147, 148, 154, 156, 160, 161, 166, 171, 172, 177, 181, 184, 186
World Soul, 7, 124, 186
Zemler-Cizewski, W., 8
Zerbi, P., 21

www.ingramcontent.com/pod-product-compliance
Lightning Source LLC
Chambersburg PA
CBHW070254230426
43664CB00014B/2525